SANDS OF TIME

Sands Of Time

The Gulf's Rich Tapestry Before Oil

GEW SCIENCES SOCIALES GROUP

Hichem Karoui (Ed.)

Global East-West (London)

Contents

ABOUT THE AUTHORS

About This Series

This book is the first volume in a series of 12 that will be released successively. The series is "Knowledge of the Gulf".

"Knowledge of the Gulf" is an indispensable series that delves into the rich and intricate tapestry of the Gulf region, offering readers a profound reexamination of its past and a thoughtful contemplation of its future. This comprehensive collection, spread across twelve meticulously crafted books, opens up alternative narratives often overlooked in mainstream discourse. Each book provides a lens through which readers can view different facets of the Gulf's history, uncovering hidden stories and addressing contemporary issues.

The series stands out for its commitment to authenticity and depth, presenting well-researched insights that resonate with both the seasoned historian and curious layperson alike. By confronting real concerns citizens face today—such as socio-economic challenges, cultural identity, and environmental sustainability—the series offers practical knowledge that equips readers to contribute meaningfully to their communities' futures. It's not just about understanding where people come from; it's about shaping where they're headed.

Moreover, "Knowledge of the Gulf" emphasizes intergenerational dialogue by shedding light on topics crucial for children's future. The narrative balance between historical reflection and futuristic vision encourages informed discussions within families and communities. Through these pages, readers will find themselves armed with wisdom vital for fostering progress while honoring heritage—a necessary blend for navigating today's complex world.

The Editor.

Chapter 1

The Ancient Civilization: Tracing the Origins

The study of ancient civilizations in the Gulf region holds profound significance in understanding the development of human societies and the intricate tapestry of cultural evolution. As we embark on this journey of exploration, it is imperative to recognize the pivotal role of these early Gulf civilizations in shaping history. Delving into the depths of time, archaeological evidence becomes our guiding light, offering glimpses of an era shrouded in mystery and grandeur. The methodologies employed in uncovering and interpreting such evidence are crucial in reconstructing the narratives of ancient civilizations, breathing life into their stories once more. This chapter unravels the enigma of the Gulf's ancient past, resonating with echoes of forgotten empires and bustling city-states. Setting the stage for a comprehensive examination, it beckons us to traverse the annals of time and venture into the realms of antiquity. By comprehensively exploring the material remains and remnants left behind by our forebears, we endeavor to piece together the mosaic of early Gulf civilizations, illuminating their complex socio-cultural landscapes and vibrant heritage. Through meticulous study and analysis, we aim to shed light on the multifaceted aspects of ancient life, from economic systems and urban developments to religious beliefs, artistic expressions, and interactions with neighboring cultures. This pursuit enables us to comprehend the rich historical tapestry that has laid the groundwork for the contemporary Gulf, underscoring the enduring legacy of its ancient inhabitants. In unraveling the chronicles of the past, we bridge the temporal chasm between antiquity and modernity, seeking to foster a deeper appreciation for the cultural continuum that defines the Gulf's ancient civilizations.

Archaeological Evidence and Methodologies

The study of ancient civilizations in the Gulf region relies heavily on meticulously analyzing archaeological evidence and applying various methodologies. Archaeology serves as a crucial tool for unraveling the mysteries of the past, enabling us to piece together the intricacies of early human societies and their interactions with the environment. Through the systematic excavation of sites and the careful scrutiny of material remains, researchers gain valuable insights into ancient peoples' lifestyles, beliefs, and technological advancements. Exploring archaeological sites has proven instrumental in expanding our understanding of the complexities inherent in ancient civilizations in a region as rich in history as the Gulf. Archaeologists utilize various scientific techniques to uncover and interpret historical artifacts, structures, and settlements. Excavations offer a window into bygone eras, shedding light on how early inhabitants navigated their surroundings, built communities, and cultivated resources. Moreover, examining

stratigraphy, soil composition, and environmental changes provides essential context for comprehending the chronology of
human occupation in the Gulf. By meticulously documenting
and cataloging findings, archaeologists can construct narratives that piece together the fragmented remnants of the past,
allowing modern audiences to appreciate the depth of cultural
heritage embedded within the region. Furthermore, the dating of archaeological materials through radiocarbon analysis,
thermoluminescence, and other sophisticated dating methods
facilitates the establishment of temporal frameworks, allowing
researchers to trace the evolution of settlements and activities
across millennia. This detailed temporal precision is invaluable
in reconstructing historical sequences and discerning societal
development patterns, trade networks, and influences from
neighboring regions. Additionally, remote sensing technologies,
such as LiDAR and ground-penetrating radar, have revolutionized the identification of sub-surface features and previously
undiscovered sites, significantly enhancing our ability to comprehend ancient settlements' spatial organization and extent.
The depth and breadth of archaeological knowledge continue
to expand through the concerted efforts of interdisciplinary
collaboration, incorporating specialists in fields ranging from
geology and botany to anthropology and conservation. Integrating traditional fieldwork with cutting-edge technological
innovations ensures that the past is preserved and dynamically
re-imagined, fostering a richer appreciation for the enduring
legacies of the ancient Gulf civilizations.

Early Human Settlements and Migration Patterns

The study of early human settlements and migration
patterns in the Gulf region is a fascinating exploration of
our ancient ancestors' movements and adaptations to their

environment. Understanding how people first arrived in this region and the subsequent development of communities provides valuable insights into the dynamics of human civilization. The vast expanses of the Gulf landscape, with its varied terrain and climatic conditions, played a pivotal role in shaping early inhabitants' migration patterns and settlement strategies. As we delve into the intricate tapestry of prehistoric human activities, we uncover the complexities of migration routes, settlement locations, and the societal implications of these ancient movements. From the fertile crescents to the river valleys and coastal regions, the Gulf witnessed an array of settlement strategies shaped by the availability of resources, environmental challenges, and interactions with neighboring cultures. These early settlers navigated through changing landscapes, utilizing their knowledge of natural phenomena and seasonal rhythms to establish sustainable habitats. Their diverse migratory paths reflect the resilience and adaptability of human societies and spotlight the rich cultural mosaic that emerged across the Gulf over millennia. By examining the archaeological remnants and artifacts left behind by these early settlers, we gain valuable perspectives on their subsistence strategies, technological advancements, and social organizations. The interplay between climatic shifts, resource abundance, and communal dynamics significantly influenced the establishment and dispersal of settlements, leaving an indelible mark on the historical landscape of the Gulf. Furthermore, the gradual evolution of migration patterns and settlement structures provides valuable evidence of human ingenuity and problem-solving capabilities in response to the challenges encountered in new territories. Analyzing the spatial distribution of early settlements and deciphering the demographic trends embedded within the archaeological record enhances our understanding of the sociocultural fabric that shaped the ancient Gulf communities. It invites us to unravel the intricate narratives of cultural exchanges, communal resilience, and adaptive strategies that reverberate across the annals of human history in the Gulf.

Development of Urban Centers in Antiquity

Urban centers played a pivotal role in the ancient civilizations of the Gulf region, serving as hubs of innovation, cultural exchange, and economic activity. The development of these urban centers marked significant milestones in advancing human societies, reflecting antiquity's complex social, political, and economic dynamics. As populations grew and agricultural practices evolved, the emergence of urban centers became synonymous with consolidating power, establishing trade networks, and flourishing artistic and intellectual pursuits. The layout and architecture of these early cities reflected their inhabitants' ingenuity and organizational skills, showcasing intricate infrastructural designs, monumental structures, and communal spaces that facilitated social interaction and communal activities. From the strategic positioning of defensive walls to constructing elaborate temples and administrative buildings, urban planning in antiquity demonstrated a sophisticated understanding of spatial organization and resource management. The urban landscape also bore testament to the interconnectedness of ancient societies, with evidence of cultural diffusion and the assimilation of diverse traditions discernible in the material remains unearthed by archaeological excavations. The thriving trading activities within these urban centers enriched local economies and fostered cultural exchange, enriching and diversifying artistic expressions, craftsmanship, and religious practices. Moreover, specialized artisan quarters and marketplaces attested to the division of labor and the vitality of commercial transactions within these bustling urban environments. Establishing governance structures

and administrative institutions delineated the power structures that governed these urban centers, shedding light on the
sociopolitical organization and the enforcement of laws and
regulations. Beneath the grandeur of these ancient cities lay
the daily lives of diverse communities, each contributing to
the tapestry of urban life through their distinct social roles,
religious observances, and participation in civic affairs. Exploring the development of urban centers in antiquity offers profound insights into the complexities of ancient societies, their
aspirations, and their enduring legacies that continue to shape
the modern Gulf region.

*Economic Foundations: Trade, Agriculture, and
Craftsmanship*

The economic landscape of the ancient Gulf civilization
was underpinned by a complex web of trade, agriculture, and
craftsmanship, laying the foundations for the flourishing society that emerged in antiquity. Trade was pivotal in connecting
the Gulf region with distant lands, facilitating the exchange of
goods, ideas, and cultural practices. The Gulf's abundant natural resources and strategic location propelled it into a prominent position within the broader network of ancient trade
routes. Traders from neighboring regions sought the valuable
commodities produced in the Gulf, such as pearls, spices,
incense, and luxury textiles, fuelling a thriving commercial
exchange that influenced societal structures and cultural dynamics. Alongside trade, agriculture formed the backbone of
the Gulf's economic stability, with ingenious irrigation systems
enabling the cultivation of crops and sustaining settlements
amidst arid landscapes. The agricultural surplus supported
local communities and contributed to the sustenance of urban
centers and trading hubs. Moreover, cultivating dates, grains,

and fruits fostered a sense of self-sufficiency and resourceful-ness among the inhabitants. Craftsmanship also flourished in the ancient Gulf civilization, with artisans honing their skills to produce exquisite pottery, intricate jewelry, textiles, and other artifacts coveted locally and abroad. The mastery of metallurgy and woodworking further enriched the repertoire of crafts, showcasing the ingenuity and creativity of the Gulf's artisans. Such skilled craftsmanship not only served practical purposes but also held symbolic significance, reflecting the artistic and cultural sophistication of the civilization. Further-more, the synergistic relationship between trade, agriculture, and craftsmanship formed a robust economic ecosystem that laid the groundwork for sustained growth and prosperity. The multifaceted nature of economic activities instilled resilience and adaptability within the ancient Gulf society, fostering an environment where innovation and enterprise thrived. As we delve into the nuanced interplay of trade, agriculture, and craftsmanship, a deeper appreciation emerges for the intricate tapestry of economic foundations that underpinned the an-cient civilization of the Gulf.

Social Hierarchies and Governance

In exploring the ancient civilizations of the Gulf, it becomes evident that social hierarchies played a pivotal role in shaping communal dynamics. These hierarchies were often structured around familial lineages, with prominent tribes and clans sig-nificantly influencing their respective communities. At the apex of these social structures were esteemed leaders who wielded authority in governance, justice, and resource alloca-tion. Governance within these ancient societies was multifac-eted, encompassing formal institutional systems and informal customary practices. The governance framework facilitated coordination among various social groups and ensured the maintenance of order and stability. Central to this structure were councils comprised of respected elders and influential individuals whose wisdom and experience were highly valued in decision-making processes. Furthermore, the division of labor and specialization within these civilizations gave rise to distinct social classes. While some members of society engaged in agricultural pursuits, others honed their skills as artisans, traders, or administrative functionaries. This diversification contributed to the stratification of society, creating a complex web of interdependent roles and responsibilities. The allocation of resources and access to privileged positions were often determined by one's societal status and contributions to the community. Moreover, the enforcement of laws and codes of conduct in these early Gulf civilizations bore testament to a developing legal system to preserve social harmony. Disputes were adjudicated through established judicial mechanisms, with mediators and arbitrators playing crucial roles in resolving conflicts. Sanctions, such as fines or public admonishments, were imposed to maintain order and discourage transgressions against societal norms. As these ancient societies evolved, so too did the structures of governance and hierarchical arrangements. The confluence of external influences, technological advancements, and cultural exchanges precipitated shifts in power dynamics and social stratification. Moreover, the interplay between social hierarchies and governance underscored the intricate tapestry of human interactions, reflecting the complexities inherent in organizing communal life.

Religious Beliefs and Ritual Practices

The study of religious beliefs and ritual practices among the ancient civilizations of the Gulf offers profound insights into the spiritual and cultural fabric that defined these societies. In examining the religious landscape of this region, one encounters a diverse tapestry of faith traditions and ceremonial observances that reflect the complex interplay between the natural environment, social structures, and human aspirations. The inhabitants of the Gulf were deeply attuned to the rhythms of nature, finding spiritual significance in the ebb and flow of tides, the cycle of seasons, and the celestial movements. These observations created a rich pantheon of deities and spirits, each associated with specific elements and phenomena. Moreover, religious rituals permeated daily life, shaping communal gatherings, rites of passage, and cyclical festivities. From solemn processions honoring fertility goddesses to elaborate ceremonies invoking the protection of sea deities for successful voyages, the rites performed by the ancients underscored their reverence for the unseen forces that governed earthly existence. Artifacts and archaeological findings further illuminate the material expressions of religious devotion, including intricately crafted idols, votive offerings, and sacred architectural spaces. The convergence of trade networks and cultural exchanges played a pivotal role in the transmission and syncretism of religious ideologies, resulting in a fascinating fusion of belief systems and cosmological narratives. Thus, the exploration of religious beliefs and ritual practices enriches our understanding of the Gulf's ancient civilizations and serves as a testament to the enduring human quest for transcendence and interconnectedness with the divine.

Artistic Expressions and Cultural Achievements

The artistic expressions and cultural achievements of the ancient civilizations that flourished around the Gulf region are a testament to the vibrancy and creativity of these societies. Art played a fundamental role in shaping the identity and heritage of these cultures, reflecting their values, beliefs, and aspirations. From intricate pottery and ceramics to stunning jewelry and metalwork, the material culture of the Gulf's ancient civilizations exemplifies sophisticated craftsmanship and artistic skill. These artifacts serve as aesthetic masterpieces and provide valuable insights into these ancient people's daily lives, societal structures, and spiritual practices. The utilization of various artistic mediums, such as rock engravings, wall paintings, and relief sculptures, allowed the ancient inhabitants of the Gulf to express narratives of mythology, rituals, and historical events. Each artistic creation encapsulated these cultures' unique perspectives and experiences, illuminating their worldview and symbolism. Furthermore, the architectural marvels of ancient cities and settlements, with their intricate layouts and monumental structures, speak volumes about these societies' advanced engineering and design prowess. Beyond mere practical purposes, the built environment was a canvas for conveying power, grandeur, and communal identity. Cultural achievements extended beyond visual arts and architecture, encompassing literature, poetry, and oral traditions. The rich oral heritage of the Gulf's ancient civilizations passed down through generations, conveyed wisdom, moral teachings, and historical chronicles. Poetic compositions, with their rhythmic verses and evocative imagery, captivated the hearts and minds of listeners, preserving the collective memory and ethos of these societies. The emergence of script and written language further propelled the documentation and dissemination of knowledge, fostering intellectual and literary pursuits amongst scholarly circles. Moreover, the innovative advancements in technological and scientific domains underscore these ancient cultures' intellectual curiosity and problem-solving abilities. From astronomy and navigation techniques to agricultural practices and irrigation systems, the ingenuity of the Gulf's ancient civilizations manifested in practical innovations that contributed to the prosperity and resilience of their communities. The exchange of knowledge and expertise with neighboring civilizations fostered a dynamic environment of cultural diffusion, leading to the cross-pollination of ideas and practices. In conclusion, the ancient Gulf civilizations' artistic expressions and cultural achievements epitomize a legacy of ingenuity, creativity, and human ingenuity. By delving into the diverse array of artistic artifacts and cultural accomplishments, we gain a profound appreciation for the enduring impact of these civilizations on the tapestry of human history.

Interactions with Neighboring Civilizations

The ancient civilizations of the Gulf were not isolated entities; they actively interacted with neighboring societies, contributing to the rich tapestry of cultural exchange and trade that shaped the region. Interactions with Mesopotamia, the Indus Valley, and the ancient civilizations of Iran and Central Asia were pivotal in influencing the development of the Gulf's cultural identity. The exchange of goods, ideas, and technologies fostered a dynamic environment where diverse cultures coexisted and thrived. The Mesopotamian influence, particularly from the Sumerians and Babylonians, can be observed in the archaeological record of the Gulf region, reflecting a history of trade and diplomatic ties. The sophisticated irrigation techniques and agricultural practices of Mesopotamia left a lasting impact on the agricultural landscape of the Gulf, transforming it into a flourishing center of food production. Additionally, the Mesopotamian influence extended to religious beliefs and mythologies, as evidenced by shared motifs and deities across the two regions. The maritime trade routes connecting the Gulf with the Indus Valley civilization facilitated the exchange of precious commodities such as copper, pottery, and semiprecious stones. This interaction facilitated economic prosperity and led to the transfer of knowledge in metallurgy and urban planning. The robust trade networks across the Arabian Sea empowered the Gulf's civilizations to engage in mutually beneficial exchanges, enriching their cultural and material assets. Furthermore, the historical connections between the Gulf and the civilizations of Iran and Central Asia were integral in shaping the artistic and architectural expressions of the region. The distinct motifs and stylistic elements found in artifacts and structures point to a cross-pollination of artistic traditions, highlighting the interconnectedness of the ancient world. Diplomatic relations and alliances with neighboring civilizations also played a crucial role in establishing strategic partnerships and fostering peaceful coexistence. The art of diplomacy and cultural exchange fostered an atmosphere of mutual respect and collaboration, laying the groundwork for enduring relationships that transcended geographical boundaries. Through these intricate interactions, the Gulf's ancient civilizations emerged as vibrant cultural diversity and innovation hubs, demonstrating the profound impact of cross-cultural exchanges on societal evolution.

Reflecting on the Legacy of the Gulf's Ancients

The enduring legacy of the ancient civilizations that thrived in the Gulf region continues to captivate and inspire contemporary scholars and enthusiasts alike. As we reflect on the rich tapestry of their achievements, it becomes evident that the foundations laid by these ancestral societies have significantly shaped the cultural, economic, and social dynamics of the modern Gulf states. One of the most remarkable legacies of the Gulf's ancients lies in their interactions with neighboring civilizations. The exchange of ideas, goods, and technologies across ancient trade routes not only facilitated prosperity but also fostered a cross-pollination of cultures that left an indelible mark on the region's collective identity. Through extensive archaeological evidence, we gain insight into the complex network of trade and diplomacy that linked the Gulf with Mesopotamia, the Indus Valley, and beyond. This interconnectedness highlights the Gulf as a pivotal hub in the ancient world, where diverse cultures converged and co-alesced. Furthermore, the artistry and cultural achievements of the Gulf's ancients continue to resonate profoundly. From intricate pottery and jewelry to monumental architecture and expressive artworks, the creativity and craftsmanship of these societies are enduring testaments to human ingenuity. The aesthetic sensibilities and technical prowess exhibited in their creations serve as timeless sources of inspiration, fostering a deep appreciation for past artistic traditions. Beyond material culture, the ancients' religious beliefs and ritual practices offer profound insights into their cosmological worldview and spiritual pursuits. Temples, tombs, and sacred sites witness the symbolic significance attributed to the natural world and celestial phenomena. This provides a glimpse into the rites and ceremonies that underscored the ancient peoples' quest for transcendence and meaning. In conclusion, the legacy of the Gulf's ancients is an invaluable inheritance that connects the past with the present, inviting us to ponder the continuity of human endeavors and the enduring influence of ancient wisdom. By delving into the annals of antiquity, we unravel the mysteries of bygone eras and enrich our understanding of the cultural mosaic that defines the contemporary Gulf. The profound impact of the Gulf's ancients resonates through the ages, reminding us of the timeless relevance of their innovations, aspirations, and interconnectedness.

Chapter 2

The Gulf of Beginnings: Geographical and Historical Overview

The Gulf region is prominent at the crossroads of continents, making it a vital link between diverse cultures and economies. Situated at the crossroads of Europe, Asia, and Africa, the Gulf has historically been a critical maritime route facilitating trade and cultural exchange between these continents. The strategic geographic positioning of the Gulf has not only shaped its unique identity but has also influenced the development of civilizations far beyond its shores. This geographical importance has been pivotal in defining the Gulf's historical, cultural, and economic significance. Moreover, the Gulf's access to the Indian Ocean and the Arabian Peninsula has made it an area of immense strategic value, drawing the interest of ancient empires and modern superpowers alike. Its positioning at the mouth of the Persian Gulf, with its proximity to the vast Eurasian continent, has contributed to the region's

status as a vital hub for global commerce and cultural interchange. Understanding the Gulf region's physical geography
and climatic characteristics is crucial for comprehending its
historical trajectory, economic activities, and environmental
sustainability. The unique landforms and climatic conditions
have not only shaped the natural habitat and biodiversity of
the Gulf but have also influenced human settlement patterns,
economic activities, and cultural practices. As such, delving
into the details of the Gulf's physical geography offers profound insights into the intricate interconnectedness of nature
and human societies within this region.

Physical Geography: Landforms and Climate

The Gulf region, situated in the Middle East, is characterized by a diverse and captivating physical geography that
has profoundly impacted its development and cultural identity. Enclosed by vast desert expanses and dotted with rugged
mountain ranges, the landforms of the Gulf region have played
a pivotal role in shaping the unique environmental conditions
and sustaining the indigenous flora and fauna. The jewel-toned
waters of the Gulf provide a striking contrast to the arid landscapes that envelop its shores, fostering a delicate ecosystem
and supporting marine life vital to the livelihoods of coastal
communities.

The climatic conditions in the Gulf region are notably extreme, with scorching temperatures during the long summer
months and minimal precipitation throughout the year. The
relentless sun beats down upon the undulating sand dunes
and rocky outcrops, creating an otherworldly panorama that
has captivated travelers and inhabitants for centuries. Additionally, the region experiences frequent dust storms and

occasional hurricanes, further testament to the formidable forces of nature at play.

The varying landscapes of the Gulf region encompass sprawling deserts, such as the Rub'al Khali and the Arabian Desert, as well as fertile oases that provide sustenance and respite for both humans and wildlife. Mountains, including the Al Hajar range and Jebel Jais, punctuate the horizon, offering breathtaking vistas and valuable natural resources. These geographical features have influenced settlement patterns, trade routes, and cultural practices, contributing to the vibrant tapestry of societies thriving in this unique environment.

It is essential to recognize the intricate interaction between the Gulf region's landforms and climate and the customs, traditions, and economic activities of its inhabitants. A deep appreciation of these elements will offer valuable insights into how the natural environment has shaped the region's historical trajectory, from early human settlements to the present day. Furthermore, understanding the delicate balance of this ecosystem is imperative for fostering sustainable practices and ensuring the preservation of this rich and complex heritage for generations to come.

Historical Significance: From the Stone Age to the Islamic Era

The Gulf region's historical significance stretches back through the annals of time, encompassing a rich tapestry of human civilization. From the Stone Age to the Islamic Era, the Gulf has witnessed the evolution of societies, cultures, and trade routes, leaving an indelible mark on the historical landscape.

Evidence of early human habitation in the region dating back to the Stone Age provides a glimpse into the prehistoric roots of Gulf civilization. The discovery of ancient tools, rock art, and burial sites attests to the presence of early human communities, shedding light on their way of life and technological advancements.

As millennia passed, the Gulf became a pivotal crossroads for various empires, serving as a melting pot of diverse cultures and traditions. The rise and fall of Mesopotamian, Persian, Greek, and Roman influences left a lasting imprint on the region, shaping its political, social, and economic dynamics. The convergence of these great empires led to a cultural renaissance that connected East and West and fostered an exchange of ideas, knowledge, and innovation.

The advent of Islam heralded a new era in the Gulf's history, bringing profound changes in governance, religion, and societal norms. The spread of Islam across the Arabian Peninsula transformed the Gulf into a hub of Islamic civilization, characterized by the establishment of prosperous trade networks, architectural marvels, and learning centers. The Islamic Era ushered in an era of enlightenment, scientific exploration, and artistic expression, culminating in intellectual pursuits and cultural achievements flourishing.

Furthermore, the legacy of the Islamic Golden Age continues to resonate in the Gulf's heritage, as evidenced by the preservation of ancient mosques, madrasas, and souks that bear testament to the region's enduring Islamic legacy—this period of history laid the groundwork for the vibrant cultural identity and socioeconomic prosperity that defines the modern-day Gulf.

In essence, the historical significance of the Gulf from the Stone Age to the Islamic Era encapsulates a narrative of resilience, adaptation, and the enduring spirit of human endeavor, providing invaluable insights into the region's multifaceted heritage and enduring impact on global civilization.

Cultural Intersection: The Meeting of Empires

The Gulf region has long been a significant crossroads where various empires and cultures have converged, interacted, and coexisted. This cultural melting pot has led to a rich tapestry of influences, traditions, and practices that have shaped the identity of the Gulf throughout history. From the ancient Mesopotamians and the influence of the Babylonian Empire to the great Persian civilizations, the Gulf served as a hub for trade, exchanging ideas, and blending customs and beliefs. The legacy of these interactions can still be seen today in the region's architecture, art, language, and social structures. The arrival of Islam in the 7th century further shaped the cultural landscape of the Gulf, bringing with it new forms of governance, arts, and sciences. The Islamic Golden Age witnessed a flourishing of learning and intellectual pursuits, with scholars from diverse backgrounds contributing to advancing knowledge. This era's economic prosperity and intellectual achievements left an indelible mark on the Gulf, fostering an environment that encouraged open dialogue and collaboration among different cultures. The Gulf's position as a pivotal trading hub attracted the attention of European powers during the Age of Exploration, leading to further cultural exchanges and the introduction of Western influences. The colonial era brought about significant changes in governance, legal systems, and trade patterns, leaving a lasting impact on the region's social fabric. This confluence of diverse cultural elements has contributed to forming a cosmopolitan identity within the Gulf, characterized by a synthesis of traditions worldwide. Today, the Gulf remains a dynamic melting pot, embracing its rich heritage while simultaneously adapting to the forces of globalization. The intertwining of different cultural threads has woven a captivating narrative of resilience, adaptability, and coexistence, positioning the Gulf as a vibrant center of cultural diversity and intercultural dialogue.

Economic Development Through the Ages

Throughout history, the Gulf region has been intertwined with a tapestry of economic development that has withstood the test of time. From the earliest civilizations to the modern era, the economic landscape of the Gulf has continually evolved and adapted to the changing tides of commerce and trade. In ancient times, the region was a thriving hub for exchanging goods, where caravans traversed vast deserts laden with precious cargo, connecting distant lands and cultures. The advent of maritime trade further fueled economic growth as ancient sailing vessels, such as dhows, plied the azure waters, carrying exotic wares and fostering cross-cultural exchanges. These early commercial endeavors laid the foundation for the Gulf's enduring tradition as a crossroads of global trade. The region's strategic location between East and West made it a focal point for intercontinental commerce, leading to prosperous trading ports and bustling markets that drew merchants and voyagers from far-flung corners of the world. The convergence of different economic systems, from the agrarian economies of ancient settlements to the sophisticated mercantile networks of medieval empires, enhanced the region's standing as an economic powerhouse. As centuries passed, the Gulf continued to thrive as a nexus of commerce, witnessing the ebb and flow of empires that left indelible imprints on its economic landscape. The symbiotic relationships forged between various civilizations led to the amalgamation of diverse economic practices, creating a dynamic marketplace where goods, ideas, and technologies were incessantly traded and diffused. The discovery of oil in the 20th century catalyzed a monumental shift in the economic dynamics of the Gulf, propelling the region into a new era of unparalleled prosperity. This transformative resource not only reshaped the economic fortunes of the Gulf but also reverberated across the globe, opening new frontiers of trade and investment. The influx of wealth from oil exports triggered unprecedented infrastructural developments, propelling the Gulf states onto the global stage as modern economic powerhouses. Amidst this modernization, the region has balanced traditional economic pursuits with contemporary innovations, nurturing a diversified economy encompassing finance, tourism, and technological advancements. The Gulf's economic resilience and adaptability testify to its enduring legacy as a vibrant crucible of commerce and innovation, sculpted by the winds of time and tempered by the rich tapestry of its historical heritage.

Significant Cities and Sites of Import

The Gulf region is replete with a tapestry of historically significant cities and archaeological sites, each bearing testament to the many cultures and civilizations that have graced its lands. One such city of immense historical importance is Uruk, often regarded as one of the world's first actual cities. As a pivotal urban center of ancient Mesopotamia, Uruk's legacy extends far beyond the vast ruins that now stand as evidence of its former grandeur. Its influence reached the ancient world, shaping early urban development and social organization. Another notable site is the majestic city of Tyre, renowned in antiquity for its maritime prowess and position as a key trading hub in the Mediterranean. The remnants of Tyre's port and acclaimed purple dye industry provide invaluable insights into the commerce and cultural exchanges of the ancient maritime world. As we shift focus to the Arabian Peninsula, the city of

Mecca emerges as an unparalleled focal point of religious significance and pilgrimage. Its historical and contemporary importance as the spiritual center of Islam renders it an essential site to study for understanding the convergence of faith, trade, and societal dynamics. Equally noteworthy is the ancient Iranian city of Pasargadae, established by Cyrus the Great and serving as the capital of the Achaemenid Empire. This historical site encapsulates the rich heritage of Persian civilization, showcasing remarkable architectural feats and royal palaces. Furthermore, the island of Failaka in present-day Kuwait is a captivating repository of ancient Greek and Mesopotamian influences, evidenced by its archaeological artifacts and temple ruins. The diversity of these cities and sites underscores the multifaceted history of the Gulf, inviting us to delve deeper into the interconnected narratives of human civilization, trade, and cultural exchange.

Ecological Biodiversity: Flora and Fauna

The Gulf region is a striking testament to the stunning ecological diversity of flora and fauna. The unique ecological landscape of the Gulf is a harmonious blend of desert, coastal, and marine ecosystems, allowing for an astonishing richness of biodiversity. The arid desert plains are adorned with hardy, drought-resistant plant species such as acacia trees, thyme, and date palms, showcasing nature's adaptive brilliance in extreme climatic conditions. Moving towards the coast, one encounters mangroves, salt marshes, and tidal flats that serve as critical nurseries for various marine life. These critical coastal ecosystems play a vital role in terrestrial and aquatic food chains, supporting countless species and ensuring the fragile balance of the local environment. The Gulf's marine environment further dazzles with its kaleidoscopic array of underwater life.

The rich coral reefs harbor a mesmerizing tapestry of fish, mollusks, crustaceans, and other marine creatures, contributing to the unparalleled splendor of the Gulf's underwater world. From the majestic humpback whales and dugongs to the tiny nudibranchs and seahorses, the Gulf's waters are teeming with life, each organism playing an indispensable part in the complex web of marine biodiversity. However, this remarkable biodiversity faces ever-increasing threats from human activities. Urbanization, industrialization, overfishing, and climate change pose significant challenges to the delicate balance of the Gulf's ecosystems. Efforts to conserve and protect the Gulf's biodiversity have gained momentum recently, with initiatives focusing on sustainable development, marine conservation areas, and awareness campaigns. By understanding and appreciating the irreplaceable ecological treasures of the Gulf, it is our collective responsibility to ensure the preservation of this exceptional natural heritage for future generations.

Socioeconomic Impacts: Past to Present

The Gulf region's socioeconomic landscape has been intricately shaped by its historical development, serving as a melting pot of diverse cultures and an epicenter of global trade. From ancient times to the present day, the region's economic prosperity has been intricately intertwined with its social dynamics, influencing and being influenced by the ebb and flow of civilizations. At the heart of this prosperity lies the strategic geographical positioning of the Gulf, which has facilitated trade routes connecting East and West, fostering a rich tapestry of cultural exchange that continues to define the region today.

ARCHAEOLOGICAL CONTRIBUTIONS: UNCOVERING
HISTORY

Exploring the Gulf's archaeological landscape has been
fascinating, shedding light on the region's rich and complex
history. Archaeological endeavors have played a pivotal role
in unraveling the mysteries of civilizations past, providing invaluable insights into ancient societies' cultural, social, and
economic dynamics. Archaeologists have pieced together a
narrative that spans millennia through the meticulous excavation of sites, the recovery of artifacts, and the interpretation
of historical records.

One of the most significant contributions of archaeological
research in the Gulf region has been the discovery and documentation of ancient trade routes, which facilitated the exchange of goods, ideas, and technologies across vast distances.
Identifying caravan paths, maritime routes, and commercial
centers has deepened our understanding of the interconnectedness of ancient societies and the mechanisms through
which commerce thrived in the region. This has enriched our
knowledge of the past and offered valuable lessons for contemporary economic and cultural exchanges.

Moreover, archaeological investigations have unearthed evidence of early human settlements, providing crucial evidence
of the Gulf's prehistoric inhabitants and their ways of life.
Researchers have reconstructed the daily routines, social organization, and technological advancements of early civilizations by studying ancient dwellings, tools, pottery, and other
material remains. These discoveries have illuminated ancient
peoples' adaptive strategies and resilience in coping with environmental challenges and harnessing natural resources for
sustenance and development.

The preservation and restoration of archaeological sites
have been instrumental in fostering a sense of cultural identity

and heritage among the inhabitants of the Gulf region. By safe-guarding the tangible remains of past civilizations, communities have connected with their ancestors, acknowledging the enduring legacies of their forebears and embracing a shared historical consciousness. Furthermore, these efforts have attracted scholarly attention, tourism, and international recognition, contributing to the promotion of cultural tourism and the appreciation of the Gulf's historical significance globally.

The Gulf's archaeological contributions have expanded our comprehension of ancient societies and enriched contemporary discourse on heritage conservation, historical narratives, and cross-cultural interactions. By unearthing the relics of the past, archaeology has woven together the threads of history, illuminating the diverse tapestry of human experiences and shaping a deeper appreciation for the enduring legacy of the Gulf's ancient civilizations.

Conclusion: Integrating History with Modernity

The archaeological contributions discussed in the preceding section have shed light on the rich history of the Gulf region. As we delve into the annals of time, it becomes increasingly evident that the nexus between history and modernity is a crucial aspect shaping the region's identity and trajectory. The convergence of historical narratives and contemporary progress presents a compelling juxtaposition informing the Gulf societies' collective consciousness.

Integrating history with modernity requires a deep understanding and appreciation of the past while embracing the present era's opportunities and challenges. It necessitates a delicate balance between preserving the heritage and traditions that have withstood the test of time and innovatively adapting to the dynamic demands of globalization and technological advancements.

With an astute recognition of the historical groundwork laid by our predecessors, the contemporary Gulf society stands on the shoulders of its forebears, drawing inspiration from their resilience, creativity, and global interactions. The preservation of ancient landmarks, artifacts, and cultural practices serves as a testament to our commitment to honoring and safeguarding the legacy of our ancestors, acting as a bridge that connects us to our roots while propelling us forward into the modern age.

Moreover, integrating history with modernity fosters a sense of cultural continuity that transcends temporal boundaries. By acknowledging and embracing our historical heritage, we reinforce a shared sense of identity and belonging among the diverse communities of the Gulf, fostering unity and cohesion amidst the ever-evolving societal landscape.

At the same time, we must recognize the imperative for adaptability and progressive thinking in the face of contemporary challenges. Embracing modernity entails harnessing technological advancements, education, and governance to ensure sustainable economic development, social welfare, and environmental stewardship. By leveraging the lessons of history, we are empowered to craft innovative solutions and strategic approaches that align with the global standards of excellence while upholding the unique ethos of the Gulf region.

In conclusion, the harmonious integration of history with modernity emboldens the Gulf societies to traverse the intricate tapestry of time with sophistication and purpose. By upholding our venerable legacy and responding adeptly to the demands of the present age, we pave the way for a future that resonates with the wisdom of antiquity while embracing the promise of progress.

Chapter 3

Desert Nomads: The Bedouin Culture

The Bedouin way of life is intricately woven with the harsh and unforgiving conditions of the desert. Their existence in the arid and barren landscapes has cultivated unique characteristics that embody resilience, adaptability, and resourcefulness. Originating from the vast deserts of the Arabian Peninsula, Bedouins have historically thrived in an environment where survival is a daily challenge. Their historical background is deeply rooted in the nomadic lifestyle, characterized by a constant quest for sustenance and shelter amidst the shifting sands. The resilience of the Bedouin people is evident in their ability to navigate through the inhospitable terrain, enduring extreme temperatures and scarce water sources. This unwavering determination to overcome the adversities of the desert has shaped their culture and traditions, fostering a sense of self-reliance and independence. The historical tapestry of the Bedouin heritage is interwoven with tales of bravery, perseverance, and a deep connection to the land they traverse. Their ancestral roots stretch back centuries, evolving alongside the challenges posed by nature, forging a legacy of resilience that permeates every aspect of their existence. The rich history of the Bedouin tribes is a testament to their ability to adapt to ever-changing circumstances while upholding their traditional values and customs. The intricate balance between tradition and adaptation is a hallmark of Bedouin life, as they deftly navigate the modern world without compromising the essence of their heritage. As we delve deeper into the facets of Bedouin culture, it becomes evident that their enduring spirit and adaptability stand as a beacon of inspiration, carrying forward a legacy crafted by centuries of resilience amidst the harsh desert landscape.

Origins and Historical Background

The origins of Bedouin culture are deeply rooted in the history of the Arabian Peninsula, dating back to ancient times. The term 'Bedouin' is derived from the Arabic word 'badawi', which refers to those living in the desert. The historical background of the Bedouin people is characterized by a nomadic way of life shaped by the harsh desert environment and a complex web of tribal relations. Scholars believe that the Bedouin culture evolved over thousands of years, influenced by various factors such as climatic conditions, geographical features, and interactions with neighboring civilizations.

Historical records indicate that the Bedouin tribes played a significant role in the trade routes of the ancient world, serving as guides and providers of essential goods to caravans traversing the desert. This network of trading relationships facilitated cultural exchanges and contributed to the rich tapestry of Bedouin heritage. The legacy of the Bedouin is intertwined with the region's history as they navigated through periods of prosperity, conflict, and transition.

The Bedouins' nomadic lifestyle enabled them to adapt to the challenges of the desert, relying on their deep understanding of seasonal changes, water sources, and survival skills. Their resilience and mobility allowed them to traverse vast distances in search of pastures for their herds and sustainable living conditions. This history of migration and settlement is embedded in the collective memory of the Bedouins, shaping their identity and traditions.

Furthermore, the historical background of the Bedouin is marked by a tradition of oral storytelling, preserving myths, legends, and historical accounts passed down through generations. This oral tradition has been a cornerstone of Bedouin culture, providing insights into their ancestral narratives and the interconnectedness of tribal lineages. The tales of heroism, adventure, and wisdom have woven a rich tapestry of folklore that continues to resonate in Bedouin communities today.

Delving into the origins of the Bedouin reveals an intricate and profound historical background, reflecting the endurance of a people bound by tradition, reverence for the land, and a deep connection to their ancestral past.

Social Structure and Tribal Organization

As the mesmerizing tapestry of Bedouin culture unfolds, one cannot overlook the intricate social structure and tribal organization that form the very fabric of their society. The nomadic nature of the Bedouin lifestyle has fostered a unique system where tribes are the cornerstone of social order. Within each tribe, a complex web of interconnected families and lineages dictates social standing, rights, and responsibilities. Authority is often decentralized, with chiefs or sheikhs typically holding leadership roles, maintaining an air of respect and wisdom within the community. This hierarchy is not rigid but somewhat fluid, adapting to the demands of the environment and the challenges encountered in the desert. Mutual support and cooperation define the intricate ties among members, creating a sense of unity and survival in the harsh desert terrain. While some tribes assert territorial boundaries, others embrace a more fluid approach, allowing intertribal interaction and exchange. Despite the seemingly isolated existence in the vast desert expanse, communication and alliances between tribes play a pivotal role in ensuring security, trade, and the preservation of cultural traditions. These communal dynamics exemplify the resilience and adaptability inherent in the Bedouin social structure, showcasing a rich tapestry of interconnectedness and interdependence.

Traditional Dress and Ornamentation

The traditional dress and ornamentation of the Bedouin people hold great significance, reflecting their cultural heritage and nomadic way of life. Distinctive attire and adornments serve practical purposes and symbolize identity, social status, and cultural pride within the Bedouin community. The attire of the Bedouins is designed to protect the harsh desert environment while allowing freedom of movement essential for their nomadic lifestyle. Men wear loose-fitting robes such as the thobe or dishdasha, often in neutral tones to camouflage against the desert landscape. These garments also feature intricate embroideries and embellishments that denote regional variations and clan affiliations. Likewise, women's attire includes flowing dresses adorned with elaborate patterns and vibrant colors, with veils and headscarves offering protection from the sun and sand. Natural fibers like wool, cotton, and silk reflect the Bedouins' resourcefulness and adaptation to their surroundings. Ornamentation is pivotal in Bedouin culture, with jewelry and accessories as wealth, status, and familial ties markers. Silver and gold jewelry, often adorned with semi-precious stones, are cherished possessions passed down through generations, signifying heritage and lineage. Each piece holds symbolic meaning, representing prosperity, fertility, protection, and spirituality. Intricately woven camel hair cords and tassels are incorporated into clothing and accessories, showcasing the craftsmanship and artistry of the Bedouin people. Furthermore, the intricate patterns and motifs adorning their traditional garments and jewelry convey narratives of their history, traditions, and beliefs. As the Bedouin way of life evolves in the modern era, a concerted effort exists to preserve and promote the significance of traditional dress and ornamentation. Artisans continue to uphold age-old techniques, ensuring the continuation of skilled crafts such as embroidery, weaving, and metalwork. Amidst contemporary influences, the Bedouin people endeavor to maintain the integrity and authenticity of their cultural attire and adornments, celebrating their rich heritage amidst societal change and globalization challenges.

Nomadic Lifestyle and Seasonal Movements

The nomadic lifestyle of the Bedouin people is intricately linked to their seasonal movements across the desert terrain. These movements are carefully planned and strategically carried out to ensure the community's and livestock's well-being. The cyclical nature of their migrations is driven by the need to find suitable grazing pastures and water sources for their herds and escape harsh environmental conditions. Each phase of the nomadic journey holds significance in shaping the cultural identity and resilience of the Bedouin tribes.

With the arrival of spring, the Bedouin nomads embark on a significant rite of passage, known as 'Razfa,' marking the start of their seasonal migration. This period sees the community packing their tents, belongings, and essential supplies and setting off towards the cooler highlands where fresh veg-etation and water can be found. The rhythmic trekking of the nomadic caravans across the vast deserts becomes a testament to the strength and adaptability of the Bedouin culture.

As summer approaches, the Bedouin tribes gradually move to higher ground for cooler temperatures and greener pastures. Their extensive knowledge of the land allows them to navigate through rugged terrains and scorching heat with unparalleled precision. During this season, the nomads establish temporary settlements, creating a harmonious coexistence with nature while tending to their flocks. The bond between the Bedouins and their environment is evident in their sustainable practices, ensuring minimal impact on the delicate ecosystem.

The transition to autumn heralds the return journey as the Bedouin tribes return to the lower plains, guided by the changing landscapes and weather patterns. Their resilience and astute understanding of natural indicators enable them to anticipate potential challenges and take pre-emptive mea-sures. The nomadic lifestyle instills a deep sense of unity and collaboration within the community as they face the trials of their arduous yet purposeful journey together.

In winter, the Bedouin nomads seek out sheltered valleys and fertile plains to rest and replenish their resources before the cycle begins anew. This season of respite provides an op-portunity for reflection and social bonding as stories are shared around campfires, traditions are upheld, and skills are handed down through generations. Within this hushed tranquility, the essence of the Bedouin spirit resonates, echoing the timeless wisdom of their ancestors amidst the vast expanse of the desert.

Economic Activities: Herding and Hunting

The economic activities of herding and hunting have been integral to the traditional Bedouin way of life, providing sustenance, livelihoods, and a deeper connection to the natural environment. Herding, primarily of camels, goats, and sheep, has been a central focus of the Bedouin economy, allowing them to thrive in the harsh desert landscapes. The nomadic lifestyle necessitated a deep understanding of animal husbandry and the ability to navigate vast stretches of arid terrain in search of grazing grounds. This intimate knowledge of the land and its resources has been passed down through generations, shaping the cultural identity of the Bedouin people. Furthermore, the importance of herding extends beyond the practical aspects of food and resource acquisition; it is intricately linked to social customs and traditions, forming the foundation of communal values and kinship ties among the tribes. In addition to herding, hunting played a complementary role in sustaining the Bedouin communities. While the scarcity of wildlife in the desert presented challenges, skilled hunters were revered for their prowess and resourcefulness. Hunting expeditions provided meat and hides and honed the survival skills essential for thriving in the rugged desert environment. The interplay between herding and hunting encapsulates the resilience and adaptability of the Bedouin people, illustrating how they have harmonized with the natural world and utilized its offerings for their sustenance. Despite the evolution of modernization and external influences, the enduring significance of herding and hunting remains a testament to Bedouin culture's enduring legacy.

Cultural Traditions: Poetry, Music, and Dance

Enriched by their nomadic lifestyle, the Bedouin culture is a tapestry woven with the threads of poetry, music, and dance.

These expressive traditions serve as profound chronicles of the Bedouin way of life, symbolizing their identity and preserving their history across generations. Primarily an oral culture, poetry is revered among the Bedouins, embodying their emotions, values, and collective memory. The melodic rhythm of traditional verse echoes across the desert, carrying tales of love, courage, and tribal heritage. This poetic tradition entertains and serves as a platform for discussing social issues, conveying wisdom, and commemorating significant events. Furthermore, music is central in Bedouin communal gatherings, enhancing celebratory occasions and daily routines. The haunting melodies of traditional instruments such as the rabab and the mir created an unmistakable ambiance, fostering solidarity and shared experiences among the community. Accompanying the musical rhythms, traditional dances exemplify the Bedouin's vibrant cultural spirit and deep sense of unity. These spirited movements, often inspired by elements of nature and wildlife, convey narratives of bravery, endurance, and harmony with the environment. Whether in joyful festivities or moments of hardship, these dance forms bind the Bedouin together, forging strong bonds and reinforcing their collective consciousness. Overall, the cultural traditions of poetry, music, and dance entertain and uplift the spirit and serve as vital vessels for transmitting the essence of the Bedouin culture, fostering continuity, and strengthening their communal identity.

Spiritual Beliefs and Practices

The spiritual beliefs and practices of the Bedouin culture are deeply rooted in their nomadic way of life, reflecting a profound connection to the desert environment and an intricate understanding of natural elements. Central to the Bedouins' spiritual worldview is monotheism, with a strong emphasis on the worship of a single, all-powerful deity. This monotheistic faith forms the core of Bedouin spirituality, guiding their daily actions, rituals, and social interactions. The belief in the unity of God encompasses all aspects of Bedouin life and underscores their reverence for the natural world.

In the vast expanse of the desert, the celestial bodies hold immense significance in Bedouin spiritual beliefs. The sun, moon, and stars are manifestations of divine power, serving as celestial guides that influence the rhythms of Bedouin life. The movements and positions of these celestial bodies shape important ceremonial and practical activities, such as determining prayer times, marking seasonal transitions, and guiding nomadic journeys through the desert. Bedouin spiritual leaders, known as 'shaykhs,' play a pivotal role in interpreting celestial omens and guiding the community in adhering to traditional beliefs and practices.

Moreover, the desert itself is viewed as a sacred realm, embodying both the trials and blessings of the Bedouin existence. The Bedouins' spiritual grit and resilience are honed within this austere landscape. The stark beauty of the desert, with its shifting sands and undulating dunes, serves as a poignant reflection of the cyclical nature of life, evoking contemplation and introspection. Within this setting, Bedouin spiritual practices often manifest in communal rituals, prayers, and invocations, expressing gratitude for the sustenance provided by the desert and seeking protection from its formidable challenges.

The ethos of hospitality is intricately interwoven with Bedouin spirituality, epitomizing the noble virtues of generosity, compassion, and solidarity. The practice of welcoming strangers reflects the belief in the interconnectedness of all beings and the divine mandate to provide mutual support in the face of adversity. This profound sense of hospitality extends beyond social conventions, resonating with the spiritual principle of benevolence and goodwill towards others. Such acts of kindness and empathy are considered sacred duties, fostering a sense of harmony and equilibrium within the community.

As the winds sweep across the desert and the stars illuminate the night sky, the spiritual tapestry of the Bedouin culture continues to thrive, preserving ancient traditions while embracing the evolving rhythms of modernity. The fusion of spiritual beliefs and practices with the enduring legacy of the desert creates a timeless testament to the resilience and wisdom of the Bedouin people, transcending the boundaries of time and space.

Adaptations to Desert Environment

The Bedouin people have long thrived in the harsh desert environment, demonstrating remarkable adaptations that allow them to survive and flourish amidst seemingly inhospitable conditions. One of the most striking adaptations is their profound knowledge of the desert terrain. Over generations, they have intimately understood the land, water sources, vegetation, and animal movements. This knowledge is passed down through oral tradition, ensuring the perpetuation of expertise in navigating and utilizing the desert environment.

Furthermore, the Bedouins have developed ingenious techniques for water conservation and storage. Utilizing underground cisterns, known as 'jub,' and constructing elaborate falaj irrigation systems, they have efficiently managed scarce water resources. Additionally, their mastery of camel husbandry has played a pivotal role in their ability to traverse vast distances across the desert, as these resilient animals provide transportation and a source of sustenance in the form of milk and meat.

In terms of shelter, the portable and versatile nature of the Bedouin tents reflects their adaptation to the transient lifestyle necessitated by their nomadic existence. These black goat-hair tents, known as 'beit al-sha'ar,' are well-ventilated, providing relief from the sweltering heat during the day and offering warmth during cold desert nights. Moreover, the strategic positioning of these encampments allows for protection against wind and sandstorms, illustrating the thoughtful adaptation of their living spaces to the challenging environmental conditions.

The Bedouins' dietary habits also reflect their adaptation to the desert environment. Their cuisine primarily consists of staple foods that can withstand the arid climate, such as dates, grains, and dairy products. Preserving food items using traditional methods, like dehydration or fermentation, enables them to mitigate the scarcity of fresh produce in the desert. Furthermore, their resourcefulness in utilizing every part of an animal following a hunt demonstrates their sustainable approach to procuring sustenance from the limited resources available in the desert.

Despite the rapid modernization sweeping across the region, the Bedouin people remain resilient, preserving their deep-rooted knowledge and adaptive skills that have sustained their existence for centuries. While contemporary influences are inevitable, the continued practice of these time-honored adaptations underscores the connection between the Bedouins and their ancestral desert environment.

Impact of Modernization on Bedouin Culture

The harsh demands of the desert environment have long shaped the rugged and timeless traditions of Bedouin culture. However, in recent decades, the rapid modernization and urbanization sweeping across the region have brought profound changes to the traditional way of life for the Bedouin people. Modernization's impact on Bedouin culture is a complex and multi-faceted phenomenon that touches upon every aspect of their daily existence.

One of the most notable effects of modernization on Bedouin culture pertains to the nomadic lifestyle. Historically, Bedouins were known for their mobile and adaptive way of life, following seasonal migration patterns and herding across vast expanses of desert terrain. However, with the increasing encroachment of urban development and national borders, many Bedouin tribes have been compelled to settle in more permanent dwellings, disrupting age-old migratory routes and altering the dynamics of tribal organization.

Furthermore, the traditional economic activities of herding and hunting have also undergone significant transformation due to modernization. With the expansion of commercial agriculture, increased government regulations, and changing land tenure systems, the availability of grazing lands and hunting grounds has dwindled, forcing many Bedouins to seek alternative means of livelihood and integrate into the mainstream economy.

Modernization has also impacted the spheres of cultural expression, such as poetry, music, and dance. While these art forms have deep roots in Bedouin heritage, the influence of global media and changing social dynamics has gradually eroded traditional folk arts as younger generations are increasingly drawn to modern entertainment and popular culture.

Moreover, the ongoing influence of modern education and access to advanced healthcare services has introduced new perspectives on individual aspirations, community dynamics, and gender roles within Bedouin society. This has led to a re-evaluation of traditional values and customs, sparking debates about retaining cultural identity in the face of external influences.

In conclusion, the impact of modernization on Bedouin culture is a story of continuous adaptation and transformation.

It is a narrative that encapsulates the challenges and opportunities faced by the Bedouin people as they navigate the complexities of preserving their heritage while embracing the benefits of progress and development.

Chapter 4

Desert Nomads: The Bedouin Culture

The Bedouin way of life is intricately woven with the harsh and unforgiving conditions of the desert. Their existence in the arid and barren landscapes has cultivated unique characteristics that embody resilience, adaptability, and resourcefulness. Originating from the vast deserts of the Arabian Peninsula, Bedouins have historically thrived in an environment where survival is a daily challenge. Their historical background is deeply rooted in the nomadic lifestyle, characterized by a constant quest for sustenance and shelter amidst the shifting sands. The resilience of the Bedouin people is evident in their ability to navigate through the inhospitable terrain, enduring extreme temperatures and scarce water sources. This unwavering determination to overcome the adversities of the desert has shaped their culture and traditions, fostering a sense of self-reliance and independence. The historical tapestry of the Bedouin heritage is interwoven with tales of bravery, perseverance, and a deep connection to the land they traverse. Their ancestral roots stretch back centuries, evolving alongside the challenges posed by nature, forging a legacy of resilience that permeates every aspect of their existence. The rich history of the Bedouin tribes is a testament to their ability to adapt to ever-changing circumstances while upholding their traditional values and customs. The intricate balance between tradition and adaptation is a hallmark of Bedouin life, as they deftly navigate the modern world without compromising the essence of their heritage. As we delve deeper into the facets of Bedouin culture, it becomes evident that their enduring spirit and adaptability stand as a beacon of inspiration, carrying forward a legacy crafted by centuries of resilience amidst the harsh desert landscape.

Origins and Historical Background

The origins of Bedouin culture are deeply rooted in the history of the Arabian Peninsula, dating back to ancient times. The term 'Bedouin' is derived from the Arabic word 'badawi', which refers to those living in the desert. The historical background of the Bedouin people is characterized by a nomadic way of life shaped by the harsh desert environment and a complex web of tribal relations. Scholars believe that the Bedouin culture evolved over thousands of years, influenced by various factors such as climatic conditions, geographical features, and interactions with neighboring civilizations.

Historical records indicate that the Bedouin tribes played a significant role in the trade routes of the ancient world, serving as guides and providers of essential goods to caravans traversing the desert. This network of trading relationships facilitated cultural exchanges and contributed to the rich tapestry of Bedouin heritage. The legacy of the Bedouin is intertwined with the region's history as they navigated through periods of prosperity, conflict, and transition.

The Bedouins' nomadic lifestyle enabled them to adapt to the challenges of the desert, relying on their deep understanding of seasonal changes, water sources, and survival skills. Their resilience and mobility allowed them to traverse vast distances in search of pastures for their herds and sustainable living conditions. This history of migration and settlement is embedded in the collective memory of the Bedouins, shaping their identity and traditions.

Furthermore, the historical background of the Bedouin is marked by a tradition of oral storytelling, preserving myths, legends, and historical accounts passed down through generations. This oral tradition has been a cornerstone of Bedouin culture, providing insights into their ancestral narratives and the interconnectedness of tribal lineages. The tales of heroism, adventure, and wisdom have woven a rich tapestry of folklore that continues to resonate in Bedouin communities today.

Delving into the origins of the Bedouin reveals an intricate and profound historical background, reflecting the endurance of a people bound by tradition, reverence for the land, and a deep connection to their ancestral past.

Social Structure and Tribal Organization

As the mesmerizing tapestry of Bedouin culture unfolds, one cannot overlook the intricate social structure and tribal organization that form the very fabric of their society. The nomadic nature of the Bedouin lifestyle has fostered a unique system where tribes are the cornerstone of social order. Within each tribe, a complex web of interconnected families and lineages dictates social standing, rights, and responsibilities. Authority is often decentralized, with chiefs or sheikhs typically holding leadership roles, maintaining an air of respect and wisdom within the community. This hierarchy is not rigid but somewhat fluid, adapting to the demands of the environment and the challenges encountered in the desert. Mutual support and cooperation define the intricate ties among members, creating a sense of unity and survival in the harsh desert terrain. While some tribes assert territorial boundaries, others embrace a more fluid approach, allowing intertribal interaction and exchange. Despite the seemingly isolated existence in the vast desert expanse, communication and alliances between tribes play a pivotal role in ensuring security, trade, and the preservation of cultural traditions. These communal dynamics exemplify the resilience and adaptability inherent in the Bedouin social structure, showcasing a rich tapestry of interconnectedness and interdependence.

Traditional Dress and Ornamentation

The traditional dress and ornamentation of the Bedouin people hold great significance, reflecting their cultural heritage and nomadic way of life. Distinctive attire and adornments serve practical purposes and symbolize identity, social status, and cultural pride within the Bedouin community. The attire of the Bedouins is designed to protect the harsh desert environment while allowing freedom of movement essential for their nomadic lifestyle. Men wear loose-fitting robes such as the thobe or dishdasha, often in neutral tones to camouflage against the desert landscape. These garments also feature intricate embroideries and embellishments that denote regional variations and clan affiliations. Likewise, women's attire includes flowing dresses adorned with elaborate patterns and vibrant colors, with veils and headscarves offering protection from the sun and sand. Natural fibers like wool, cotton, and silk reflect the Bedouins' resourcefulness and adaptation to their surroundings. Ornamentation is pivotal in Bedouin culture, with jewelry and accessories as wealth, status, and familial ties markers. Silver and gold jewelry, often adorned with semi-precious stones, are cherished possessions passed down through generations, signifying heritage and lineage. Each piece holds symbolic meaning, representing prosperity, fertility, protection, and spirituality. Intricately woven camel hair cords and tassels are incorporated into clothing and accessories, showcasing the craftsmanship and artistry of the Bedouin people. Furthermore, the intricate patterns and motifs adorning their traditional garments and jewelry convey narratives of their history, traditions, and beliefs. As the Bedouin way of life evolves in the modern era, a concerted effort exists to preserve and promote the significance of traditional dress and ornamentation. Artisans continue to uphold age-old techniques, ensuring the continuation of skilled crafts such as embroidery, weaving, and metalwork. Amidst contemporary influences, the Bedouin people endeavor to maintain the integrity and authenticity of their cultural attire and adornments, celebrating their rich heritage amidst societal change and globalization challenges.

Nomadic Lifestyle and Seasonal Movements

The nomadic lifestyle of the Bedouin people is intricately linked to their seasonal movements across the desert terrain. These movements are carefully planned and strategically carried out to ensure the community's and livestock's well-being. The cyclical nature of their migrations is driven by the need to find suitable grazing pastures and water sources for their herds and escape harsh environmental conditions. Each phase of the nomadic journey holds significance in shaping the cultural identity and resilience of the Bedouin tribes.

With the arrival of spring, the Bedouin nomads embark on a significant rite of passage, known as 'Razfa,' marking the start of their seasonal migration. This period sees the community packing their tents, belongings, and essential supplies and setting off towards the cooler highlands where fresh vegetation and water can be found. The rhythmic trekking of the nomadic caravans across the vast deserts becomes a testament to the strength and adaptability of the Bedouin culture.

As summer approaches, the Bedouin tribes gradually move to higher ground for cooler temperatures and greener pastures. Their extensive knowledge of the land allows them to navigate through rugged terrains and scorching heat with unparalleled precision. During this season, the nomads establish temporary settlements, creating a harmonious coexistence with nature while tending to their flocks. The bond between the Bedouins and their environment is evident in their sustainable practices, ensuring minimal impact on the delicate ecosystem.

The transition to autumn heralds the return journey as the Bedouin tribes return to the lower plains, guided by the changing landscapes and weather patterns. Their resilience and astute understanding of natural indicators enable them to anticipate potential challenges and take pre-emptive measures. The nomadic lifestyle instills a deep sense of unity and collaboration within the community as they face the trials of their arduous yet purposeful journey together.

In winter, the Bedouin nomads seek out sheltered valleys and fertile plains to rest and replenish their resources before the cycle begins anew. This season of respite provides an opportunity for reflection and social bonding as stories are shared around campfires, traditions are upheld, and skills are handed down through generations. Within this hushed tranquility, the essence of the Bedouin spirit resonates, echoing the timeless wisdom of their ancestors amidst the vast expanse of the desert.

Economic Activities: Herding and Hunting

The economic activities of herding and hunting have been integral to the traditional Bedouin way of life, providing sustenance, livelihoods, and a deeper connection to the natural environment. Herding, primarily of camels, goats, and sheep, has been a central focus of the Bedouin economy, allowing them to thrive in the harsh desert landscapes. The nomadic lifestyle necessitated a deep understanding of animal husbandry and the ability to navigate vast stretches of arid terrain in search of grazing grounds. This intimate knowledge of the land and its resources has been passed down through generations, shaping the cultural identity of the Bedouin people. Furthermore, the importance of herding extends beyond the practical aspects of food and resource acquisition; it is intricately linked to social customs and traditions, forming the foundation of communal values and kinship ties among the tribes. In addition to herding, hunting played a complementary role in sustaining the Bedouin communities. While the scarcity of wildlife in the desert presented challenges, skilled hunters were revered for their prowess and resourcefulness. Hunting expeditions provided meat and hides and honed the survival skills essential for thriving in the rugged desert environment. The interplay between herding and hunting encapsulates the resilience and adaptability of the Bedouin people, illustrating how they have harmonized with the natural world and utilized its offerings for their sustenance. Despite the evolution of modernization and external influences, the enduring significance of herding and hunting remains a testament to Bedouin culture's enduring legacy.

Cultural Traditions: Poetry, Music, and Dance

Enriched by their nomadic lifestyle, the Bedouin culture is a tapestry woven with the threads of poetry, music, and dance. These expressive traditions serve as profound chronicles of the Bedouin way of life, symbolizing their identity and preserving their history across generations. Primarily an oral culture, poetry is revered among the Bedouins, embodying their emotions, values, and collective memory. The melodic rhythm of traditional verse echoes across the desert, carrying tales of love, courage, and tribal heritage. This poetic tradition entertains and serves as a platform for discussing social issues, conveying wisdom, and commemorating significant events. Furthermore, music is central in Bedouin communal gatherings, enhancing celebratory occasions and daily routines. The haunting melodies of traditional instruments such as the rabab and the mir created an unmistakable ambiance, fostering solidarity and shared experiences among the community. Accompanying the musical rhythms, traditional dances exemplify the Bedouin's vibrant cultural spirit and deep sense of unity. These spirited movements, often inspired by elements of nature and wildlife, convey narratives of bravery, endurance, and harmony with the environment. Whether in joyful festivities or moments of hardship, these dance forms bind the Bedouin together, forging strong bonds and reinforcing their collective consciousness. Overall, the cultural traditions of poetry, music, and dance entertain and uplift the spirit and serve as vital vessels for transmitting the essence of the Bedouin culture, fostering continuity, and strengthening their communal identity.

Spiritual Beliefs and Practices

The spiritual beliefs and practices of the Bedouin culture are deeply rooted in their nomadic way of life, reflecting a profound connection to the desert environment and an intricate understanding of natural elements. Central to the Bedouins' spiritual worldview is monotheism, with a strong emphasis on the worship of a single, all-powerful deity. This monotheistic faith forms the core of Bedouin spirituality, guiding their daily actions, rituals, and social interactions. The belief in the unity of God encompasses all aspects of Bedouin life and underscores their reverence for the natural world.

In the vast expanse of the desert, the celestial bodies hold immense significance in Bedouin spiritual beliefs. The sun, moon, and stars are manifestations of divine power, serving as celestial guides that influence the rhythms of Bedouin life. The movements and positions of these celestial bodies shape important ceremonial and practical activities, such as determining prayer times, marking seasonal transitions, and guiding nomadic journeys through the desert. Bedouin spiritual leaders, known as 'shaykhs,' play a pivotal role in interpreting celestial omens and guiding the community in adhering to traditional beliefs and practices.

Moreover, the desert itself is viewed as a sacred realm, embodying both the trials and blessings of the Bedouin existence. The Bedouins' spiritual grit and resilience are honed within this austere landscape. The stark beauty of the desert, with its shifting sands and undulating dunes, serves as a poignant reflection of the cyclical nature of life, evoking contemplation and introspection. Within this setting, Bedouin spiritual practices often manifest in communal rituals, prayers, and invocations, expressing gratitude for the sustenance provided by the desert and seeking protection from its formidable challenges.

The ethos of hospitality is intricately interwoven with Bedouin spirituality, epitomizing the noble virtues of generosity, compassion, and solidarity. The practice of welcoming strangers reflects the belief in the interconnectedness of all beings and the divine mandate to provide mutual support in the face of adversity. This profound sense of hospitality extends beyond social conventions, resonating with the spiritual principle of benevolence and goodwill towards others. Such acts of kindness and empathy are considered sacred duties, fostering a sense of harmony and equilibrium within the community.

As the winds sweep across the desert and the stars illuminate the night sky, the spiritual tapestry of the Bedouin culture continues to thrive, preserving ancient traditions while embracing the evolving rhythms of modernity. The fusion of spiritual beliefs and practices with the enduring legacy of the desert creates a timeless testament to the resilience and wisdom of the Bedouin people, transcending the boundaries of time and space.

Adaptations to Desert Environment

The Bedouin people have long thrived in the harsh desert environment, demonstrating remarkable adaptations that allow them to survive and flourish amidst seemingly inhospitable conditions. One of the most striking adaptations is their profound knowledge of the desert terrain. Over generations, they have intimately understood the land, water sources, vegetation, and animal movements. This knowledge is passed down through oral tradition, ensuring the perpetuation of expertise in navigating and utilizing the desert environment.

Furthermore, the Bedouins have developed ingenious techniques for water conservation and storage. Utilizing underground cisterns, known as 'jub,' and constructing elaborate falaj irrigation systems, they have efficiently managed scarce water resources. Additionally, their mastery of camel husbandry has played a pivotal role in their ability to traverse vast distances across the desert, as these resilient animals provide transportation and a source of sustenance in the form of milk and meat.

In terms of shelter, the portable and versatile nature of the Bedouin tents reflects their adaptation to the transient lifestyle necessitated by their nomadic existence. These black goat-hair tents, known as 'beit al-sha'ar,' are well-ventilated, providing relief from the sweltering heat during the day and offering warmth during cold desert nights. Moreover, the strategic positioning of these encampments allows for protection against wind and sandstorms, illustrating the thoughtful adaptation of their living spaces to the challenging environmental conditions.

The Bedouins' dietary habits also reflect their adaptation to the desert environment. Their cuisine primarily consists of staple foods that can withstand the arid climate, such as dates, grains, and dairy products. Preserving food items using traditional methods, like dehydration or fermentation, enables them to mitigate the scarcity of fresh produce in the desert. Furthermore, their resourcefulness in utilizing every part of an animal following a hunt demonstrates their sustainable approach to procuring sustenance from the limited resources available in the desert.

Despite the rapid modernization sweeping across the region, the Bedouin people remain resilient, preserving their deep-rooted knowledge and adaptive skills that have sustained their existence for centuries. While contemporary influences are inevitable, the continued practice of these time-honored adaptations underscores the connection between the Bedouins and their ancestral desert environment.

Impact of Modernization on Bedouin Culture

The harsh demands of the desert environment have long shaped the rugged and timeless traditions of Bedouin culture. However, in recent decades, the rapid modernization and urbanization sweeping across the region have brought profound changes to the traditional way of life for the Bedouin people. Modernization's impact on Bedouin culture is a complex and multi-faceted phenomenon that touches upon every aspect of their daily existence.

One of the most notable effects of modernization on Bedouin culture pertains to the nomadic lifestyle. Historically, Bedouins were known for their mobile and adaptive way of life, following seasonal migration patterns and herding across vast expanses of desert terrain. However, with the increasing encroachment of urban development and national borders, many Bedouin tribes have been compelled to settle in more permanent dwellings, disrupting age-old migratory routes and altering the dynamics of tribal organization.

Furthermore, the traditional economic activities of herding and hunting have also undergone significant transformation due to modernization. With the expansion of commercial agriculture, increased government regulations, and changing land tenure systems, the availability of grazing lands and hunting grounds has dwindled, forcing many Bedouins to seek alternative means of livelihood and integrate into the mainstream economy.

Modernization has also impacted the spheres of cultural expression, such as poetry, music, and dance. While these art forms have deep roots in Bedouin heritage, the influence of global media and changing social dynamics has gradually eroded traditional folk arts as younger generations are increasingly drawn to modern entertainment and popular culture.

Moreover, the ongoing influence of modern education and access to advanced healthcare services has introduced new perspectives on individual aspirations, community dynamics, and gender roles within Bedouin society. This has led to a re-evaluation of traditional values and customs, sparking debates about retaining cultural identity in the face of external influences.

In conclusion, the impact of modernization on Bedouin culture is a story of continuous adaptation and transformation. It is a narrative that encapsulates the challenges and opportunities faced by the Bedouin people as they navigate the complexities of preserving their heritage while embracing the benefits of progress and development.

Chapter 5

Pearls of The Past: The Ancient Pearling Industry

The history of pearl diving in the Gulf region dates back thousands of years, intertwining with the cultural and economic tapestry of societies along these ancient shores. The allure of pearls has captivated civilizations since time immemorial, serving as symbols of wealth, status, and beauty. Across the Gulf, from the coasts of Bahrain and Qatar to the shores of the United Arab Emirates and Kuwait, pearl diving emerged as a cornerstone of maritime trade and local livelihoods. The pearling industry contributed to the region's economic prosperity and played a pivotal role in shaping the social and cultural dynamics of Gulf communities. Furthermore, pearl diving fostered intricate knowledge of marine environments, navigation techniques, and sustainable resource management, showcasing the profound expertise of the seafaring peoples of the Gulf.

Pearling was not merely a profession; it embodied a way of life, forging deep-rooted connections between communities and the sea. The seasonal rhythms of pearl diving dictated the ebb and flow of coastal settlements, as entire populations would mobilize for the annual expeditions to harvest the treasures of the ocean depths. The shared experiences of venturing into the unknown waters, facing the perils of the deep, and reaping the rewards of nature's bounty instilled a sense of camaraderie and unity among the divers and their families, reflecting the collective resilience and determination intrinsic to maritime cultures across the Gulf. The association of pearl diving with tradition and heritage further enriched its significance, as rituals, songs, and stories linked successive generations to the timeless legacy of this venerated maritime pursuit.

As the pearl diving industry flourished, it became integral to the Gulf's identity, fostering intercultural exchange and global trade networks. The priceless gems harvested from the depths of the Gulf found their way to distant markets, transcending geographical boundaries and enriching diverse societies with their natural splendor. Furthermore, the prestige of Gulf pearls elevated the region to prominence internationally, solidifying its reputation as a hub of luxury and opulence. The enduring legacy of pearling is a testament to the ingenuity, resilience, and enduring spirit of the Gulf's seafaring communities, echoing through the annals of history and resonating with timeless allure.

The Origins of Pearl Diving

Pearl diving dates back to ancient times and is significant in maritime history. The practice originated from pursuing natural treasures hidden beneath the ocean's depths. It is believed to have taken root in various coastal communities worldwide, including those nestled along the shores of the Persian Gulf.

The early pearl divers were driven by the allure of uncovering these precious gems, whose lustrous beauty fascinated civilizations.

Historical accounts reveal that pearl diving was not merely a means of livelihood; it was deeply intertwined with cultural and social traditions. For many ancient societies, pearls held immense symbolic value and were associated with wealth, purity, and spiritual significance. The trade and commerce of pearls contributed to the prosperity of these coastal settlements, often catalyzing economic growth and cultural exchange.

Ancient manuscripts and folklore from the region shed light on the legendary tales of pearl diving, with stories passed down through generations. These narratives depict the bravery and resilience of the divers as they ventured into the ocean's depths in search of these prized jewels. The practice of pearl diving became an essential part of the cultural identity of the coastal communities, shaping their way of life and influencing their artistic expressions, customs, and belief systems.

Moreover, the art of pearl diving mirrored the intimate relationship between humankind and the ocean. It required a profound understanding of tides, currents, and marine ecosystems, as well as specialized techniques and tools for navigating the underwater terrain. The ancient divers honed their skills over generations, developing unique methods for harvesting pearls while fostering a deep respect for the marine environment.

As societies evolved, pearl diving continued to thrive, becoming a cornerstone of the regional economy and a symbol of maritime heritage. Its legacy endures through the centuries, leaving an indelible mark on the cultural tapestry of the Gulf region and beyond.

Techniques and Tools: The Craft of Pearl Diving

Pearl diving, an ancient practice that has shaped the cultural and economic landscape of the Gulf region, requires a mastery of specialized techniques and unique tools. The craft of pearl diving is a testament to the tenacity and skill of the divers who ventured into the depths in search of these precious gems. The process of pearl diving begins with preparing the divers and their equipment. Divers undergo rigorous training to build stamina and breath-holding capabilities, which are essential for extended dives. In addition to physical training, divers receive instruction on recognizing oyster beds and understanding underwater currents. The traditional tools used in pearl diving are rooted in centuries-old practices, reflecting the divers' ingenuity and deep connection to the sea. The most iconic tool is the 'nakhidha,' a weighted stone tied to a rope that helps divers descend rapidly to the oyster beds. Once at the desired depth, divers employ a 'fawakh' – a flat, oval-shaped basket woven from palm fronds – to collect oysters. These baskets are carefully designed to allow water to drain out while retaining the oysters. The baskets are then hoisted to the surface using ropes attached to the diving vessel. The process of retrieving the oysters involves finesse and precision, as excessive force can damage the delicate shells and compromise the pearls within. After the oysters are brought up, the harvest is painstakingly sorted, with each specimen examined for the presence of a pearl. This meticulous approach highlights the significance of quality and the craftsmanship of pearl diving. Furthermore, the communal aspect of pearling is evident as divers work together in synchronized routines, fostering a sense of unity and shared purpose. The divers return to the surface as the sun sets on the horizon, bringing the fruits of their labor. The craft of pearl diving is not merely a source of livelihood; it is a cultural tradition that binds communities and honors the legacy of the sea. The intricacies of the techniques and tools utilized in pearl diving underscore the enduring heritage and expertise of those who have mastered this timeless art form.

Socio-Economic Impact of Pearling

Pearling has had a profound socio-economic impact on the Gulf region, shaping communities and economies for centuries. The flourishing pearling industry was pivotal in sustaining livelihoods, fostering trade relations, and influencing cultural practices. As pearl diving evolved into a sophisticated craft, its economic significance became increasingly pronounced, transforming the social fabric of coastal settlements and contributing to the expansion of commercial networks—the allure of pearls as a commodity fostered complex market dynamics, driving local and international demand. The influx of wealth from pearl trading engendered social stratification, creating a class of prosperous merchants whose affluence left an indelible mark on the region's history. The economic prosperity generated by pearling reverberated through various spheres of life, from the development of infrastructure and the patronage of arts and craftsmanship to the establishment of vibrant marketplaces that attracted traders and artisans from diverse cultures. Additionally, the reliance on pearling instilled a sense of communal interdependence, as families and communities were intricately linked to the success of each dive. Moreover, the economic cycles of pearling dictated seasonal rhythms, rendering it a cornerstone of the region's cultural tapestry. However, the decline of natural pearl reserves and the advent of cultured pearls ushered in a new era, reshaping the socio-economic landscape. This transformation precipitated shifts in traditional livelihoods and trade patterns, catalyzing the emergence of alternative industries. While the legacy of pearling endures in contemporary Gulf societies, its socio-economic impact serves as a poignant testament to the enduring influence of this ancient industry.

Major Pearling Sites in the Gulf

The Gulf region has a rich history of pearl diving, with numerous sites serving as renowned hubs for this ancient industry. One of the most prominent sites is the island of Bahrain, which has been celebrated for its pearling heritage for centuries. The pristine waters surrounding Bahrain provided ideal conditions for oysters to produce high-quality pearls, attracting divers and traders from far and wide. Another significant pearling site is the coast of Qatar, where the art of pearl diving was deeply intertwined with the local culture and economy. Qatar's strategic location along the Gulf made it a vital center for pearl trading, contributing to the region's prosperity. Additionally, the shores of the United Arab Emirates, particularly in areas such as Ras Al Khaimah and Abu Dhabi, were esteemed for their pearl-rich waters, drawing skilled divers and merchants seeking these precious gems. The historical significance of these sites extends beyond their economic impact, as they became focal points of cultural exchange and interaction, weaving together the diverse communities that engaged in the pearling trade. The allure of these major pearling sites in the Gulf emanates from their natural wealth and the stories of resilience, craftsmanship, and exploration that continue to resonate through the ages. From the glimmering coastlines of Bahrain to the captivating waters off the shores of the UAE and Qatar, these sites embody the enduring legacy of pearl diving and stand as testaments to the enduring human quest for beauty and prosperity within the embrace of the Gulf's maritime landscape.

Seasonal Rhythms and Pearl Diving

In the ancient pearling industry, the seasonal rhythms played a significant role in determining the success and safety of pearl diving expeditions. The journey into the depths of the Gulf waters was intricately linked with the natural cycles that governed the marine environment. As the seasons shifted, so did the conditions for pearl diving, shaping the traditions and practices of this revered profession.

The onset of the diving season marked a time of anticipation and preparation for the diving communities along the Gulf coasts. As the temperature and water conditions became more favorable, divers readied themselves to embark on their expeditions in search of the elusive treasures beneath the waves. The timing of these expeditions was crucial, often aligning with the calmer seas and clearer waters that typified the seasonal transitions.

Furthermore, the seasonal migration patterns of marine life also influenced pearl diving activities. Divers had to be attuned to the movements of various species, as they often indicated the presence of oysters and, ultimately, pearls. Understanding the migratory behaviors of marine creatures allowed divers to plan their expeditions strategically, maximizing their chances of successful harvests.

Beyond the natural elements, the seasonal rhythms also brought forth a set of rituals and customs within the pearl diving communities. Traditions associated with the commencement and conclusion of the diving season reflected the deep-rooted connection between human endeavors and the ebb and flow of nature. From ceremonial blessings to communal feasts, each phase of the seasonal cycle was marked by traditions celebrating the enduring spirit of pearl diving.

The interplay between seasonal rhythms and pearl diving extended beyond the practical aspects, permeating deep into the cultural fabric of the Gulf societies. Legends and folklore were intricately woven around seasonal transitions, attributing symbolic meanings to the changing tides and currents. Songs and stories passed down through generations encapsulated the reverence for the seasonal rhythms and their profound significance for the pearl diving communities.

However, the seasonal rhythms also brought inherent risks and challenges, as the unpredictable forces of nature could swiftly transform the tranquil waters into tempestuous torrents. Divers navigated the fine line between seizing the opportune moments and safeguarding themselves against the perils lurking in the changing seasons. This delicate balance between risk and reward underscored the resilience and expertise of the pearl diving communities.

The seasonal rhythms shaped the practical strategies of pearl diving and fostered a profound ethos of respect and harmony with the natural world. The art of pearl diving unfolded within the timeless cadence of the seasons, embodying a harmonious blend of human ingenuity, tradition, and the elemental forces that governed the Gulf waters.

Cultural Significance of Pearls

Pearls hold a deep cultural significance in many societies across the globe, and this is particularly evident in the Gulf region. The allure of pearls has transcended time, symbolizing purity, beauty, and sophistication. In many ancient cultures, including those around the Gulf, pearls were revered as precious treasures, often associated with royalty, power, and divinity.

The pearls in adornments and regal attire signified wealth, status, and elegance, cementing their position as prized possessions. The artistry involved in crafting jewelry and ornaments with pearls further elevated their value, fostering a tradition of craftsmanship and innovation. Beyond their material worth, pearls carried symbolic weight, representing love, fertility, and protection in various cultural narratives within Gulf communities. Furthermore, pearls featured prominently in religious and spiritual practices, serving as offerings and talismans believed to bring good fortune and ward off negative energies. This rich tapestry of beliefs and customs underscored the integral role of pearls in the daily lives and traditions of Gulf inhabitants. Moreover, the exchange of pearls across ancient trade routes facilitated the interweaving of diverse cultural influences, cultivating an environment of cross-cultural exchange and mutual enrichment. The cultural significance of pearls has endured through the ages, permeating art, literature, and folklore, and continues to resonate in the heritage and ethos of the Gulf. Even as the pearling industry has evolved, the cultural reverence for pearls remains a memorable part of the region's identity, representing a timeless legacy reverberating through its customs and contemporary expressions.

Decline of the Pearling Industry

The decline of the pearling industry marked a significant turning point in the economic and cultural landscape of the Gulf region. As the demand for pearls began to wane, largely due to the emergence of cultured pearls and shifting consumer preferences, the traditional art of pearl diving faced a rapid decline. This decline had profound implications for the economy and the social fabric of the communities that had long relied on pearl diving as a primary source of livelihood.

The shift from natural to cultured pearls, which began in the early 20th century, led to a sharp decline in the value and market demand for natural pearls. This decline was exacerbated by global economic trends, changing fashion tastes, and geopolitical shifts, all of which contributed to the downturn of the pearling industry. The economic repercussions were felt deeply across the Gulf region, with many pearl diving communities facing hardship and economic instability. The dwindling economic prospects led to significant changes in traditional ways of life, as many families sought alternative sources of income and employment. The once vibrant and bustling pearling hubs began to witness a gradual exodus of skilled divers and craftsmen, further contributing to the industry's decline. The decline of the pearling industry also profoundly impacted the Gulf communities' cultural identity. As pearling had been intricately woven into these societies' social fabric and heritage for centuries, the fading of this ancient tradition led to a sense of loss and nostalgia. Many efforts were made to preserve the memory of the pearling era through museums, cultural initiatives, and oral history projects, reflecting the pearling heritage's deep emotional and cultural significance. Despite the decline, the legacy of pearl diving continues to be cherished and celebrated, serving as a poignant reminder of the resilience and adaptability of the Gulf communities in the face of economic and cultural challenges.

Pearling and Global Commerce

The history of the pearling industry in the Gulf region has had a profound impact on global commerce. From ancient times, the pearls harvested from the pristine waters of the Arabian Gulf were highly sought after by traders from distant lands. The allure of the lustrous Gulf pearls captivated the hearts and minds of merchants, creating a flourishing network of trade that stretched across continents and seas.

As the pearl diving industry thrived, the Gulf region became a central hub for international transactions, attracting merchants from as far as India, China, and Europe. The demand for Gulf pearls transcended cultural and geographical boundaries, shaping the dynamics of global commerce during that era. The exquisite pearls served as a currency of prestige often exchanged for spices, textiles, and other exotic commodities. This trade enriched the economies of the Gulf civilizations and fostered cultural exchanges and diplomatic relations among nations.

Furthermore, the pearls sourced from the Gulf played a significant role in developing maritime trade routes, with merchant ships navigating treacherous waters to transport these valuable treasures to distant markets. The economic significance of the pearling industry extended beyond regional borders, influencing the global flow of goods and contributing to the interconnectedness of ancient trade networks. The legacy of this trade reverberates through the annals of history, illustrating the enduring impact of the Arabian Gulf on the tapestry of global commerce.

The influence of pearls from the Gulf reverberated through the ages, leaving an indelible mark on the evolution of global commerce. Gulf pearls' cultural and historical significance continues to resonate in the realm of luxury trade and artisanal craftsmanship. Their coveted reputation persists, inspiring contemporary designers and merchants to uphold the legacy of these iridescent jewels within the modern marketplace.

In essence, the pearling industry in the Gulf region serves as a testament to the enduring connection between local enterprises and the wider global economy. Its historical implications span centuries, showcasing the pivotal role played by the Gulf in shaping the diverse tapestry of global commerce.

The allure of Gulf pearls continues to captivate connoisseurs and collectors worldwide, perpetuating the timeless legacy of pearling and global commerce.

Modern Revival and Cultural Legacy

In recent decades, the ancient tradition of pearl diving has experienced a remarkable resurgence in the Gulf region. This modern revival of the pearling industry reflects a growing appreciation for pearls' cultural legacy and historical significance in the Gulf's heritage. With advancements in technology and sustainable practices, the pearl industry has transformed, reclaiming its position as a symbol of luxury and prestige in the global market. The reemergence of pearl farming has revitalized the economy and rekindled a sense of pride and connection to tradition among the communities along the coast. Through strategic partnerships and innovative methods, the Gulf has once again established itself as a prominent player in the world's pearl market, offering high-quality cultured pearls to an international clientele. Embracing traditional knowledge and contemporary techniques, the modern pearling industry has struck a delicate balance between honoring centuries-old customs and adapting to the demands of a rapidly changing world. This harmonious blend has led to economic prosperity and contributed to the preservation of cultural heritage. The craft of pearl diving, once endangered by the rise of synthetic pearls and shifting societal values, has now become a celebrated art form that encapsulates the resilience and adaptability of the region's people. The pearling industry's revival has brought about economic gains and sparked a renaissance of cultural expression and identity. Through public initiatives and private investments, the Gulf has embraced its rich heritage, establishing museums, cultural centers, and educational programs dedicated to promoting the legacy of pearling. These efforts have served to foster a deeper understanding of the historical significance of pearls and their intrinsic connection to the identity of the Gulf. Furthermore, the modern revival of pearling has facilitated cross-cultural exchanges and collaborations, bridging the past with the present and creating new avenues for artistic and commercial partnerships. As the pearl industry continues to thrive in the 21st century, it stands as a testament to the enduring impact of ancient traditions and the ability of communities to evolve while preserving their rich cultural tapestry.

Chapter 6

Nets and Knots: Fishing Traditions Across the Gulf

For centuries, fishing has been an integral part of the Gulf communities' daily lives and cultural identity. The historical integration of fishing into these societies stems from a deep-rooted reliance on the bountiful marine resources that sustained their livelihoods and enriched their traditions. The ancient inhabitants of the Gulf region recognized the significance of the sea as a consistent source of sustenance, shaping their belief systems, customs, and social structures around the rhythms of the tides and the abundance of marine life. The connection between the people and the sea was not solely utilitarian; it was also deeply spiritual, as rituals and ceremonies often accompanied fishing to honor the ocean's bounties. The exchange of fishing knowledge and techniques was passed down through generations, serving as a vital link between past and present, reinforcing the interconnectedness of Gulf communities with the sea. As time progressed, these traditions evolved and adapted to changing environmental conditions and societal needs, demonstrating a resilience that continues to characterize Gulf fishing traditions. The harmony between the people and the sea has left an indelible imprint on the cultural fabric of the Gulf, fostering a profound appreciation for the fishing heritage and its enduring impact on the region's identity.

Historical Overview of Fishing in the Gulf

Fishing has been integral to the Gulf region's history, shaping its cultural and economic landscape for centuries. The ancient inhabitants of the Gulf coastline relied on fishing as a primary food source and livelihood, with evidence of fishing practices dating back thousands of years. Early civilizations such as the Sumerians, Phoenicians, and Persians established thriving fishing communities along the Gulf's shores, utilizing sophisticated techniques to harvest the rich marine resources. These ancient fishing traditions laid the foundation for developing the Gulf's maritime culture and trade networks, shaping the region's identity and economic prosperity. Over time, fishing evolved from a subsistence activity into a sophisticated industry, driving the growth of coastal settlements and influencing the cultural heritage of the Gulf. The historical record reveals a tapestry of fishing practices, from traditional handline and net fishing to the construction of intricate fish traps and weirs that reflected the ingenuity of the Gulf's early fishermen. Furthermore, the interplay between fishing and trade led to the exchange of knowledge and technologies across the Gulf, fostering a dynamic network of maritime activities that transcended geographical boundaries. As seafaring civilizations interacted and traded with one another, fishing became intertwined with the broader cultural and commercial dynamics of the Gulf, leaving a lasting imprint on the region's historical narrative. The arrival of foreign influences, such as Portuguese and British colonial powers, introduced new fishing methods and technologies to the Gulf, reshaping the traditional practices while contributing to the diversification of the Gulf's fishing industry. Despite these transformative shifts, many of the foundational principles and techniques of Gulf fishing have endured through the ages, reflecting the resilience and adaptability of the region's fishing traditions. Today, the historical legacy of fishing in the Gulf continues to resonate through contemporary practices, serving as a testament to the enduring significance of this ancient maritime pursuit.

Types of Fish and Seasonal Patterns

The Gulf region is home to a diverse array of marine species, each playing a crucial role in the traditional fishing practices that have been upheld for centuries. The seasonal patterns and migration behaviors of these fish have been deeply intertwined with the lives of the fishermen who rely on them for sustenance and livelihood. Throughout the year, the waters of the Gulf witness the rhythmic ebb and flow of various fish species, each following their unique patterns dictated by environmental factors such as water temperatures, currents, and food availability.

During the cooler winter months, the Gulf experiences a surge in species populations like groupers, snappers, and emperor fish. These cold-loving species thrive in the nutrient-rich waters, attracting fishermen to strategic locations where they congregate. As spring arrives, an abundance of pelagic fish such as mackerel, tuna, and sardines can be found migrating through the Gulf waters, presenting opportunities for fishermen to cast their nets with great anticipation.

The scorching heat of summer heralds the arrival of species like kingfish, barracuda, and trevally, seeking refuge in the slightly cooler depths of the Gulf. This shift in the fish population prompts the fishermen to adapt their techniques and strategies, attuning themselves to the changing ecosystem. As the searing summer transitions into milder autumn, the Gulf witnesses the return of the earlier cold-water species, completing the cyclical nature of the regional fishery.

Understanding these seasonal patterns is fundamental to the sustainability of Gulf fishing traditions. It allows the fishermen to plan their operations in harmony with the natural rhythms of the marine ecosystem, ensuring that the delicate balance between human activity and the biodiversity of the Gulf remains preserved. Furthermore, this knowledge has been passed down through generations, becoming an integral part of the cultural heritage associated with the fishing communities of the Gulf region.

From this deep understanding of the ocean's seasonal dance, the art of fishing in the Gulf emerges. It encapsulates a profound respect for nature and an intricate comprehension of the interconnectedness between seasonal patterns and marine life's behavior.

Traditional Fishing Techniques and Tools

Fishing in the Gulf has been a cornerstone of the region's culture and economy for centuries, shaped by its unique geographical features, climate, and rich marine biodiversity. Traditional fishing techniques and tools have evolved, reflecting the resourcefulness and ingenuity of the communities that have relied on the sea for sustenance and livelihood.

One of the most prominent traditional fishing techniques in the Gulf is hand-thrown nets. Crafted with meticulous precision, these nets are designed to efficiently capture fish while minimizing impact on the surrounding marine ecosystem. Fishermen skillfully maneuver these nets to encircle schools of fish, demonstrating an intimate understanding of the underwater terrain and the behavior of different species.

In addition to hand-thrown nets, another prevalent method is using fish traps, ingeniously constructed from locally sourced materials such as palm fronds and bamboo. These traps are strategically placed in areas where fish congregate, capitalizing on tidal movements and natural pathways to optimize the catch. The craftsmanship in constructing these traps is a testament to the knowledge passed down through generations, combining practicality with sustainable fishing practices.

Furthermore, traditional fishing expeditions often involve dhows, which are traditional sailing vessels integral to maritime activities in the Gulf. Dhows facilitate access to prime fishing grounds and provide a platform for deploying nets and traps with precision. The art of navigating and maintaining these vessels requires expertise and a deep connection to the sea, marking the significance of maritime traditions in the fabric of Gulf societies.

Apart from the techniques themselves, the tools utilized in traditional Gulf fishing are emblematic of the fishermen's resourcefulness. Each tool serves a distinct purpose, from handmade hooks and lines to intricately carved harpoons, and embodies the fusion of functionality and cultural craftsmanship. The utilization of natural resources reflects a harmonious relationship with the environment, showcasing a sustainable approach to fishing that has sustained coastal communities for millennia.

As modernization and technological advancements continue to shape the fishing industry, there is a growing appreciation for the enduring wisdom of these traditional techniques and tools. They stand as a testament to the resilience and adaptability of Gulf fishermen, embodying a legacy that transcends mere subsistence to encompass a profound respect for the sea and its bountiful offerings.

The Art of Knot Tying

Knot tying is an essential skill and art form passed down through generations in the Gulf fishing traditions. The adeptness in tying various knots is a hallmark of expertise for fishermen, reflecting their practical knowledge and mastery of their craft. Each knot serves a specific purpose, whether to secure nets, fasten lines, or connect different parts of the fishing gear. These intricate knots are a testament to the ingenuity and resourcefulness of the Gulf fishermen, who have honed their skills to navigate the challenging conditions of the sea. Knot tying is not just about functionality; it embodies a deep understanding of the maritime environment and the need for reliability and durability in the face of nature's unpredictability.

A rich repertoire of knots is used in Gulf fishing, each with its unique characteristics and applications. From the simple yet sturdy square knot to the elaborate and specialized bowline, each knot is designed to withstand the rigors of the marine environment and fulfill its role with utmost precision. The knot-tying process is imbued with reverence and tradition, as experienced fishermen take pride in teaching and passing these techniques to the younger generation. It is a way of preserving the legacy of seafaring culture and ensuring that the artistry of knot-tying endures through time. Beyond its practical utility, the art of knot tying also holds symbolic significance, representing the interconnectedness of the fishing community and the harmonious relationship between man and the sea.

The meticulous and deliberate manner in which these knots are tied reflects the values of patience, perseverance, and attention to detail deeply ingrained in the fabric of Gulf fishing traditions. This traditional knowledge is upheld with great respect, as it forms an integral part of the cultural identity and heritage of the Gulf region. Furthermore, the aesthetic beauty of these knots, with their intertwining patterns and elegant symmetry, is a testament to the artistic sensibilities of the fishermen, who infuse creativity and finesse into their utilitarian craftsmanship. It manifests the marriage between function and form, where practicality meets artistry in maritime livelihoods.

In essence, knot tying encompasses more than just securing ropes; it encapsulates the wisdom, resilience, and cultural significance woven into the fabric of Gulf fishing traditions. As the tradition continues to thrive and adapt amidst modernization, the enduring relevance of knot tying as a symbol of heritage and expertise is a poignant reminder of the timeless customs and skills that bind the Gulf's fishing communities together.

Social and Economic Impact of Fishing

Fishing has played a pivotal role in shaping Gulf communities' social and economic dynamics for centuries. The reliance on the bounties of the sea has not only sustained livelihoods but has also fostered a deep sense of camaraderie and interdependence among the fishing communities along the Gulf Coast.

From a social perspective, fishing has been more than just an occupation; it has been a way of life deeply ingrained in these coastal societies' cultural fabric. It has provided a means for communities to bond over shared experiences and challenges, creating a strong sense of unity and mutual support. The communal nature of fishing activities has given rise to traditions and rituals that are passed down through generations, further strengthening the social cohesion within these communities.

Furthermore, the economic impact of fishing extends beyond sustenance to encompass trade and commerce. The abundance of marine resources has historically fueled trade networks and economic exchange, allowing fishing communities to engage in barter and trade with inland settlements, fostering economic growth and development. The trade of fish and other maritime products has not only provided a source of income for the fishermen and their families but has also contributed to the overall prosperity of these regions.

Moreover, fishing has served as a catalyst for interconnectedness between different communities, both locally and regionally. The exchange of goods and cultural practices resulting from fishing activities has facilitated cultural diffusion and the cross-pollination of diverse traditions, further enriching the cultural tapestry of the Gulf.

In contemporary times, the social and economic impact of fishing continues to be a driving force behind the sustainability and resilience of Gulf communities. However, modern challenges such as overfishing, environmental degradation, and fluctuating market demands have necessitated innovative approaches to ensure the continued prosperity of fishing communities.

Efforts towards sustainable fishing practices, conservation initiatives, and the integration of modern technology aim to preserve the socio-economic significance of fishing while safeguarding the marine ecosystem for future generations. Recognizing the intrinsic value of traditional fishing practices, there is a growing emphasis on promoting cultural heritage and preserving the time-honored rituals associated with fishing, thereby reinforcing the social and economic foundations shaped by this ancient maritime tradition.

Cultural Significance and Rituals

The cultural significance of fishing in the Gulf is deeply rooted in the traditions and rituals of the coastal communities. Fishing is not merely a means of livelihood but a way of life intertwined with spiritual beliefs, customs, and social structures. Across generations, the act of casting nets and setting sail has been enshrined in folklore and oral traditions, symbolizing the unity between humans and the sea. Rituals associated with fishing often involve prayers and supplications to ensure bountiful catches and safe voyages. These rituals reflect the profound respect and reverence the communities hold for the marine environment, acknowledging their dependence on its resources. Furthermore, traditional ceremonies and festivals mark key stages of the fishing calendar, amplifying the communal bond and pride in the age-old practices. Stories and myths related to legendary catches and mythical sea creatures are passed down from elders, adding a layer of mystique and wonder to the daily lives of the fisherfolk. The rhythm of the tides and the changing seasons dictate the time for fishing expeditions and the timing of these cultural celebrations, reinforcing the interconnectedness between nature and human activity. Additionally, the crafts and skills associated with fishing, such as boat-building and net-making, are imbued with cultural symbolism and represent a vital link to the history and identity of the communities. These practices carry profound traditional knowledge and wisdom, representing an intangible cultural heritage that shapes the collective memory and ethos of the coastal societies. The rituals and cultural significance of fishing in the Gulf convey a sense of symbiosis, reciprocation, and gratitude towards the marine ecosystem, exemplifying the enduring legacy of artisanal fishing and the conservation of cultural heritage.

Conservation and Sustainability Practices

In the face of modern challenges such as overfishing and environmental degradation, the need for conservation and sustainability practices in Gulf fishing has become increasingly urgent. The delicate balance of the marine ecosystem in the Gulf demands a thoughtful and proactive approach to ensure the preservation of traditional fishing practices for future generations. Key strategies for conservation and sustainability include the establishment of marine protected areas, the implementation of catch quotas and size limits, and the promotion of sustainable fishing techniques. By designating specific areas as marine protected areas where fishing activities are regulated or prohibited, authorities can safeguard crucial habitats and protect vulnerable species from overexploitation. Moreover, imposing catch quotas and size limits for specific fish species helps maintain population levels and prevents the depletion of critical marine resources. These measures are vital in sustaining the ecological integrity of the Gulf's waters. Adhering to sustainable fishing techniques is equally important in safeguarding the long-term viability of the Gulf's fisheries. Encouraging selective fishing gear, such as traps and hooks that minimize bycatch, can reduce unintended harm to non-targeted marine organisms. Additionally, endorsing the practice of responsible fishing methods, like seasonal closures to allow fish populations to replenish, further supports the conservation of marine biodiversity. To enforce adherence to these principles, education and outreach programs are pivotal in raising awareness and fostering a sense of stewardship among

fishermen and the wider community. Collaborative efforts between governmental agencies, scientific institutions, and local
fishing communities are essential in implementing effective
conservation and sustainability measures. Furthermore, integrating traditional ecological knowledge into contemporary
management approaches can offer valuable insights into the
historical relationship between humans and the marine environment, serving as a foundation for informed decision-
making. Embracing technological innovations that promote
sustainable fishing practices, such as GPS tracking to monitor
fishing vessels and satellite imaging to assess marine resource
abundance, represents a significant leap forward in advancing
conservation efforts. These advancements enable more efficient resource management and contribute to the protection
of fragile marine ecosystems. Adopting a holistic approach
that combines scientific research, policy development, and
community engagement is fundamental in ensuring the longevity of Gulf fishing traditions while safeguarding the region's
natural wealth. By incorporating conservation and sustainability practices into the fabric of Gulf fishing, we can aspire to
preserve the rich heritage of this ancient tradition and secure
the marine environment for generations to come.

Technological Advances in Modern Gulf Fishing

In recent years, technological advancements have significantly impacted the fishing industry across the Gulf region.
Incorporating modern tools and techniques has revolutionized traditional fishing practices, enhancing efficiency and
sustainability. One notable innovation is electronic navigation
systems, allowing fishermen to locate fishing grounds and navigate safely through the waters precisely. This optimizes the
catch, reduces fuel consumption, and minimizes the impact on

marine ecosystems. Furthermore, advanced sonar technology enables fishermen to accurately identify schools of fish, leading to more targeted and responsible harvesting.

The utilization of modern materials and equipment has also redefined the fishing process. Lightweight and durable synthetic nets have replaced traditional organic fiber nets, offering improved performance and longevity. Additionally, introducing specialized fishing gear, such as automated longline systems and hydraulic reel winches, has streamlined the hauling and retrieval process, reducing physical strain on the fishermen while increasing productivity.

Moreover, satellite communication systems have revolutionized fishing operations, enabling real-time weather updates and vessel tracking. This advancement enhances safety at sea and facilitates swift responses to changing environmental conditions. Additionally, remote monitoring technologies allow authorities to enforce regulations effectively, combating illegal, unreported, and unregulated (IUU) fishing activities.

Integrating modern data collection methods and analytics has also had a transformative impact. Real-time monitoring of catch sizes and species compositions provides valuable insights for sustainable resource management. Fishermen can now make informed decisions based on accurate data, contributing to conserving marine biodiversity and ecosystems.

Furthermore, emerging innovations in aquaculture and fish farming have offered new opportunities for diversification within the fishing industry. Controlled environment aquaculture facilities have been developed, allowing for the sustainable cultivation of various fish species, reducing pressure on wild stocks, and providing alternative seafood sources for the market.

In conclusion, technological advances have reshaped the landscape of Gulf fishing, promoting sustainable practices, improving operational efficiency, and ensuring the preservation of traditional fishing heritage in the face of modern challenges.

Conclusion: Preserving Traditions in a Modern Era

Preserving the rich fishing traditions of the Gulf in the modern era is paramount to maintaining the cultural identity and heritage of the region. While technological advances have revolutionized the fishing industry, there is a growing awareness of the importance of safeguarding traditional fishing practices. The sustainability of marine resources and the preservation of centuries-old customs are now at the forefront of conservation efforts.

In an era of rapid globalization and industrialization, it is imperative to recognize the intrinsic value of traditional fishing methods. These methods ensure the replenishment of fish stocks and uphold the delicate ecological balance of the Gulf's marine habitats. The intergenerational transmission of knowledge about fishing traditions carries profound significance - it serves as a testament to Gulf communities' enduring resilience and adaptability.

Furthermore, preserving traditional fishing practices contributes to the region's overall cultural tapestry. Fishing rituals, folklore, and communal customs associated with these age-old practices showcase the profound connection between the people of the Gulf and their natural environment. These customs serve as a living link to the past while simultaneously shaping the region's contemporary identity.

The convergence of traditional wisdom and modern technology has led to innovative approaches to preserving fishing traditions. Conservation initiatives, sustainable fishing practices, and community-driven efforts underscore the commitment to ensuring that these cherished customs endure for future generations. By harmonizing the wisdom of the past with the present advancements, the Gulf region is rewriting the traditional narrative, ensuring its relevance in the modern era.

As we navigate the complexities of the 21st century, it is evident that preserving traditional fishing customs is not merely a local concern but a global imperative. The ripple effects of nurturing these traditions resonate beyond the shores of the Gulf, contributing to the collective ethos of cultural diversity and heritage conservation worldwide. At its core, the preservation of Gulf fishing traditions serves as a poignant reminder of the timeless wisdom Indigenous communities hold and their invaluable contributions to the broader global heritage.

In conclusion, the harmonious coexistence of age-old fishing traditions and modern advancements is essential for the sustained prosperity of the Gulf. By embracing this synergy, the region can celebrate its heritage while forging a more sustainable and culturally enriched future.

Chapter 7

The Oasis Treasures: Trade Routes of the Desert

Desert trade routes have been pivotal in shaping history, serving as conduits for cultural exchange, economic development, and spreading ideas across vast and barren landscapes. The historical significance of these ancient arteries of commerce is immense, as they facilitated the movement of goods, people, and knowledge, fostering connections between distant civilizations. Caravans traversing these arid expanses were not mere merchandise conveyors but agents of change, fueling the growth of societies and empires. The impact of desert trade routes on civilizations was profound, with the flow of commodities such as spices, silk, precious metals, and agricultural produce enriching both the traders and the lands they reached. Moreover, the intermingling of diverse cultures along these routes engendered a cross-pollination of ideas, beliefs, and practices, leading to the evolution of art, literature, and technology. This interconnectedness forged resilient networks of mutual dependence, challenging the prevailing notion of desolate isolation attributed to desert regions. The endurance and ingenuity exhibited by those involved in sustaining these trade routes reflect the resourcefulness required to overcome the formidable obstacles nature poses, further solidifying the significance of these pathways in human history. In this diverse tapestry of exchanges, desert trade routes emerged as epicenters of innovation, where different civilizations left indelible imprints on one another, inciting a rich tapestry of shared legacies. As we embark on a journey through the annals of desert trade, it becomes evident that these routes not only shaped the past but continue to exert their influence on the present and future, serving as testaments to humankind's enduring resilience and adaptability amidst the harshest of terrains.

Geography of the Oasis: Vital Stops for Caravans

The geography of an oasis is as fascinating as it is vital to the trade routes that crisscross the desert. These lush and fertile spots amid arid landscapes offer a lifeline for caravans traversing the vast expanse of the desert. The strategic positioning of oases directly impacts the success and safety of these ancient trade routes.

Oases provide essential waypoints where travelers and their pack animals can rest, resupply, and seek shelter from the harsh elements of the desert. As such, oasis locations have determined the establishment of specific trade corridors, shaping the fabric of commerce and cultural exchange in the old world. Among the most renowned of these vital stops are the legendary oases of Al-Hasa, Siwa, and Al Ain, each playing a pivotal role in sustaining the flow of goods and ideas across the desert.

Furthermore, the geographical features surrounding these oases, such as towering sand dunes, rocky outcrops, or rugged mountains, not only contribute to the allure of these sites but also pose formidable challenges to the caravans that must navigate through them. Navigating these natural obstacles demands expertise in interpreting the signs of the desert and an intimate knowledge of the topography of oasis surroundings.

In addition to their practical importance, the oases often boast remarkable natural beauty and unique ecosystems. Lush date palm groves, babbling springs, and cool, shaded alcoves are treasures of respite and rejuvenation amid the unforgiving desert landscape. This natural grandeur has inspired countless poets, artists, and explorers throughout history, adding a layer of allure and mystique to these vital stopping points.

Overall, the geography of the oasis serves as a testament to human ingenuity and endurance in the face of extreme conditions. It showcases the ability of ancient civilizations to adapt to and thrive in their environment while also providing a tangible glimpse into the extraordinary trading networks that once connected distant lands. The significance of the oasis as a vital stop for caravans cannot be overstated, as it embodies the intersection of natural wonders, human cooperation, and economic enterprise in the heart of the desert.

Goods on the Move: What Traveled Through the Oasis

As caravans traversed through the vast deserts, they carried a diverse array of goods across the oasis, serving as vital hubs for trade. The coveted commodities that journeyed through these arid landscapes encapsulated the essence of ancient commerce and cultural exchange. Precious spices from the Far East, including cinnamon, pepper, and cardamom, intermingled with the intoxicating fragrances of Arabian incense, myrrh, and frankincense. These valuable treasures symbolized opulence and held deep religious and ceremonial significance. Fabrics crafted from luxurious silks, cotton, and wool were carefully packed onto the camel caravans, embodying exquisite craftsmanship and reflecting the intricate weaving traditions of distant lands. The alluring sparkle of gemstones, such as rubies, sapphires, and emeralds, added a glimmer of allure to the cargo. At the same time, precious metals like gold, silver, and copper gleamed under the scorching desert sun, representing wealth and prosperity. Agricultural products, including dates, figs, and grains, spoke of sustenance and agricultural prowess, illustrating the resilience of farming communities in the face of challenging environmental conditions. Moreover, exotic fauna and flora, such as perfumed oils, rare animal pelts, and medicinal herbs, lent the cargo an air of mystique and allure. Additionally, as the caravans converged at the oasis, cultural artifacts, manuscripts, and oral traditions were shared, allowing for the exchange of knowledge and ideas that transcended geographical boundaries. The goods' diversity and richness traversing through the oasis underscored the intricate web of connectivity that defined ancient trade routes, fostering mutual understanding and symbiotic relationships between distant civilizations.

The Caravan Leaders: Figures of Authority and Navigation

In the vast expanse of the desert, the role of caravan leaders transcended mere navigation; they were revered as figures of authority, possessing a deep understanding of the complexities and nuances of leading their respective caravans through treacherous terrains and harsh conditions. These leaders were often seasoned veterans of desert travel, well-versed in the art of reading the shifting sands and celestial bodies to guide their caravans toward safety. Their expertise extended beyond mere geographical knowledge, encompassing the ability to negotiate with various tribes and communities along the routes, ensuring the smooth passage of goods and personnel. Caravan leaders carried significant responsibilities for the success of the trade missions and the safety and well-being of their fellow travelers. Beyond their navigational acumen, these leaders held the trust and respect of all involved, fostering a sense of unity and purpose amidst the grueling journeys. They provided guidance during sandstorms, arranged nightly camps, managed available resources, and mediated disputes, exhibiting exceptional leadership qualities that extended far beyond the boundaries of traditional leadership roles. The tales of their exploits became woven into the fabric of desert lore, elevating the stature of these individuals to heroic proportions in the collective imagination of the desert-dwelling societies. Through their brave and bold endeavors, these stalwart leaders forged the vital connections that sustained the intricate web of trade routes and cultural exchanges, leaving an indelible mark on the historical tapestry of the desert civilizations.

Oasis as Socioeconomic Centers

In the arid and unforgiving landscapes of the desert, oases emerge as vital centers of socioeconomic activity, playing a pivotal role in sustaining life and facilitating trade. These verdant havens represent far more than just water sources in an otherwise parched environment; they serve as bustling hubs of commerce, culture, and social interaction, fostering a unique sense of community and shared purpose. At the heart of these oases lie bustling marketplaces where goods from distant lands converge, creating a vibrant tapestry of trade that weaves together the threads of different cultures and traditions. The economic significance of these oases cannot be overstated, as they provide a livelihood for communities and act as key nodes in the intricate web of desert trade routes. Moreover, inter-mingling diverse peoples within oasis communities sparks a rich exchange of ideas, beliefs, and customs, shaping the social fabric in profound ways. The intricate networks of irrigation and agricultural practices developed around these oases fur-ther underscore their role as socio-economic pillars, enabling the sustainable cultivation of crops and fostering a sense of stability and prosperity amid geographical adversity. As cen-ters of learning, artistry, and innovation, the oases have been instrumental in preserving and transmitting cultural legacies through generations, embodying the resilience and adaptabil-ity of human civilization in even the harshest environments. From the architectural marvels that stand as testaments to human ingenuity to the lively bustle of bazaars teeming with exotic wares' sights, sounds, and aromas, the oases reverberate with the pulse of thriving economies and vibrant communi-ties. Indeed, the oases stand as timeless symbols of endurance and interconnectedness, exemplifying these socioeconomic centers' profound impact on shaping the narrative of desert civilizations.

Water Engineering: Sustaining Life in Arid Regions

The unforgiving desert landscapes posed monumental chal-lenges to the sustainability of life in ancient civilizations. However, through incredible feats of water engineering, these communities were able to thrive in these arid regions. The development and maintenance of intricate irrigation systems are a testament to their innovative solutions for sustaining life. Ancient engineers utilized various techniques such as qanats, falaj, and khettara to capture and distribute precious water resources efficiently. These systems harness natural water sources, utilizing gravity to transport water across vast distances, providing essential sustenance for agriculture, human consumption, and livestock. The cultural significance of these water engineering marvels extended beyond mere functionality. They served as communal gathering points, promoting social cohesion, trade, and knowledge exchange. Additionally, these structures represented a profound and harmonious relationship between humans and their environment, embodying a deep respect for the delicate balance of nature. Examining these remarkable achievements not only unveils an advanced understanding of hydrology and hydraulic principles but also sheds light on the resourcefulness and resilience of ancient societies. Their meticulous planning, precise craftsmanship, and enduring legacy continue to inspire contemporary water management practices and sustainability efforts in arid regions worldwide.

Architectural Marvels: Structural Ingenuity in Harsh Climates

The architectural marvels that emerged from the harsh climates of ancient desert trade routes stand as a testament to human ingenuity and perseverance. In the unforgiving landscape of the desert, where extreme temperatures and scarce resources posed significant challenges, ingenious architectural designs were developed to provide shelter, promote trade, and facilitate cultural exchange. Structures in the form of caravanserais, fortresses, and trading posts dotted the vast desert landscapes, strategically positioned along the trade routes to accommodate and service the needs of the traveling merchants and their caravans. These architectural marvels served practical functions and showcased the artistic and engineering prowess of the civilizations that thrived amidst the desolate terrain. The architecture of these structures was influenced by a blend of cultural exchanges, reflecting the diverse traditions and techniques brought by traders and travelers from across the borders. Blending architectural styles and construction methods resulted in unique and innovative designs that harmoniously integrated with the environment while providing essential refuge and support for transient populations. Adapting building materials, such as earth, stone, and palm wood, allowed for sustainable construction that complemented the natural surroundings. These structures' intricate designs and layouts also reflected the social, economic, and political dynamics of the flourishing trade networks traversing the deserts. They represented symbols of power, safety, and hospitality, embodying the enduring spirit of commerce and intercultural engagement. As we delve into the study of these architectural masterpieces, we gain insight into the resourcefulness and resilience of ancient societies, uncovering the enduring legacy of their innovation and adaptive capability. Furthermore, the preservation and restoration of these architectural remnants serve as a bridge between the past and the present, offering a profound connection to our shared history and the remarkable endeavors of those who navigated and thrived in the challenging desert environments.

Cultural Exchanges: Influence Beyond Borders

Cultural exchanges have shaped the rich tapestry of traditions and beliefs across the Arabian desert. The expansive trade routes cutting through the heart of the desert not only facilitated the exchange of goods and served as conduits for the cross-fertilization of ideas, languages, and cultural practices. These interactions between diverse civilizations left an indelible mark on the social landscape, spawning a vibrant fusion of customs and traditions.

The Arabian desert was a melting pot of cultures and ethnicities, with caravans serving as mobile microcosms of diversity. The encounter between Bedouin nomads, traders from distant lands, and indigenous communities fostered an atmosphere of mutual learning and assimilation. Languages echoed through the shifting dunes as traders bartered wares while sharing tales of faraway lands, sowing the seeds of linguistic evolution and hybrid dialects.

Religious ideologies also mingled along the trade routes, leading to a mosaic of belief systems that coexisted and interwove, giving rise to a tolerant and inclusive ethos. From the teachings of Islam to the enduring influence of Christianity and Judaism, the desert became a canvas upon which various faiths painted their mark, engendering an environment where spiritual exchange flourished amidst the arid expanse.

Another hallmark of cultural intermingling was the exchange of knowledge and technologies. The transmission of agricultural practices, architectural techniques, and medicinal remedies brought about by the encounter of diverse communities led to innovations that enhanced the resilience and prosperity of settlements within the harsh desert environment. The cross-pollination of these practices resulted in the emergence of harmonized structures and sustainable agricultural systems that endured for generations.

Art and craftsmanship bore the unmistakable imprint of cultural exchanges, as artisans drew upon myriad influences to imbue their creations with a distinctive blend of styles. From intricate pottery patterns to the mesmerizing motifs woven into textiles, the artistic expressions born from transcultural interactions reflected the shared aesthetics and inspirations distilled from many societies.

In conclusion, the interchange of cultures along the ancient desert trade routes was an enriching process that left a legacy of interconnectedness and mutual enrichment. The crossroads of civilizations facilitated the amalgamation of diverse elements, leading to a multifaceted cultural panorama characterized by resilience, adaptability, and inclusivity.

Security and Conflict: Protecting the Trade Lanes

The deserts were not just vast wastelands filled with trade caravans and peaceful exchanges. Behind the veils of shimmering heat were hidden threats and perilous risks that came with protecting the trade lanes. One of the primary challenges of maintaining these vital routes was safeguarding against banditry and raids from opportunistic marauders. The caravan leaders and their retinues had to be vigilant and resourceful, often resorting to complex military strategies and defensive formations to deter and fend off potential assailants. Guarding the merchandise and ensuring the safety of the traders and their invaluable cargoes became a constant struggle, shaping the very fabric of desert trade.

Furthermore, as trade routes grew in significance, they attracted the attention of ambitious empires and rival city-states seeking to control and monopolize these arteries of commerce. Thus, the desolate landscapes witnessed conflicts fueled by territorial disputes, power struggles, and assertions of dominance over lucrative trade opportunities. These clashes led to the fortification of key strategic points along the routes, giving rise to fortified waystations and citadels that served as bastions of defense and safe havens for weary travelers. Such sites transformed into centers of cultural diffusion, where ideas, languages, and traditions intermingled amidst the fusion of defensive architecture and indigenous customs.

In addition to external threats, internal friction among the diverse communities navigating the trade lanes also posed immense risks. Tensions arising from differences in languages, religious beliefs, and societal customs often erupted into confrontations, endangering the smooth flow of goods and the overall harmony of the trade network. It necessitated the establishment of codes of conduct and arbitration mechanisms to mitigate internal conflicts and ensure the sustained vitality of the trade routes.

As the passage of time brought progress and technological advancements, security measures evolved to combat the perils besetting the trade lanes. Innovations such as mounted patrols, signaling systems, and intelligence networks emerged as crucial components of safeguarding the flow of commerce. Invariably, the history of securing the trade lanes epitomizes the remarkable resilience and adaptability of those committed to sustaining the lifelines of desert trade.

Transition to Modern Trade: From Ancient Routes to Contemporary Roads

The transition from ancient trade routes to contemporary roads marks a pivotal shift in the Gulf's economic landscape. Traditional desert trade routes have evolved with modern transport and infrastructure to support the region's burgeoning economy. This transition has facilitated the movement of goods and services and spurred economic growth, technology integration, and cultural exchange. The once perilous journeys through unforgiving terrain have been replaced by efficient highways, railways, and ports, connecting the Gulf to the global marketplace.

Modern trade routes have redefined the concept of trade, creating a network that is seamlessly integrated with international commerce. The Gulf's strategic location at the crossroads of major continents has made it an indispensable hub for global trade. Transitioning from camel caravans to container ships, the region has embraced technological advancements to streamline logistics, improve efficiency, and reduce transit times.

Moreover, the modernization of trade routes has opened up new opportunities for economic diversification and sustainable development. As old trade paths gave way to modern infrastructure, businesses flourished, and new industries emerged. The introduction of modern trade corridors has transformed remote villages into thriving commercial centers and unleashed the entrepreneurial spirit of the region.

Beyond its economic implications, the transition to modern trade routes has catalyzed social and cultural transformations. It has enabled the Gulf to engage with the world on its own terms, facilitating cultural exchanges and fostering greater understanding between nations. The cosmopolitan nature of the modern trade landscape has led to the convergence of diverse traditions, languages, and customs, enriching the fabric of society.

As the Gulf navigates this transition, it faces new challenges and opportunities. By embracing sustainable practices, investing in green technologies, and promoting collaboration among nations, the region aims to build resilient and future-ready trade networks. The transition to modern trade routes represents a paradigm shift—a testament to the region's ability to adapt, innovate, and thrive in the ever-evolving global trade arena.

Chapter 8

Silhouettes of Trade: The Routes That Connected Worlds

In antiquity, the vast interwoven web of trade routes was fundamental in forging connections between distant lands and diverse civilizations. These ancient pathways were not merely channels for exchanging goods; they were arteries through which ideas, beliefs, and customs flowed. The network of trade routes was a vital conduit for cultural diffusion, enabling the cross-pollination of artistic, intellectual, and spiritual traditions among peoples separated by great distances. They provided a platform for the convergence of languages, knowledge sharing, and the fusion of varied lifestyles. The meticulous crisscrossing of these paths facilitated interactions between individuals of differing ethnicities, fostering an environment where mutual understanding and cooperation could thrive. The routes became melting pots of diversity, where merchants, travelers, and explorers interacted, leading to hybrid cultures that incorporated elements from distant lands. Through this inter-connected web, the world witnessed the harmonious merging of various cultural legacies, allowing for the emergence of new artistic expressions, philosophical concepts, and societal structures. As a result, the trade routes played a pivotal role in shaping the identities and worldviews of the societies they in-tersected. This section explores the profound impact of these ancient trade routes as catalysts for the confluence of diverse cultures, emphasizing their contribution to the rich tapestry of human civilization.

Mapping the Routes: Glimpses of Ancient Pathways

The ancient trade routes that connected distant lands across the Gulf region are a testament to human ingenuity, en-durance, and the quest for prosperity. These pathways form an intricate web weaving through deserts, mountains, and seas, facilitating the exchange of goods, ideas, and cultures. Map-ping these routes offers us intriguing glimpses into the lives of those who traversed these ancient pathways. The caravan routes, such as the Incense Route and the Silk Road, carved their way through unforgiving terrain, linking the Arabian Pen-insula with the Mediterranean, Central Asia, and the Indian subcontinent. These paths were not mere trails; they served as conduits of knowledge, where civilizations met and exchanged goods, technology, and beliefs. As we trace the routes, we uncover the historical significance of strategic locations, such as oases, which provided crucial rest stops for weary travelers and bustling marketplaces for trade. The route maps reveal the interconnectedness of seemingly distant lands and highlight the resourcefulness of those who braved the arduous journeys. Studying these ancient pathways allows us to appreciate the enduring human spirit that thrived along these trade routes, leaving behind a legacy that inspires awe and admiration.

Trade Goods: From Silk to Spices

The bustling ancient trade routes facilitated the exchange of a myriad of goods that would profoundly impact the interconnected civilizations. From China in the East to the Mediterranean in the West, many commodities traversed the expansive network of routes, shaping economic landscapes and cultural trends. One of the most sought-after merchandise was silk, which originated from the sophisticated Chinese civilization and was revered for its luxurious texture and vibrant colors. The allure of this fabric fueled significant trade, leading to the fabled Silk Road becoming synonymous with prosperity and enlightenment.

While silk held a special allure, spices were equally coveted and played a pivotal role in the ancient trade. The aromatic treasures such as cinnamon, cardamom, pepper, and saffron added rich flavors to cuisines and possessed medicinal and preservative qualities. Traders journeyed far and wide to procure these exotic spices, navigating treacherous terrains and transcending cultural barriers. Their arrival in distant markets sparked culinary and alchemical revolutions, enriching local cuisines and providing a tantalizing glimpse into far-off lands.

Beyond luxury goods, essential commodities like salt, precious metals, and gemstones were also vital to ancient trade. Salt, often called 'white gold,' held practical significance as a preservative, flavor enhancer, and symbol of wealth. Precious metals such as gold and silver served as currency and represented opulence and power, adorning monarchs and temples across the trading routes. Gemstones, renowned for their rarity and beauty, captivated hearts and minds, adorning jewelry and ceremonial objects while also being valued as symbols of status and prestige.

Furthermore, the flow of trade goods was not merely a commercial undertaking; it was an intricate tapestry woven with cultural threads. The exchange of goods fostered cross-cultural encounters, leading to the assimilation and dissemination of knowledge, traditions, and artistic influences. As goods changed hands, so did ideas, philosophies, and religious beliefs, sparking intellectual awakenings and igniting the beacon of human progress. The vibrancy and diversity of the goods traversing the ancient trade routes mirrored the intricacies of human interaction, shaping the destiny of civilizations and echoing through the annals of history.

Cultural Exchanges Along the Routes

Encompassing a tapestry of diverse peoples, the ancient trade routes connected distant lands and facilitated cultural exchanges that left an indelible mark on the societies they touched. As caravans traversed vast expanses and ships sailed across treacherous waters, they transported goods and served as conduits for exchanging ideas, beliefs, traditions, and knowledge. The fusion of cultures along these routes shaped unique identities and fostered cosmopolitan environments where a rich amalgamation of customs and practices flourished.

The Silk Road, for instance, was instrumental in disseminating religious beliefs such as Buddhism, Christianity, and Islam, leading to the construction of diverse religious sites and architecture. Ideas about governance, literature, art, and philosophy were also interwoven into the fabric of societies, laying the groundwork for intellectual advancements and cross-cultural collaborations. Furthermore, the exchange of culinary traditions and agricultural practices contributed to diversifying diets and cultivation techniques, enriching the culinary land-scape and enhancing agricultural productivity.

Concomitantly, the maritime trade routes witnessed the convergence of seafaring communities, engendering thriving port cities teeming with vibrant marketplaces and bustling docks. With the influx of foreign commodities, indigenous artistry and craftsmanship transformed, giving rise to inno-vative techniques and designs that combined various cultural aesthetics. Moreover, languages and dialects meshed during commercial interactions, resulting in the evolution of pidgin languages and lingua franca, which eased communication and fostered cross-cultural understanding.

Yet, these cultural exchanges were not devoid of conflicts and struggles. Tensions arising from differing belief systems, competition for resources, and complex geopolitical dynamics occasionally led to diplomatic standoffs and sporadic con-frontations. However, efforts towards diplomacy and collabo-ration often prevailed, underscoring the resilient bonds forged through trade and cultural integration.

The interconnected trade routes catalyzed a profound intermingling of customs and traditions, fostering a globalized ethos that transcended geographical boundaries. This cross-pollination of cultures laid the foundation for the colorful tapestry of human heritage we see today, where remnants of centuries-old interactions still resonate in contemporary soci-eties' rituals, arts, and societal norms.

Historical Impacts on Local Economies

The historical trade routes profoundly impacted the local economies of their traversed regions. As goods and ideas flowed along these ancient pathways, they brought about sig-nificant economic changes for the communities along their routes. Trade led to the development of specialized industries and the growth of urban centers that served as pivotal hubs for commerce and cultural exchange. These economic transformations fueled innovation, entrepreneurial spirit, and diverse ecosystems of production and consumption. The exchange of goods enriched local economies and fostered intercultural cooperation and understanding of the environment.

Furthermore, expanding trade networks brought prosperity to previously isolated regions, effectively integrating them into the global economy. This integration led to new trading cities and mercantile centers, attracting talent, capital, and expertise worldwide. As a result, these once-remote areas became hotbeds of economic activity, serving as crossroads where merchants, artisans, and entrepreneurs converged to engage in lucrative trade ventures.

The influx of wealth from trade also had a cascading effect on the social structure of these local economies. It gave rise to thriving merchant classes and facilitated the patronage of the arts, architecture, and scholarship. This economic prosperity allowed for establishing educational institutions, cultural amenities, and public infrastructure that enhanced the overall quality of life within these burgeoning commercial centers. Additionally, wealth accumulation through trade created opportunities for philanthropy and civic development, leaving enduring legacies in charitable endowments, public works, and communal spaces.

However, it is essential to recognize that economic prosperity also came with the challenges of managing wealth, ensuring fair trade practices, and mediating disputes arising from commercial interactions. The historical impacts on local economies underscore the complex dynamics of trade, power, and socioeconomic change that unfolded throughout the ancient world, leaving indelible marks on the fabric of society and shaping the narratives of generations to come.

Architectural Footprints: Marketplaces and Caravanserais

The historical trade routes that connected worlds left behind a lasting legacy in the form of architectural marvels such as marketplaces and caravanserais. These structures were pivotal in facilitating trade, providing essential rest stops and shelter for weary travelers and their pack animals. The architectural footprints of marketplaces and caravanserais tell a compelling story of the bustling commercial activities and cultural exchanges that defined ancient trade networks.

Marketplaces, often located at key junctures along trade routes, were vibrant hubs where merchants from distant lands converged to showcase and exchange an array of goods. These bustling centers of commerce were characterized by a blend of architectural styles, reflecting the diverse origins of the traders and the products they brought with them. These marketplaces' striking facades and intricate designs stand as a testament to the opulence and sophistication of ancient trading communities. Visitors would have been greeted by a sensory spectacle of sights, sounds, and scents as exotic wares from far-off lands were proudly presented for eager buyers.

On the other hand, Caravanserais served as vital waystations for caravan travelers crossing long stretches of arid terrain. These imposing structures were strategically positioned along the trade routes, offering secure lodging, animal stabling, and storage facilities for goods. The architecture of caravanserais was designed to protect against the harsh elements and the potential threat of banditry, featuring sturdy walls, inner courtyards, and often intricate geometric patterns decorating the interiors. The very layout of these caravanserais, with their central courtyards and surrounding chambers, spoke to the practical yet elegant design principles that catered to the needs of weary travelers.

Moreover, the architectural footprints of marketplaces and caravanserais bear witness to the cultural fusion and creative synthesis that resulted from the interaction between different civilizations. Ornate motifs, structural elements, and decorative details showcased a remarkable blending of artistic traditions, serving as physical manifestations of the interconnectedness of distant societies through trade. As such, these architectural marvels not only served practical purposes but also acted as symbolic embodiments of unity and cooperation across boundaries.

In recounting the history of marketplaces and caravanserais, we gain profound insight into the ingenuity and adaptability of ancient traders and the enduring legacy of their economic and cultural exchanges. Exploring these architectural footprints allows us to envision the vibrant tapestry of the past, where the convergence of trade routes transcended mere transactions, giving rise to enduring monuments that tell the timeless tale of interconnected civilizations.

Influential Traders: Biography Snippets

1.   Amr ibn Hind (580-665 AD): was a prominent Arabian merchant known for his extensive trade network across the Arabian Peninsula and beyond. His proficiency in navigating the challenging terrains of the desert enabled him to establish key trading routes connecting distant regions. His keen business acumen and diplomatic skills secured lucrative partnerships and alliances, solidifying his status as one of the most influential traders of his time.

2. Shihab al-Din Abu'l Abbas Ahmad ibn Fadlallah al-'Umari (1300-1384 AD): Hailing from Damascus, Shihab al-Din was renowned for his contributions to travel literature and his insights on maritime trade in the Indian Ocean. As a seasoned voyager himself, his writings provided invaluable details on the bustling trade hubs and cultural exchanges along the maritime routes, shedding light on the diverse interactions between different civilizations.

3. Fatima bint Sa'd al Khair (1631-1699 AD): was a prominent female trader from Mecca whose astute business acumen and shrewd negotiation skills propelled her to great success. She played a pivotal role in overseeing the trade of luxury goods, fostering diplomatic ties, and advocating for women's economic empowerment in the trading sphere. Her legacy inspires future generations of female entrepreneurs in the Gulf region and beyond.

4. Yusuf Ali Khoory (1867-1930 AD): emerged as a prominent figure in the modern era, significantly contributing to the expansion of trade networks in the Gulf region during the early 20th century. His innovative approaches to diversifying trade commodities and exploring new markets were instrumental in shaping the region's economic landscape. Khoory's entrepreneurial ventures and philanthropic endeavors left an indelible mark on the trajectory of trade and commerce in the Gulf, earning him widespread admiration and respect.

Risks and Rewards: Perils of Ancient Trade

Ancient trade routes were not merely pathways for exchanging goods and ideas; they were perilous yet essential arteries that facilitated the movement of caravans, ships, and traders across vast and often treacherous landscapes. The allure of exotic goods from distant lands was met with great risk as merchants navigated through unfamiliar terrains and faced a myriad of challenges along their journeys.

One of the foremost risks inherent in ancient trade was the threat of banditry and piracy. With valuable cargo and lucrative profits at stake, traders became targets for opportunistic raiders and maritime marauders seeking to plunder their goods. Caravans traversing remote desert expanses encountered the constant fear of ambush, while merchant vessels sailing through uncharted waters contended with the ever-looming specter of piracy. These threats necessitated the formation of protective caravans, armed escorts, and intricate alliances and pacts among trading communities to deter and combat such perils.

The unpredictable forces of nature also posed significant risks to ancient traders. Journeys across desolate deserts were fraught with extreme temperatures, scarce water sources, and the looming specter of sandstorms and dust clouds. Maritime expeditions grappled with stormy seas, fierce storms, and unpredictable winds, with the absence of modern navigation technologies amplifying the danger. Such environmental hazards made every trade expedition a test of resilience, resourcefulness, and endurance.

Moreover, the fluctuating political landscape of antiquity added another layer of uncertainty to trade ventures. Interactions with foreign kingdoms and empires entailed navigating intricate webs of diplomacy, allegiances, and feuds. Border disputes, shifting power dynamics, and intermittent conflicts could disrupt trade routes, leading to unforeseen detours, delays, or even outright embargoes. These geopolitical intricacies imbued ancient trade with an element of geopolitical gambit, where success hinged on the quality of goods, the astuteness of diplomatic negotiations, and adaptability in the face of geo-political shifts.

In light of these multifaceted perils, ancient trade's rewards were monumental and transformative. Unraveling the tapestry of ancient commerce reveals a narrative of risk and opportunity, where daring traders thrived amidst adversity and reshaped the course of history through their tenacity, enterprise, and vision.

The Decline of Trade Routes: Causes and Consequences

Trade routes that had thrived for centuries gradually declined due to many factors, each leaving its mark on the interconnected global commerce network. One of the primary causes was the shift in geopolitical power, as empires rose and fell, disrupting established trade patterns. The rise of new powers often brought along trade alliances and policy changes, impacting the flow of goods across ancient routes. Similarly, the discovery of sea routes and advancements in maritime technology diverted trade away from traditional land-based routes, altering the dynamics of global commerce.

Economic shifts also precipitated the decline of trade routes. Changes in demand for specific goods, alongside fluctuations in production and supply, led to the reevaluation of trade pathways. Moreover, with the evolution of trade practices and the emergence of new market centers, traditional routes lost their significance, resulting in their gradual abandonment. Additionally, the prevalence of conflicts and wars posed significant threats to the security of trade caravans and maritime vessels, deterring merchants from utilizing established routes.

Consequently, the decline of trade routes bore extensive consequences. Once-prosperous cities along these routes faced economic downturns, leading to urban decay and the loss of cultural vibrancy. Communities that had relied on trade as their lifeblood encountered social and political upheavals, as the diminishing flow of goods disrupted established power structures and societal norms. Furthermore, the decline of trade routes strained diplomatic relations between regions, affecting economic ties, cultural exchanges, and the spread of knowledge and ideas.

Amidst these repercussions, numerous historical lessons emerged, emphasizing the fragility and resilience of trade routes. The decline of ancient trade routes underscored the intricate interplay of economic, political, and social factors in global connectivity. It also highlighted the need for adaptability and innovation in evolving trade landscapes. These profound legacies echo through modern-day globalization as poignant reminders of trade's endurance and transformative nature.

The Enduring Legacy of Trade

The intricate network of ancient trade routes has left an indelible mark on the civilizations it interconnected, fostering cultural exchange, economic prosperity, and technological advancements. Despite the decline of these routes over time, their legacy endures in the shared traditions, languages, and customs that persist across regions. The enduring legacy of trade is evident in the vibrant tapestry of art, architecture, and knowledge that continues to bridge communities and nations today. Beyond the tangible remnants of marketplaces and caravanserais, the intangible impact of trade echoes through time, shaping the ethos and identity of societies along these ancient pathways. This enduring legacy transcends the boundaries of geography and time, serving as a testament to the resilience and adaptability of human connectivity. Furthermore, the lessons learned from the historical decline of trade routes provide invaluable insights into the dynamics of globalization and economic interconnectedness in our modern world. By understanding the causes and consequences of this decline, we gain perspective on the fragility and significance of the systems that sustain international trade today. As we reflect on the enduring legacy of trade, we are reminded of its pivotal role in shaping the ancient world's cultural, economic, and social landscapes. Through this lens, we recognize the vital importance of preserving and celebrating the historical legacies of trade, acknowledging their impact on contemporary societies. The enduring legacy of trade beckons us to cherish and honor the interconnectedness that has shaped humanity, inviting us to seek common ground amidst diversity and embrace the richness of our shared heritage.

Chapter 9

Land of Myths: Legends and Folklore of the Gulf

Legends and folklore play a pivotal role in shaping and pre-serving the cultural identity of the Gulf region. These tales have been passed down orally through generations, embodying the collective wisdom, experiences, and beliefs of the Gulf's diverse communities. They serve as repositories of historical knowledge, moral teachings, and societal norms, offering in-valuable insights into the region's rich heritage. The enchant-ing narratives found within Gulf legends and folklore are not merely stories; they encapsulate the essence of the Gulf's tra-ditions, values, and deeply rooted customs. Moreover, they act as foundational pillars upon which the region's cultural, spiri-tual, and social fabric is woven. These tales provide profound glimpses into the perspectives, aspirations, and fears of the people who call the Gulf their home. Examining these legends and folklore unveils the intricate tapestry of influences that have shaped the Gulf's worldview, contributing to its distinct and cherished cultural identity. As such, delving into Gulf legends and folklore allows for a deeper understanding of the intrinsic connections between tradition, community, and the human experience. Through these captivating narratives, the heartbeat of Gulf culture resonates—beckoning us to explore the marvels and mysteries enshrined within the annals of time.

Mythical Origins: Creation Tales Across the Gulf

In exploring the rich tapestry of Gulf legends and folklore, one cannot ignore the profound significance of creation tales that permeate the collective consciousness of its inhabitants. These narratives hold the key to understanding the Gulf societies' cultural, spiritual, and existential underpinnings, providing a glimpse into the beliefs and values that have shaped generations. The diversity of creation myths across the region reflects the multifaceted nature of Gulf identity, with each tale serving as a testament to the enduring human quest for meaning and origin. From the shimmering sands of the desert to the azure depths of the sea, these timeless stories offer insights into the complex relationship between humanity and the natural world. The creation tales speak of the universe's origins and illuminate the intrinsic connections between the past, present, and future. Each myth weaves a narrative that transcends time, offering a window into the collective psyche of Gulf communities. One encounters tales of cosmic entities fashioning the world from primordial chaos, celestial beings shaping the earth, and divine interventions that set the course of human destiny. The symbolic imagery and allegorical motifs within these narratives serve as a repository of wisdom, morality, and metaphysical contemplation, enriching the cultural landscape of the Gulf. Storytelling becomes an art form, a sacred tradition where elders impart knowledge, virtues, and truths to the younger generations, ensuring the preservation of cherished legacies. As we delve deep into these creation tales, we embark on a journey through the realms of antiquity, where the boundaries between myth and reality blur and where the essence of existence unfolds through the prism of imagination and lore. Through understanding the diverse creation myths that define the Gulf, we gain valuable insights into the roots of belief systems, social structures, and the fabric of everyday life. These myths continue to echo through the corridors of time, resonating in the customs, rituals, and artistic expressions of contemporary Gulf society, affirming the enduring legacy of these ancient narratives.

Heroes and Heroines: Archetypes in Gulf Mythology

In the rich tapestry of Gulf mythology, heroes and heroines emerge as timeless archetypes, embodying humanity's virtues, vices, and struggles. These mythic figures serve as beacons of inspiration and guidance, reflecting Gulf societies' cultural values and aspirations through the ages. From tales of brave warriors to wise and benevolent rulers, Gulf mythology has diverse archetypes that resonate with the region's collective consciousness. Heroes are often depicted as valiant champions, undertaking epic quests to defeat evil forces or uphold justice and honor. They symbolize courage, resilience, and determination, offering moral lessons and exemplifying noble conduct for generations. Similarly, heroines in Gulf mythology are portrayed as ideals of grace, wisdom, and compassion, wielding their inner strength and intellect to overcome adversity and shape destinies. Whether warrior princesses leading armies into battle or enigmatic goddesses guiding mortals through trials, these female archetypes embody the multifaceted nature of femininity and inspire admiration and reverence. The tales of heroes and heroines in Gulf mythology also reflect the complex interplay between mortal existence and the divine realm. Many narratives depict protagonists as intermediaries between gods and humans, bridging the gap between the earthly domain and the transcendent spheres. Their transformative journeys mirror the spiritual evolution of individuals, emphasizing the pursuit of enlightenment and the quest for transcendence. Moreover, these mythic archetypes often serve as cultural touchstones, fostering a sense of collective identity and shared heritage among the peoples of the Gulf. Through oral traditions, visual arts, and performing arts, the stories of heroes and heroines have endured, imparting moral teachings and instilling a profound appreciation for the cultural legacy. These archetypes continue to exert a profound influence in contemporary society, shaping artistic expressions, ethical frameworks, and societal aspirations. The enduring appeal of Gulf mythological archetypes lies in their ability to resonate with universal themes of human experience, offering timeless wisdom and insight into the complexities of existence.

Sacred and Profane: Spiritual Narratives and Practises

Within the rich tapestry of Gulf culture, we find a convergence of sacred narratives and rituals woven into every facet of daily life. From ancient times to the modern era, spiritual beliefs and practices have held a profound significance for the peoples of the Gulf. These narratives often intersect with the profane, offering a holistic view of existence that acknowledges both the divine and the mundane. The spiritual heritage of the region is characterized by a myriad of enchanting tales and revered customs, each serving as a testament to the enduring power of faith. Whether through symbolic rites or ethereal storytelling, the spiritual narratives of the Gulf epitomize the inherent connection between the material and the metaphysical.

At the heart of these traditions lie stories illuminating the human quest for meaning, depicting encounters with spirits, jinn, and other mystical beings inhabiting unseen realms. Such narratives entertain and convey moral lessons, thus imbuing them with an educational significance that transcends generations. Moreover, the performance of sacred rituals serves as a tangible expression of devotion and reverence, creating a communal bond that unites the inhabitants of the Gulf in shared reverence. Each gesture, prayer, and invocation is a thread in the intricate fabric of belief that binds individuals and communities alike.

Beyond mythology and folklore, the Gulf's spiritual customs reflect a diversity of religious and philosophical influences, echoing a history shaped by trade and cultural exchange. Whether honoring deities, saints, or ancestors, the practice of venerating the divine exemplifies the plurality and adaptability of Gulf spirituality. Furthermore, the sanctity attributed to natural elements within these narratives, such as oases, mountains, and celestial bodies, signifies a harmonious relationship between humanity and the environment, emphasizing deep-seated respect for the earth and its abundance. This interconnectedness underscores the intrinsically holistic nature of spiritual life in the Gulf, where the imprint of tradition resonates with the innovation of the present day. Through this lens, one can perceive how spiritual narratives continue to inform and influence the ethos of contemporary Gulf society, shaping values and guiding aspirations in a world pulsating with change.

Tales of the Sea: Lore of Mariners and Monsters

The Gulf region has a rich tapestry of maritime lore woven through generations, captivating the imaginations of seafarers and land-dwellers alike. These tales of the sea are as diverse as the waters they emerge from, encompassing a wide array of narratives that evoke wonder and trepidation. The folklore of mariners in the Gulf is intertwined with the daily lives of fishermen, pearl divers, and traders who have braved the tumultuous seas for centuries. These stories often portray the inherent risks of seafaring, showcasing the bravery and resilience required to navigate the unpredictable tides and weather conditions. Moreover, the oral traditions carry accounts of mythical creatures that dwell beneath the waves, stirring both fascination and fear among those who traverse the expansive aquatic realm. From majestic sea serpents to elusive merfolk, these fantastical beings populate the sailors' folklore, adding an aura of mystique to the maritime domain. Through these captivating narratives, cultural values and maritime expertise are imparted from generation to generation, cultivating a profound respect for the sea and its mysteries. Furthermore, the tales serve as cautionary reminders, highlighting the perils of hubris and the importance of humility before the unfathomable forces of nature. By delving into these enchanting stories, one gains insight into the symbiotic relationship between the Gulf's people and the ocean's boundless expanse. As such, the lore of mariners and monsters in the Gulf entertains and enthralls, and preserves timeless wisdom and reverence for the elemental forces that shape the maritime world.

Desert Whispers: Bedouin Legends and Survival Stories

The oral tradition of Bedouin culture is rich with captivating legends and survival stories passed down through generations. These tales provide a glimpse into the Bedouin way of life, reflecting their deep reverence for the desert and its challenges. Bedouin folklore often revolves around resilience, adaptation, and the interconnectedness of nature and humanity. One recurring motif in these narratives is the extraordinary survival skills of the Bedouin people, illustrating their ability to thrive in the harshest of environments.

These stories depict the courage and resourcefulness required to navigate the unforgiving terrain of the desert. They offer insights into the spiritual beliefs and values that guide Bedouin communities, emphasizing the importance of kinship, trust, and communal support. The legendary figures featured in these tales exemplify wisdom, fortitude, and an intimate understanding of the natural world, serving as role models for subsequent generations.

Furthermore, Bedouin legends often intertwine with practical knowledge about desert flora and fauna, encapsulating the profound symbiosis between the nomadic people and their surroundings. These stories show the significance of traditional practices, such as caravan routes, water conservation, and animal husbandry, shedding light on the intricate web of survival strategies honed over centuries.

Survival stories also underline the unpredictable and hazardous nature of the desert, highlighting encounters with sandstorms, mirages, and formidable wildlife. Such accounts offer a window into the mindset and ingenuity required to navigate these hazards, fostering a deep appreciation for the resilience and adaptability embedded within Bedouin cultural heritage.

In conclusion, the legends and survival stories of the Bedouin hold invaluable insights into the ethos of this nomadic society, offering timeless lessons in endurance, unity, and harmonious coexistence with the natural world. These narratives serve as a testament to the enduring spirit of the Bedouin people and their unwavering connection to the desert landscapes they call home.

Mystical Flora and Fauna: The Symbolism in Nature

Mystical Flora and Fauna constantly feature in the rich tapestry of Gulf folklore, imbuing the natural world with divine significance and symbolic meaning. The ancient stories and legends passed down through generations are replete with vivid depictions of plants and animals, each carrying profound symbolism. The towering date palm, with its life-sustaining fruit and sheltering fronds, is a potent symbol of fertility, rejuvenation, and hospitality in Gulf mythology. Similarly, the noble Arabian horse, revered for its strength, speed, and loyalty, embodies qualities of honor, grace, and resilience in the tales of yore. Furthermore, mystical creatures like the majestic falcon and the elusive desert oryx are revered as spiritual guides, embodying wisdom, freedom, and adaptability. These symbolic representations of flora and fauna serve as metaphorical reflections of the values, virtues, and beliefs cherished by the people of the Gulf. Moreover, the interconnectedness of human lives with the natural world is beautifully elucidated through stories that depict the respectful relationship between mankind and the environment. Delving deeper into the lore, one discovers captivating narratives that illustrate the intrinsic bond between humans and nature, emphasizing the importance of harmonious coexistence and stewardship of the land. The diverse ecosystems of the Gulf region, from the rippling dunes to the azure sea, are portrayed as living entities with their spirits, fostering a profound respect for the elements and the cycles of nature. The stories of mystical flora and fauna impart timeless wisdom, teaching valuable lessons about conservation, sustainability, and the enduring power of the natural world. As custodians of this ancient heritage, it is imperative to recognize the symbolic significance of the Gulf's natural inhabitants, preserving their physical presence and spiritual and cultural legacy.

Fables of Wealth and Woe: Morals and Messages

Throughout the rich tapestry of Gulf folklore, fables have served as powerful vessels for conveying timeless wisdom and moral guidance. These captivating stories have been woven into the Gulf culture fabric, offering profound insights into human nature's and society's complexities. Fables of wealth and woe explore the intricacies of life, presenting allegorical narratives that resonate with both young and old alike. Embedded within these tales are valuable lessons on virtue, vice, and the delicate balance between success and downfall. The allure of these fables lies in their enchanting narratives and the profound truths they unveil. Whether set amidst the bustling souks or the tranquil desert dunes, these fables mirror the universal struggles and triumphs that define the human experience. From the misfortunes of a greedy merchant to the triumph of a humble peasant, these fables transfixed audiences with vivid depictions of human folly and resilience. Through the guise of talking animals, mythical beings, and iconic figures, these stories illuminate the timeless battle between righteousness and temptation, offering poignant reflections on the consequences of one's actions. Marked by rich symbolism and allegory, these fables delve into the core values

and ethical dilemmas that have shaped Gulf society for generations. At the heart of these tales lay invaluable messages that
transcend time and place; they shed light on the enduring pursuit of contentment, the perils of ambition without principles,
and the strength of humility and compassion. The artful blend
of wit and wisdom in these narratives has ensured their lasting
significance as they continue to be passed down through generations, preserving the timeless ethos of the Gulf. Embedded
within these age-old folktales are profound insights into the
human condition and the perennial quest for spiritual fulfill-
ment. In delving into these fables of wealth and woe, readers
are beckoned to behold the intricate dance of fate, fortune, and
the irrevocable bonds that weave the tapestry of existence.

Oral Tradition: The Art of Storytelling in the Gulf

Oral tradition is an integral part of the cultural tapestry
of the Gulf region, weaving together a rich and diverse array
of stories that have been passed down through generations.
Through the art of storytelling, Gulf communities have preserved their history, values, and traditions, allowing them to
transcend time and connect with contemporary society. This
enduring practice is not merely about recounting tales; it encapsulates the collective wisdom and ethos of the Gulf people,
offering insights into their worldviews, beliefs, and aspirations.
Storytelling in the Gulf is a nuanced craft, often employing
vivid imagery, metaphor, and symbolism to convey profound
moral and ethical lessons. The storytellers, revered as guardians
of knowledge, possess the skill to captivate audiences with
their eloquence, infusing life into ancient sagas and fables.
As they weave their narratives, they transport listeners across
deserts, through bustling markets, and out onto the open sea,
leaving them enraptured by the unfolding chronicles. While

preserving historical events, the oral tradition also serves to impart societal norms and cultural heritage, ensuring that customs are perpetuated across generations.

Moreover, communal storytelling fosters a sense of unity and collective identity, strengthening social bonds and nurturing a shared consciousness among the Gulf population. Gatherings around campfires or majlises become a stage where stories come alive, igniting discussions and reflections that resonate deeply within the fabric of Gulf societies. The essence of storytelling transcends entertainment, serving as a medium for introspection, provoking contemplation on individual actions, and fostering empathy and understanding for others.

Contemporary Gulf Society continues to be profoundly influenced by the age-old art of storytelling. While modern technologies have emerged, the oral tradition persists, adapting to coexist with digital mediums. Efforts are being made to preserve this art form, recognizing its pivotal role in shaping cultural identities and fostering a sense of belonging. Encouragingly, initiatives to document these oral narratives and support storytellers are gaining traction, ensuring that future generations will inherit this invaluable resource. The timeless allure of storytelling endures, transcending generations and reaffirming its place as a cherished pillar of Gulf heritage.

Cultural Impact: How Myth Shapes Contemporary Gulf Society

The enduring presence of mythology within the Gulf region reverberates in contemporary society, significantly influencing cultural practices, artistic expressions, and societal norms. Gulf myths serve as a rich tapestry of narratives seamlessly woven into everyday life's fabric, imparting wisdom, offering moral guidance, and reinforcing collective identities. In today's Gulf society, the impact of these mythical narratives is palpable in various aspects, from language and literature to visual arts and entertainment. One pervasive influence of Gulf mythology is evident in modern storytelling traditions, where elements of ancient tales are seamlessly integrated with contemporary themes, reflecting the continuity of cultural values and beliefs. Furthermore, Gulf myths inspire a spectrum of creative endeavors, from literature and music to visual arts and architecture, infusing these creative outputs with a sense of rootedness and connection to the revered past. The ethical quandaries and subtle morals embedded within these age-old tales resonate deeply with contemporary Gulf citizens, shaping their perceptions of right and wrong, good and evil, and echoing through the moral frameworks that underpin social interactions. Moreover, the imagery and symbolism drawn from Gulf mythology often form the basis of cultural celebrations, ceremonies, and rituals, enriching these communal events with layers of significance and profound meaning. Beyond the realm of culture and the arts, the enduring heritage of Gulf mythology also exerts its influence on social structures, offering a blueprint for understanding societal roles, familial dynamics, and even governance systems. The allegorical wisdom contained within these myths serves as a source of inspiration and an anchor for navigating the complexities of contemporary life. Ultimately, the profound impact of Gulf mythology on contemporary society underscores the enduring relevance of these timeless narratives, highlighting their role as custodians of tradition, morality, and the collective imagination.

Chapter 10

Craftsmanship and Commerce: Artisans and Traders of the Gulf

Craftsmanship and commerce have been integral to the development of the Gulf region, with traditional crafts playing a pivotal role in shaping its cultural identity. The historical evolution of artisan techniques reveals a rich tapestry of skills passed down through generations, contributing to the unique heritage of the Gulf. These traditional crafts not only showcase the artistic prowess of the artisans but also represent a timeless link to the region's past, embodying the essence of cultural continuity and resilience. As societies flourished around these crafts, they became symbols of pride and distinction, reflecting the intrinsic value placed on skilled craftsmanship within the Gulf community. Artisans' intricate artistry and meticulous dedication resonate with the broader cultural fabric, illustrating the fusion of aesthetics, functionality, and tradition. Moreover, preserving indigenous crafts reflects an enduring commitment to honoring the customs, beliefs, and ethos that define the Gulf's cultural heritage. In examining the significance of traditional crafts within regional development, it becomes evident that these practices have sustained livelihoods and fostered remarkable economic growth. The exchange of artisan products has historically facilitated trade relations, creating vibrant marketplaces and commercial networks that bolstered the Gulf's economy. Furthermore, these crafts have played a central role in forging connections with neighboring regions, enriching the tapestry of cross-cultural influences in the Gulf's artistic traditions. As such, understanding the interplay of craftsmanship and commerce provides invaluable insights into the dynamic role of traditional crafts in shaping the Gulf's economic and cultural landscape. In exploring this intricate relationship, we delve into the heart of the Gulf's storied legacy, uncovering the profound impact of craftsmanship and commerce on the region's historical narrative and contemporary identity.

Historical Evolution of Artisan Techniques

Craftsmanship within the Gulf region has a rich and diverse history, shaped by centuries of evolution and innovation. The historical evolution of artisan techniques in the Gulf is a fascinating tapestry that intertwines cultural influences, technological advancements, and economic dynamics. The craftsmanship heritage of the Gulf can be traced back to ancient civilizations, where artisans honed their skills through trial and error, gradually perfecting techniques that became synonymous with the region's distinct artistic identity. From intricate weaving patterns to exquisite pottery designs and masterful metalwork, the historical evolution of artisan techniques reflects an unwavering dedication to preserving traditional craftsmanship while adapting to the changing tides of time. The interplay of trade routes, cultural exchanges, and societal dynamics has shaped and refined these artisan techniques over the centuries. As trade flourished along the ancient maritime routes, artisans were exposed to new materials, tools, and design influences, fueling a constant cycle of creativity and adaptation. Moreover, the cross-cultural interactions between civilizations introduced novel methods and designs, enriching the Gulf's artisan landscape with diverse influences. For instance, the exchange of pottery techniques between Mesopotamia and the Indus Valley civilizations contributed to developing distinctive pottery styles within the Gulf region. Similarly, weaving experienced significant transformations as Gulf artisans incorporated techniques from neighboring cultures, creating elaborate textiles that became highly sought after in trade networks. Acknowledging the integral role of technological innovations in shaping the historical evolution of artisan techniques is crucial. Advancements in metallurgy, textile production methods, and potter's wheel technology revolutionized craftsmanship, empowering artisans to achieve greater precision and intricacy. Adopting new tools and techniques catalyzed a renaissance of artistic expression, leading to the emergence of iconic craftsmanship styles that endure today. This relentless pursuit of excellence and innovation is a testament to the artisans' unwavering commitment to their craft and enduring legacy within the Gulf region.

Principal Crafts: Weaving, Pottery, and Metalwork

Craftsmanship in the Gulf region is characterized by a rich tapestry of traditional trades honed over centuries. Among the foremost crafts are weaving, pottery, and metalwork, each with its distinct heritage and significance within the local communities. Weaving is unique in Gulf culture, with techniques passed down through generations. The region's weavers are known for their intricate patterns and vibrant colors, often using locally sourced materials such as camel hair and palm fronds. These woven creations serve practical and decorative purposes, prominently in daily life and ceremonial occasions. Pottery, another time-honored craft, reflects the artistry and skill of Gulf artisans. Clay vessels, distinctive in form and design, exemplify the fusion of function and aesthetics. From utilitarian containers to ornamental pieces, Gulf pottery embodies the creative expression inherent in traditional craftsmanship. Metalwork, encompassing blacksmithing and silversmithing, has likewise played a pivotal role in the region's artisanal landscape. The forging of tools, weaponry, and ornamental items showcases the mastery of intricate metalworking techniques. Artisans employ age-old methods to shape and embellish metals, contributing to the enduring allure of Gulf metalwork. The interplay of these principal crafts underscores the cultural significance and economic value of traditional artisanal practices in the Gulf. As guardians of heritage, craftsmen continue to uphold and celebrate the legacy of weaving, pottery, and metalwork, ensuring that these time-honored traditions endure for future generations.

The Artisan Workplace: Tools and Techniques

Artisans of the Gulf have long been revered for their exquisite craftsmanship. Each trade boasts a rich tapestry of skills and techniques passed down through generations. The artisan workplace is the epicenter of creativity and production, where a skilled craftsman's mastery of tools and techniques is the hallmark. Weaving, pottery, and metalwork are central to the cultural and economic fabric of the Gulf region, each demanding a unique set of tools and methods.

Weavers, often working with traditional handlooms, meticulously intertwine vibrant threads to create intricate textiles renowned for their beauty and durability. The gentle metal clinking against metal fills the air in the workshops of skilled blacksmiths and metalworkers, where molten alloys are skillfully molded into ornate designs. Meanwhile, in the serene environs of potters' studios, the deft hands of artisans mold clay into timeless vessels reflective of the region's heritage. Each artisan's workspace teems with essential implements, be it looms, spindles, and shuttles for weavers; anvils, hammers, and chisels for metalworkers; or kilns, potter's wheels, and sculpting tools for potters, attesting to the precision and artistry synonymous with Gulf craftsmanship.

Techniques passed down through centuries are rigorously upheld, ensuring the authenticity and quality of the craft. The tools are imbued with significance, often reflecting the fusion of tradition and innovation, such as adapting modern welding equipment alongside traditional bellows in metalworking. Seasoned artisans impart their expertise on apprentices, perpetuating ancient wisdom and safeguarding the continuity of these time-honored traditions. Moreover, the artisan workplace is a haven for experimentation and evolution, as craftsmen adeptly integrate contemporary influences without compromising the integrity of their craft.

Beyond the tangible tools, the artisan workspace embodies an ethos of dedication and reverence for tradition, exuding an aura of quiet diligence and deep-rooted pride. The synergy between tools and techniques permeates every aspect of the artisan's daily ritual, from the rhythmic orchestration of the loom to the melodic resonance of forging metal. Each stroke of the brush, each turn of the potter's wheel, bears testimony

to the artisan's consummate mastery and unwavering commitment to preserving the essence of Gulf craftsmanship.

Trade Mechanisms: Barter, Coinage, and Marketplaces

Trade mechanisms in the ancient Gulf were diverse and
played a significant role in shaping economic interactions. The
exchange of goods and services was facilitated through various
systems, including barter, coinage, and marketplaces. Barter, a
prevalent method in early trade, involved directly exchanging
goods between parties without using currency. This system
relied on mutual agreement and often led to intricate networks
of trading relationships. Additionally, the introduction of stan-
dardized coinage brought a new dimension to trade by providing a universal medium of exchange. Coins served as a unit
of value and reflected the issuing authority's economic and
political stability, influencing trading patterns and alliances.
Moreover, the emergence of bustling marketplaces across the
Gulf region created vibrant commercial hubs where goods from
distant lands converged, fostering a dynamic environment for
commerce. These marketplaces became vital meeting points
for traders, artisans, and buyers, stimulating cross-cultural
interactions and economic growth. The diversity of goods
available in these marketplaces showcased the rich tapestry
of craftsmanship and trade, attracting merchants from far
and wide. The interplay of barter, coinage, and marketplaces
formed the backbone of the Gulf's economic vitality, enabling
the flourishing artisanal and trading communities to thrive.
Understanding the intricate dynamics of these trade mechanisms provides valuable insights into the historical economic
landscape of the Gulf, shedding light on the interconnectedness of diverse cultures and the evolution of trade practices.

Prominent Trading Hubs and Their Economic Impact

The Gulf region has been historically renowned for its prominent trading hubs, crucial nodes where goods, ideas, and cultures converged. These bustling centers of commerce played a pivotal role in shaping the economic landscape of the ancient world. Exploring the economic impact of these trading hubs reveals a rich tapestry of exchange, innovation, and prosperity. One such notable hub was the city of Ubar, also known as Iram of the Pillars in folklore. Ubar flourished as a vital trading post, serving as a gateway between the interior and the coastal regions. Its strategic location made it an indispensable stop along the lucrative incense trade routes, fostering economic growth and cultural exchanges. Another significant trading center was Mleiha, surrounded by fertile plains and strategically positioned along major trade routes. Mleiha stood as a beacon of commercial activity, witnessing the flow of goods and merchants from distant lands. The economic influence of these hubs extended far beyond their physical boundaries, leaving a lasting imprint on the development of civilizations and interregional interconnectedness. As commodities such as pearls, spices, textiles, and precious metals exchanged hands at these hubs, the economic impact rippled across vast territories, fueling the prosperity of nations and transforming societies. The societal dynamics within these trading hubs were equally compelling, showcasing the convergence of diverse groups and the coexistence of different cultural and ethnic identities. This melting pot of humanity created a dynamic marketplace where artisans, traders, and visitors mingled, fostering a vibrant ecosystem of commerce and cultural exchange. The economic significance of these trading hubs cannot be overstated, as they laid the groundwork for the prosperity and interconnectedness that characterized the ancient world.

These hubs facilitated the flow of goods and served as crucibles of innovation, where new ideas, technologies, and artistic developments emerged and disseminated. The intricate trade web established by these hubs formed the backbone of the Gulf's economic identity, solidifying its position as a vibrant center of global commerce and cooperation.

Artisans in Society: Status and Roles

Artisans in Gulf societies have traditionally held esteemed positions, with their skills and craftsmanship forming an integral part of the region's cultural and economic fabric. Their societal status is marked by the recognition of their expertise and the value placed on their contributions to the community. Artisans are viewed as custodians of heritage, preserving ancient techniques and passing them down through generations. Their roles extend beyond mere craftsmanship; they are storytellers, weaving narratives into their creations, and their work often reflects the collective identity of their communities. Artisans hold significant sway within this framework, shaping daily life's aesthetic and functional aspects. The prestige associated with mastery of a craft means that artisans are accorded respect and admiration and are often regarded as bearers of essential knowledge. Their involvement in trade also elevates their standing, as their goods form crucial elements of commercial exchange and cultural interactions. Furthermore, the interconnected relationship between artisans and patrons reinforces the social significance of their roles, creating networks that extend across various strata of society, from local markets to elite circles. However, artisans face challenges adapting to modern economic systems and technological advancements despite their elevated status. Preserving traditional roles while engaging with contemporary demands presents a delicate balance for many artisans. While navigating this landscape, some have embraced innovation, integrating new materials and methods into their craft and redefining their societal influence. Yet, the enduring reverence for these artisans continues to underscore their enduring role in bridging the past and the present, ensuring that the legacy of their craftsmanship remains an indelible part of Gulf societies.

Cross-Cultural Influences on Craftsmanship

Craftsmanship around the Gulf has been greatly influenced by cross-cultural exchanges, resulting in a rich tapestry of artistic expression and techniques. The intermingling of various cultural influences, such as those from the Indian subcontinent, Persia, Mesopotamia, and beyond, has played a pivotal role in shaping the region's artisanal traditions. This confluence of diverse cultures brought forth a fusion of artistic styles, materials, and techniques that continue to define the craftsmanship of the Gulf.

One notable instance of cross-cultural influence is the art of pottery. The intricate designs on Gulf pottery blend Arab, Persian, and Indian motifs, showcasing the harmonious amalgamation of diverse artistic sensibilities. Similarly, weaving techniques have been enriched by introducing new materials and patterns from neighboring regions, developing unique Gulf textile traditions.

The Gulf's metalwork also bears the imprint of cross-cultural interactions. Influences from ancient Mesopotamia and Persia can be discerned in Gulf artisans' elaborate designs and techniques. The intricate filigree work and decorative metal objects represent the assimilation of diverse artistic influences, creating a genuinely distinctive craft tradition.

The exchange of ideas and techniques within the Gulf has enriched local craftsmanship and resulted in the diffusion of Gulf artistry to other regions. The trade networks and commercial exchanges facilitated the spread of Gulf artisanal products, influencing the aesthetic sensibilities of distant civilizations and leaving a lasting impact on the global artistic landscape. Furthermore, the cultural intersections fostered innovation, leading to new artistic expression forms that continue inspiring contemporary artisans.

Recognizing the significance of cross-cultural influences on Gulf craftsmanship is essential, as it unveils the interconnectedness of human societies and the enduring legacy of artistic exchange. Embracing these influences allows for a deeper appreciation of the historical journey of Gulf artisans and provides insight into the dynamic nature of artistic traditions in the region.

Challenges Faced by Traditional Craftsmen

The traditional craftsmen of the Gulf region, revered for their exquisite skills and dedication to preserving ancient techniques, face numerous challenges in the modern era. These artisans, who have inherited their crafts from generations past, grapple with various obstacles that threaten the continuity and vitality of their traditions. One significant challenge is the diminishing interest among younger generations in pursuing traditional crafts as viable livelihoods. With the allure of modern professions and the rapid pace of technological advancement, fewer young individuals are apprenticing under master craftsmen to learn the intricate art forms handed down through centuries. This trend poses a grave concern for the sustainability of these time-honored skills. Economic pressures and shifting market demands also present formidable hurdles for traditional craftsmen. While their creations are cherished for their cultural significance, the commodification of artisanal products has led to an increasing focus on mass-produced alternatives, often undermining the value of handcrafted goods. Furthermore, globalization and the influx of cheaper, mass-manufactured imported items dilute the market for authentic handmade crafts, making it increasingly challenging for traditional craftsmen to earn a living. Another critical issue these artisans face is the scarcity of resources and raw materials essential for their craft. As urbanization encroaches upon natural environments and traditional sources of materials diminish, craftsmen struggle to preserve the authenticity of their work. Moreover, environmental concerns and restrictive regulations further restrict access to these vital resources, compounding the difficulties faced by traditional craftsmen. The lack of institutional support and recognition also poses a significant challenge. Despite their invaluable contribution to the cultural heritage of the Gulf, traditional craftsmen often find themselves marginalized in official policies and initiatives. This absence of support hampers efforts to preserve and transmit their crafts to future generations. Recognizing and addressing these challenges is crucial to ensuring the survival of traditional crafts in the Gulf. Efforts to raise awareness about traditional crafts' cultural and economic significance and measures to provide sustainable livelihoods for craftsmen will be instrumental in safeguarding these precious traditions. By fostering greater appreciation for the mastery and artistry of traditional crafts and creating platforms for collaboration and market access, strides can be made toward securing a vibrant future for the Gulf's rich heritage of craftsmanship.

Preservation and Modern Adaptations of Traditional Crafts

Preserving traditional crafts in the Gulf region is crucial for maintaining cultural identity and heritage. As globalization continues influencing societies, the need to safeguard traditional craftsmanship becomes more pronounced. Efforts are being made by various organizations, artisans, and governments to ensure the survival and continuity of these time-honored practices. Preservation initiatives often encompass documentation of techniques, materials, and processes and the transmission of knowledge from master craftsmen to younger generations. By doing so, traditional crafts are preserved and adapted to suit contemporary demands. One approach to ensuring the longevity of traditional crafts involves integrating modern technology without compromising the authenticity of these artisanal works. For example, traditional pottery techniques can be enhanced through modern kilns, preserving the handmade quality while increasing efficiency and output. Additionally, artisans are exploring new domestic and international crafts markets, leveraging e-commerce platforms and social media to showcase and market their products. This expansion of commercial avenues allows traditional crafts to flourish within a modern economic landscape. Furthermore, collaborations between traditional craftsmen and designers from diverse backgrounds have led to innovative adaptations of traditional crafts, breathing new life into age-old techniques. These collaborations introduce traditional crafts to new audiences and infuse them with fresh perspectives and design sensibilities. The result is a fusion of tradition and innovation, appealing to a broader demographic while maintaining the essence of traditional Gulf craftsmanship. Promoting traditional crafts as part of the tourism industry also plays a vital role in their preservation. Cultural centers, heritage villages, and craft fairs showcase traditional crafts to locals and tourists, fostering appreciation and understanding of these art forms. Educational programs and workshops further contribute to passing on traditional skills and knowledge to future generations. In essence, the conservation and modern adaptations of traditional crafts in the Gulf reflect a harmonious balance between honoring heritage and embracing progress. Through strategic preservation efforts and thoughtful integration of contemporary elements, traditional crafts continue to thrive and evolve, ensuring that the rich tapestry of Gulf craftsmanship endures for generations.

Chapter 11

Trade Winds and Sea Routes: Navigating the Ancient Maritime Trade

Maritime trade played a pivotal role in the socio-economic development of the ancient Gulf region, serving as the life-blood that sustained civilizations and facilitated the exchange of goods, ideas, and cultural influences across vast distances. The geographical configuration of the Gulf, with its extensive coastline and strategic location as a crossroads between the East and the West, rendered maritime trade a fundamental component of the region's prosperity. The ancient mariners who navigated these waters were not merely sailors but also pioneers of commerce, forging links between diverse communities and fostering mutual interdependence among civilizations. The reliance on maritime trade was intricately woven into the fabric of ancient Gulf societies, influencing their commercial practices, social structures, and technological advancements. The advent of maritime trade brought forth an era of economic dynamism, leading to the growth of port cities, the rise of specialized trades, and the emergence of a cosmopolitan culture enriched by the convergence of merchants, craftsmen, and intellectuals from diverse lands. The ancient Gulf region became a bustling nexus of commerce, where precious commodities such as pearls, spices, incense, and textiles traversed the seas, catalyzing economic prosperity and stimulating cultural exchanges that left an indelible mark on the historical tapestry of the region. This enriching interplay of trade dynamics fostered innovation as seafaring communities honed their navigation, shipbuilding, and maritime logistics skills, ushering in an era of unprecedented progress and global connectivity. As we embark on a journey to unravel the legacy of maritime trade in the ancient Gulf, it is imperative to appreciate the profound impact of this maritime network on the formation of cohesive societies, vibrant economies, and enduring cultural ties that continue to resonate through the annals of time.

Mapping the Wind: Understanding Seasonal Patterns

The ancient maritime trade in the Gulf relied heavily on understanding seasonal wind patterns. Mariners in the ancient world were keen observers of nature and could discern patterns in wind behavior over each season. This understanding was crucial for determining the best times for embarking on voyages and ensuring safe and efficient navigation. In this section, we will delve into the intricacies of wind patterns and how they shaped the ancient maritime trade in the Gulf region.

Seasonal patterns of wind, commonly known as monsoons, played a pivotal role in the trade dynamics of the ancient mariners. Predictably reversing winds during different seasons allowed for efficient travel between distant lands. The south-west monsoon, for example, enabled ships to sail from the Arabian Peninsula towards the Indian subcontinent, while the northeast monsoon facilitated the return journey. This reliable pattern allowed traders to confidently plan their expeditions, maximizing their opportunities for profitable trade.

By comprehending the variations in wind direction and strength across different seasons, ancient mariners became adept at adjusting their routes and strategies to capitalize on the prevailing conditions. Their mastery of these seasonal winds facilitated trade and contributed to the exchange of cultures, ideas, and technologies between distant civilizations. The interplay of wind patterns and maritime trade led to enduring commercial and cultural connections across the Gulf and beyond.

Furthermore, the influence of seasonal wind patterns extended beyond trade alone. It affected the daily lives of coastal communities, influencing agricultural practices, fishing expeditions, and even social activities. The understanding and prediction of these wind patterns were intrinsic to the survival and prosperity of ancient societies in the region. Moreover, the critical knowledge of seasonal winds also had significant implications for developing and advancing navigational techniques and tools. Mariners not only observed wind patterns but also developed navigational aids and instruments to harness the power of the winds effectively. These advancements in sailing technology and navigation are a testament to the profound impact of wind patterns on the ancient maritime trade in the Gulf.

In the next section, we will explore the navigational tools and techniques that ancient mariners employed to traverse the seas and harness the power of the winds, further unraveling the fascinating world of ancient maritime trade.

Navigational Tools and Techniques of Ancient Mariners

Ancient mariners of the Gulf were masters of navigating the waters using a range of sophisticated tools and techniques that allowed them to traverse the vast expanse of the seas. One of the fundamental instruments utilized by these mariners was the astrolabe, a device used for measuring the altitude of celestial bodies. By observing the position of the sun, moon, stars, and planets, sailors could determine their latitudes and plot their course accurately. The kamal, a simple navigational tool, was employed to measure the elevation of celestial objects above the horizon. This ingenious gadget allowed sailors to calculate their latitude based on the angle of Polaris, providing crucial guidance during night voyages. Additionally, magnetic compasses revolutionized maritime navigation, allowing sailors to maintain their heading even when out of sight of land. The development of accurate charts and maps also played a pivotal role in guiding ancient mariners across the open seas. These intricate navigational aids facilitated safe passage and contributed to the expansion of trade networks and cultural exchanges between distant shores. Furthermore, the skillful interpretation of sea and weather patterns enabled mariners to anticipate forthcoming conditions, ensuring their ability to navigate challenging environments effectively. Knowing seasonal wind patterns, such as the monsoons, allowed sailors to harness nature's forces, utilizing the winds to power their vessels across strategic trade routes. These mariners honed their understanding of the seas as guardians of precious cargo. They adopted techniques like dead reckoning to estimate distances traveled and deduce their position, enhancing their capacity to navigate without modern equipment. These extraordinary navigational tools and techniques illustrate the ingenuity and expertise of ancient mariners, underscoring their profound influence on the maritime trade that shaped the history of the Gulf.

Major Sea Routes: Pathways Connecting Continents

The ancient maritime trade in the Gulf was facilitated by a network of major sea routes that connected continents and cultures. These intricate pathways, crucial for the flow of goods and ideas, played a pivotal role in shaping the economic and social landscape of the ancient world. One of the most significant sea routes was connecting the Arabian Peninsula to the Indian subcontinent. This route, often called the Arabian Sea Route, facilitated the movement of valuable commodities such as spices, textiles, and precious stones between the two regions. It also served as a conduit for exchanging knowledge and cultural practices, contributing to the rich tapestry of cross-cultural interactions. Another prominent sea route was linking the Arabian Peninsula to East Africa. This maritime corridor allowed for transporting goods such as ivory, gold, and exotic animals, fostering trade and diplomatic relations between the region's kingdoms. Furthermore, the sea route connecting the Gulf to the Mediterranean region played a pivotal role in the diffusion of goods ranging from olive oil and wine to ceramics and glassware, enriching the material culture of societies along the route. The trade across these major sea routes contributed to the civilizations' prosperity and catalyzed the exchange of nautical knowledge, maritime technology, and strategic expertise. The interconnectedness fostered by these sea routes laid the foundation for an early form of globalization, wherein distant lands were brought into contact and collaboration. Such intercontinental ties and exchanges laid the groundwork for forming cosmopolitan societies with diverse influences and innovations. In essence, the major sea routes of the ancient maritime trade were not mere pathways for the movement of goods; they were conduits for exchanging ideas, values, and advancements that spanned continents and enriched the human experience.

Key Ports of Call: Strategic Stops Along the Trade Routes

Strategically positioned along the ancient maritime trade routes in the Gulf, key ports of call played a pivotal role in exchanging goods and ideas across continents. These strategic stops served as bustling hubs of economic activity, cultural exchange, and geopolitical significance. One such renowned port was located at the crossroads of major sea routes, welcoming traders and travelers from diverse lands.

The port was meticulously designed to accommodate a vast array of vessels, ranging from sturdy dhows to larger trading ships. Its natural harbor provided shelter from tumultuous seas, ensuring safe anchorage for merchant fleets during their often perilous journeys. Skilled seafarers and seasoned navigators would eagerly anticipate arriving at this essential waypoint, where they could replenish supplies, barter commodities, and forge new partnerships.

As merchants and sailors docked at these bustling ports, the air resonated with the melodic blend of languages and dialects, highlighting the cosmopolitan nature of these vibrant trading centers. A symphony of voices echoed through the bazaars, where exotic goods from distant lands adorned the market stalls. Spices, textiles, precious metals, and other commodities enriched the local economy, transforming these ports into veritable treasure troves of wealth from the farthest corners of the known world.

Beyond their economic significance, these key ports also served as conduits for the interweaving of cultures. Here, traditions, beliefs, and artistic expressions melded, captivating the imaginations of those who ventured ashore. Delightful aromas wafted from bustling kitchens, where culinary delights of varying origins mingled to create a fusion of flavors that enticed locals and visitors alike.

Yet, amid the allure of commerce and cultural exchange, these ports were not without challenges. At times, they fell prey to the audacious exploits of pirates and privateers, threatening the valuable cargo and esteemed travelers' safety and security. However, resilient communities, fortified by shared interests and mutual dependencies, stood united against such threats, reinforcing the resilience and ingenuity inherent in the fabric of maritime trade.

Ultimately, these key ports of call facilitated the flow of goods and commodities and became bastions of diversity, harmony, and cooperation. Their legacy endures in the tapestry of history, enriching our understanding of the ancient maritime trade and serving as timeless testaments to the enduring spirit of exploration and exchange among humanity.

Commodities Traded: The Wealth of Nations in Transit

The ancient maritime trade in the Gulf was a conduit for precious goods and a melting pot of diverse and exotic commodities. As ships traversed the azure waters, they carried the riches of nations, symbolizing economic prosperity and cultural exchange. From the opulent silks of China to the fragrant spices of India and the gleaming pearls of Arabia, each cargo held its own story of origin and craft, weaving together a tapestry of global trade. The bustling ports were a sight as merchants from distant lands bartered for goods representing their homelands' unique identity. These commodities were not merely items for trade but tangible expressions of the vibrant societies that produced them. The maritime routes of the Gulf epitomized the interconnectedness of civilizations, where treasures from far-flung corners of the world mingled and found new homes along the coastlines. The trade of such diverse goods fostered a sense of unity among nations, transcending geographical boundaries to create a shared economy of abundance. This exchange of commodities also played a pivotal role in shaping the cultural landscape, as foreign influences permeated local customs and traditions. Goods such as textiles, precious metals, and gemstones not only elevated the material wealth of the region but also elevated the artistic and artisanal endeavors of the communities that engaged in trade. The thriving commerce of these goods facilitated an environment ripe for innovation and creativity, spurring advancements in various fields, including craftsmanship, agriculture, and architecture. The sea routes were not just conduits for physical wares; they also facilitated the transfer of knowledge, ideas, and beliefs, fostering a rich tapestry of cultural exchange. As the vessels plied the seas, they brought with them the teachings and philosophies of distant lands, enriching the intellectual fabric of coastal civilizations. This exchange of commodities was not solely about transactions; it symbolized the interconnected web of human endeavor and collective progress, transforming the landscapes they touched and leaving lasting imprints on the heritage of the Gulf.

Influences on Local Economies: Impact of Sea Trade

The impact of ancient maritime trade on local economies cannot be overstated. As goods and commodities flowed across the sea routes, a profound influence was exerted on the economic landscapes of the coastal regions. The infusion of foreign products and resources enriched the markets and stimulated domestic production to meet the demand. This led to the evolution of specialized industries, such as shipbuilding, navigation, and the development of port facilities.

Moreover, the influx of wealth from successful sea trade bolstered the economic power of port cities, fostering the growth of urban centers and facilitating the rise of affluent merchant classes. These economic hubs became melting pots of ideas, cultures, and entrepreneurship, nurturing an environment conducive to innovation and exchange.

The impact of sea trade extended beyond mere economic prosperity; it fostered cultural dynamism and cosmopolitanism as ports became hubs for the convergence of diverse peoples and traditions. The intermingling of languages, customs, and belief systems enriched the social fabric and contributed to a cross-pollination of ideas, leading to the advancement of arts, sciences, and trade practices.

However, with the influx of wealth and resources came challenges and conflicts. The lure of riches attracted not only legitimate traders but pirates and raiders who sought to exploit the lucrative sea trade. This necessitated the establishment of maritime laws and security measures to protect the trade routes and ensure safe passage for merchants and their cargo. The impact of such security concerns reverberated through local economies, influencing the allocation of resources and the development of defense mechanisms.

Furthermore, the reliance on sea trade exposed coastal regions to the vagaries of nature, including storms, tidal waves, and other environmental hazards. The unpredictable forces of nature constantly threatened maritime activities, leading to periodic disruptions and losses in both lives and cargo. Over time, this necessitated the evolution of navigational techniques and the construction of sturdier vessels capable of enduring the perils of the sea.

In conclusion, ancient maritime trade's impact on local economies was multifaceted, engendering prosperity and cultural exchange as well as challenges that demanded innovative solutions. The legacies of this era continue to permeate the modern-day economic and cultural landscapes, underscoring the enduring influence of ancient sea trade on the societies it touched.

Challenges at Sea: Pirates and Natural Obstacles

Maritime trade in the ancient Gulf was not without its perils. The treacherous waters were rife with challenges, both natural and man-made, that tested the resilience and resourcefulness of seafarers. One of the most notorious threats to maritime trade was piracy. Swashbuckling raiders, often operating from hidden coves and islands, struck fear into the hearts of merchants and sailors alike. The pirates would prowl the sea routes, preying on vulnerable vessels laden with valuable goods. Their tactics ranged from swift surprise attacks to prolonged sieges, making the dangerous sea journeys even more daunting.

Beyond the threat of human adversaries, nature posed formidable obstacles to maritime trade. The Gulf's unpredictable weather patterns and fierce seasonal storms could wreak havoc on unsuspecting voyagers. Navigating through narrow straits and shallow waters required expert seamanship, while the vast stretches of open sea left ships vulnerable to sudden storms and tempests. The absence of modern navigational aids meant that ancient mariners had to rely on their knowledge of celestial bodies, winds, and currents to chart a safe passage.

In response to these challenges, maritime communities developed strategies to mitigate the risks associated with sea travel. Coastal watchtowers provided early warning of pirate activity, allowing merchant ships to alter their course or seek sanctuary in fortified harbors. Additionally, alliances were forged between regional powers to combat piracy and secure vital trade routes collectively. As for the perils posed by nature, seasoned navigators honed their skills in reading the signs of the sea and sky, allowing them to anticipate and evade potential hazards.

Despite the prevalent dangers, the allure of maritime trade persisted, driven by the promises of prosperity and cultural exchange. Merchants and sailors braved the uncertain waters, knowing that the rewards of successful voyages far outweighed the risks. The tales of triumph over adversity at sea became woven into the fabric of the Gulf's history, shaping the identities of the coastal communities and fostering resilience in the face of adversity.

Interactions and Exchanges: Cultural Impacts of Trade

The ancient maritime trade routes traversing the Gulf facilitated profound cultural interactions and exchanges among the diverse civilizations participating in this extensive network. The exchange of goods was not the sole aspect of this interaction; it also served as a conduit for the interchange of ideas, languages, religions, and societal norms, ultimately shaping the region's cultural landscape. These exchanges exposed the societies along the trade routes to new ideologies, technologies, and artistic styles, fostering a rich tapestry of cultural diversity. Moreover, the interconnectedness brought about by trade led to the blending of traditions and customs, creating hybrid cultures that bore the imprint of various civilizations. Ancient mariners and merchants carried goods and acted as conduits for transmitting knowledge, beliefs, and practices between distant lands. This cross-pollination of cultures enhanced the intellectual and creative spheres of the trading nations, enriching their respective civilizations. Furthermore, the integration of diverse cultural elements resulted in the evolution of unique artistic expressions, architectural styles, and culinary traditions, exemplifying the enduring influence of interconnected trade networks on the cultural fabric of the Gulf region. Beyond material exchanges, the cultural impact of trade can be observed in the assimilation and adaptation of religious beliefs and philosophical ideologies across different communities, culminating in the emergence of syncretic faiths and philosophical doctrines. Such syncretism reflects the tolerant and inclusive nature of the ancient trading societies, which embraced diversity and integrated varied perspectives into their cultural narratives. The enduring legacy of these cultural exchanges is evident in contemporary Gulf societies, where historical trade routes continue to serve as conduits for disseminating cultural practices and sustaining intercultural dialogue. Through examining the cultural impacts of ancient maritime trade, we gain insight into the transformative power of commerce in shaping the interconnected histories and identities of the people who inhabited the ancient Gulf region.

Conclusion: Legacy of the Ancient Maritime Trade

The ancient maritime trade routes, with their multifaceted cultural exchanges and economic intersections, have left an indelible legacy on the societies of the Gulf and beyond. As maritime trade flourished, it facilitated the exchange of goods, ideas, and belief systems, contributing to the rich tapestry of cultural diversity that characterizes the region today. The enduring impact of these ancient maritime trade routes is evident in contemporary art, architecture, cuisine, and social customs, highlighting the lasting influence of cross-cultural interactions.

The interconnectedness fostered by maritime trade created vibrant cosmopolitan centers at strategic ports of call, where merchants from distant lands converged, fostering a climate of cross-cultural pollination. From Mesopotamian pottery to Indian spices and Chinese silks, the commodities exchanged along these routes fueled economies and transcended commercial transactions to become symbols of cultural amalgamation.

Additionally, the navigational tools and techniques developed by ancient mariners continue to inform modern maritime practices, underscoring the enduring legacy of seafaring traditions. Knowledge of seasonal wind patterns and the use of celestial navigation techniques passed down through generations shaped the maritime heritage and contributed to the development of advanced nautical science. Furthermore, the legacy of the challenges faced by ancient mariners, such as piracy and natural obstacles, continues to inspire resilience and innovation in contemporary maritime security strategies.

The cultural impacts of ancient maritime trade are profound, reflected in the architectural styles, gastronomic delights, and societal norms enriched and enlivened by diverse influences. This cultural legacy serves as a testament to the enduring dynamism of societies shaped by the ebb and flow of maritime trade. Moreover, embracing cultural diversity and openness to foreign ideas and customs have become embedded in the ethos of the Gulf, perpetuating the spirit of inclusivity and tolerance that reverberates through its modern societies.

In conclusion, the historical maritime trade routes have bequeathed a legacy of cultural fusion, economic prosperity, and maritime prowess that has endured across centuries. Their impact remains palpable, echoing through the traditions, innovations, and collective memory of the societies connected by these ancient maritime highways. Understanding this enduring legacy provides invaluable insights into the resilience, adaptability, and transformative power of human interaction, marking the legacy of the ancient maritime trade as a testament to the unifying force of commerce and cultural exchange.

Chapter 12

Dhows and Decks: Maritime Vessels and Navigation Techniques

Maritime vessels have played a pivotal role in shaping the ancient world, serving as the lifeline for trade and exploration across the seas. The evolution of maritime vessels, particularly dhows, represents the ingenuity and craftsmanship of ancient civilizations that sought to harness the power of the oceans for commerce and discovery. These vessels were more than just means of transportation; they were symbols of innovation, connecting distant lands and cultures. The historical significance of maritime vessels extends far beyond their utilitarian purposes, encapsulating the spirit of adventure, entrepreneurship, and cultural exchange. As we delve into the intricate details of these vessels, it becomes evident that their impact reverberates through the annals of history and continues to shape our contemporary understanding of global interconnectedness. From the humble beginnings of early sailboats to the sophisticated designs of seafaring vessels, the narrative of maritime vessels intertwines with the human desire to conquer the unknown and expand horizons. Through this exploration, we gain a deeper appreciation for the expertise required to construct and navigate these vessels, illuminating the collaborative efforts of sailors, traders, and craftsmen. This section aims to unravel the multifaceted significance of maritime vessels, shedding light on their integral role in the progression of civilizations and the facilitation of cultural exchange. As we embark on this journey, the story of maritime vessels unfolds as a testament to mankind's relentless pursuit of knowledge, wealth, and connectivity.

Historical Evolution of Dhows

The historical evolution of dhows is a captivating narrative that embodies centuries of maritime tradition and ingenuity. Originating in the Arabian Peninsula, these elegant vessels have played a pivotal role in shaping the region's cultural and economic landscape. The story of dhows begins in ancient times when their sleek designs and robust construction enabled them to navigate the treacherous waters of the Gulf and beyond. These early shows were crafted from the finest Indigenous materials, showcasing the exceptional craftsmanship of seafaring societies. As trade flourished across the Indian Ocean, dhows evolved to meet the demands of long-distance voyages, leading to the development of distinct regional variations. Over time, technological advancements and trade interactions influenced the design and functionality of dhows, reflecting a fascinating fusion of cultures and expertise. The enduring legacy of these vessels is underscored by their continued relevance in modern maritime activities, signifying the enduring resilience of their design and construction techniques. From the iconic lateen sails to the efficient hull shapes, each aspect of dhow evolution speaks volumes about the resourcefulness and adaptability of ancient maritime communities. Furthermore, the historical evolution of dhows is closely intertwined with the progression of navigation techniques, highlighting the symbiotic relationship between vessel development and seamanship. Understanding the evolution of dhows provides valuable insights into the interconnected history of maritime trade, cultural exchange, and technological innovation in the Gulf region. It is an enthralling saga that resonates with the spirit of exploration and enterprise, reflecting the enduring legacy of the maritime heritage.

Design and Construction of Maritime Vessels

The design and construction of maritime vessels in the ancient Gulf region were works of art reflecting the seafaring communities' expertise and innovation. They were meticulous crafts incorporating traditional wisdom, local resources, and an intricate understanding of the sea.

Maritime vessels such as dhows were meticulously crafted to withstand the challenges of the Gulf's waters. These vessels were designed with a keen awareness of the prevailing winds, sea currents, and the need for stability in often unpredictable conditions. The hull designs of these vessels, shaped from various types of wood, such as teak and mahogany, were influenced by generations of accumulated knowledge and experience.

Construction began with carefully selecting materials, ensuring the wood used was durable and flexible. Skilled craftsmen, often belonging to specialized shipbuilding families, painstakingly carved and assembled the elements of the vessel. Precise measurements and calculations were made to ensure the vessel's structural integrity while considering its seaworthiness.

The design and construction of maritime vessels were pragmatic and cultural expressions. The decoration and embellishment of dhows were often intricate and carried symbolic meanings that honored the communities' traditions and beliefs. These vessels' carvings, paintings, and adornments served as visual narratives of the seafaring culture, reflecting the maritime communities' values, myths, and aspirations.

Furthermore, the construction of maritime vessels played a significant role in fostering a sense of community and identity. Shipbuilding was a communal endeavor, often involving the collective effort of families and communities. The transfer of shipbuilding knowledge occurred through apprenticeships and oral traditions, passing down the skills and techniques from generation to generation.

In conclusion, the design and construction of maritime vessels in the ancient Gulf were a testament to the region's ingenuity, craftsmanship, and deep-rooted maritime heritage. The vessels were not merely instruments of trade and transportation but living embodiments of the rich cultural tapestry of the seafaring communities, seamlessly blending form and function.

Materials Used in Shipbuilding

Shipbuilding is a craft that has evolved over centuries, requiring an intricate understanding of materials and their properties. The choice of materials used in shipbuilding profoundly impacts the vessel's structural integrity, seaworthiness, and longevity. Historically, shipbuilders relied on various materials to construct maritime vessels, each chosen for its specific qualities and suitability.

One of the primary materials used in traditional shipbuilding is wood. Different types of wood have been prized for their durability, strength, and flexibility, making them ideal for constructing various ship components, including the hull, masts, and planking. Oak, cedar, teak, and pine are among the woods commonly favored by shipbuilders due to their resistance to rot, ability to withstand the rigors of the sea, and ease of shaping.

Shipbuilders have also utilized metals in addition to wood in constructing maritime vessels. Copper and bronze, for instance, have been historically employed to sheath the hulls of ships, protecting marine organisms such as barnacles and teredos while also offering resistance to corrosion. Iron and steel have similarly played pivotal roles in shipbuilding, offering unparalleled strength and reinforcement for critical structural elements.

Furthermore, the advent of modern shipbuilding techniques has seen the integration of composite materials into the construction of maritime vessels. Fiberglass, carbon fiber, and other advanced composites have gained traction for their exceptional strength-to-weight ratio, corrosion resistance, and design flexibility. These materials have revolutionized shipbuilding, enabling the creation of vessels capable of withstanding the demands of contemporary maritime operations.

From natural materials like wood and metal to cutting-edge composites, the selection of materials used in shipbuilding reflects the dynamic interplay between tradition and innovation. A deep appreciation for the characteristics and behaviors of these materials underscores the artistry and engineering prowess inherent in the construction of maritime vessels, emphasizing the enduring significance of shipbuilding as a testament to human ingenuity and mastery over the seas.

Navigational Tools and Techniques

Maritime navigation in the ancient Gulf region relied on various tools and techniques that allowed sailors to traverse the open seas accurately and confidently. The navigational prowess of mariners was imperative, as they needed to rely on observations of celestial bodies, such as the sun and stars, as well as their understanding of wind patterns and ocean currents to steer their vessels. One essential tool used for navigation was the astrolabe, an intricate instrument that enabled sailors to determine the angle between the horizon and celestial bodies, aiding in calculating latitude. This provided crucial information for charting courses and maintaining their bearings. Additionally, the kamal, a simple device consisting of a small wooden tablet and knotted cord, was employed to measure the altitude of celestial bodies above the horizon. These tools were complemented by magnetic compasses, which offered guidance by indicating the direction of magnetic north. Moreover, knowledge of wave patterns, cloud formations, and wildlife behavior assisted seafarers in predicting weather changes, avoiding hazards, and identifying potential landmasses. Alongside these traditional methods, oral traditions and the accumulated wisdom of experienced sailors played a central role, providing invaluable insights into navigating the unpredictable waters of the Gulf. This body of knowledge, passed down through generations, formed part of the intangible heritage of maritime communities and significantly contributed to the success of their voyages. The combination of these navigational tools and techniques facilitated safe passage. It enabled the flourishing trade networks that connected distant shores and cultures, highlighting maritime navigation's crucial role in shaping the Gulf region's history and prosperity.

Roles and Skills of the Crew

The success and safety of maritime voyages in ancient times were heavily reliant on the expertise and efficiency of the crew members. Each crew member aboard a dhow or any other maritime vessel played a distinct role, requiring specific skills and knowledge to ensure the smooth operation of the vessel and the successful completion of the journey. The roles and responsibilities varied depending on the size of the vessel, the duration of the voyage, and the nature of the cargo being transported. A well-organized crew was crucial for navigating through unpredictable weather conditions and unknown waters. The captain or master of the vessel held the highest authority. He was responsible for making critical decisions concerning the direction of the voyage, handling emergencies, and overseeing the crew's performance. The first mate or chief officer assisted the captain and often managed the day-to-day operations, including supervising loading and unloading activities, managing the crew, and ensuring compliance with maritime laws and regulations. The sailors, also known as seamen or deckhands, formed the backbone of the crew, undertaking a wide range of tasks such as rigging sails, steering the vessel, hoisting cargo, and maintaining the cleanliness and orderliness of the ship. They possessed excellent physical strength and endurance, often working long hours under challenging conditions. Additionally, skilled craftsmen such as carpenters, coopers, and sailmakers were essential for maintaining and repairing the vessel, equipment, and cargo-carrying apparatus. These individuals brought specialized expertise invaluable during extended voyages when immediate access to external assistance was not feasible. Furthermore, navigators and helmsmen guided the vessel using celestial navigation, reading the stars, sun, and moon to determine the ship's position and course. Their proficiency in interpreting charts and using navigational instruments ensured the vessel stayed on course, avoiding obstacles and reaching its intended destination. As a cohesive unit, the crew needed to communicate effectively, anticipate each other's actions, and respond promptly to unforeseen challenges. The harmony and coordination among crew members were vital for successfully maneuvering the vessel through dangerous waters and ensuring the safety of all onboard. The combination of skills, expertise, and unwavering teamwork enabled ancient maritime crews to navigate the high seas, foster international trade, and contribute to exchanging cultures and knowledge across distant regions.

Famous Navigators and Their Journeys

Throughout history, the Arabian Gulf has been blessed with intrepid navigators whose journeys have left an indelible mark on maritime exploration and trade. One such legendary figure is Ahmad ibn Majid, a renowned navigator and cartographer from the 15th century. Ibn Majid played a pivotal role in shaping the region's maritime history through his extensive knowledge of navigation techniques and his daring voyages across the Indian Ocean.

Another notable navigator is Vasco da Gama, the Portuguese explorer who charted a sea route to India around the Cape of Good Hope in 1498. Da Gama's groundbreaking expedition revolutionized global trade and opened up new avenues for maritime commerce in the Arabian Gulf region.

The remarkable feats of Zheng He, the Chinese admiral and explorer, also merit mention in any discussion of famous navigators. Zheng He's voyages across the Indian Ocean during the 15th century fostered diplomatic relations. They facilitated trade between China and the lands bordering the Arabian Gulf, leaving an enduring legacy on the region's maritime history.

In addition to these luminaries, the journeys of Sinbad the Sailor, a mythical character from the collection of Middle Eastern folktales known as the One Thousand and One Nights, have captivated the imaginations of seafarers and storytellers for centuries. While the tales of Sinbad are steeped in myth and legend, they reflect the fascination with maritime exploration and the allure of distant lands that has characterized the region's seafaring heritage.

These illustrious examples underscore the profound impact of navigators and their expeditions on the interconnected history of the maritime Silk Road and the Arabian Gulf. Their experiences have enriched our understanding of ancient maritime traditions, cultural exchange, and the enduring significance of navigational prowess in shaping the course of human civilization.

Impact of Maritime Travel on Trade

Maritime travel has always been pivotal in shaping trade and commerce across the ancient world. The development of maritime vessels and navigation techniques revolutionized trade, establishing extensive trade networks that connected distant lands and cultures. The impact of maritime travel on trade was profound, influencing economies, societies, and the exchange of goods and ideas.

One key impact of maritime travel on trade was facilitating long-distance commerce. Through advanced sailing vessels such as dhows, merchants could transport large quantities of goods across the seas, reaching new markets and establishing lucrative trading routes. This led to the exchange of diverse commodities, including spices, textiles, precious metals, and exotic goods, enriching the economies of the exporting and importing regions.

Furthermore, maritime travel fostered cultural exchanges and the dissemination of knowledge and ideas. As ships plied the waters, they became conduits for the spread of languages, religions, and philosophies, contributing to a rich tapestry of cross-cultural interactions. This exchange of ideas and beliefs enriched societies and laid the foundation for future diplomatic ties and alliances between different civilizations.

The impact of maritime travel on trade also extended to technological advancements. Navigation techniques and ship-building methods were continually refined and shared among seafaring communities, leading to innovations in maritime technology. Developing more efficient vessels and navigational instruments enhanced the safety and efficiency of sea voyages. It opened up new trade routes and opportunities, further expanding the scope of global trade.

Moreover, integrating maritime travel into trade networks had far-reaching economic implications. It stimulated the growth of port cities and trading hubs, fostering urban development and infrastructure. Merchants and traders amassed wealth and established commercial enterprises, contributing to the rise of powerful mercantile classes. The wealth generated from maritime trade also fueled the patronage of arts and scholarship, nurturing cultural flourishing in various regions.

In conclusion, maritime travel's impact on trade was multifaceted, encompassing economic, cultural, and technological dimensions. It reshaped global commerce, fostered cultural exchanges, and propelled technological progress, leaving an enduring legacy that continues to shape our interconnected world today.

Conservation of Ancient Maritime Artifacts

Conserving ancient maritime artifacts is necessary for preserving our history and culture and a crucial aspect of understanding the development of maritime navigation and trade development. These artifacts, whether sunken ships, navigational instruments, or cargo items, provide invaluable insights into the techniques, materials, and skills used by ancient mariners. The conservation of these artifacts requires meticulous planning, specialized expertise, and a deep respect for our shared maritime heritage.

One of the primary challenges in conserving ancient maritime artifacts is the delicate balance between protecting the items from further degradation and creating public access for study and appreciation. Preservation efforts often involve a multidisciplinary approach, bringing together historians, archaeologists, conservationists, and environmental scientists to develop comprehensive strategies. These strategies encompass careful retrieval, documentation, analysis, and preservation processes that adhere to strict ethical and scientific standards.

The environment in which these artifacts are found plays a significant role in determining the conservation methods. For example, items recovered from underwater sites require specific treatment to prevent deterioration caused by exposure to air and pollutants. Advanced techniques such as freeze-drying, chemical stabilization, and controlled storage environments are utilized to ensure the long-term survival of these artifacts while maintaining their historical integrity.

Furthermore, the conservation process extends beyond the physical preservation of artifacts. It also involves promoting public awareness and education about the importance of these relics. Museums, research institutions, and educational programs are pivotal in showcasing and interpreting maritime artifacts, connecting people with maritime heritage, and their significance in shaping our world today. These organizations contribute to the ongoing dialogue about preserving and interpreting our maritime past through exhibitions, interactive displays, and outreach initiatives.

In the context of the Gulf, where maritime trade has played a significant role for centuries, the conservation of ancient maritime artifacts holds particular significance. It sheds light on the rich history of maritime cultures and fosters a sense of pride and connection to the region's maritime legacy. By safeguarding and celebrating these artifacts, we honor the enduring spirit of exploration, innovation, and exchange that has shaped the Gulf's identity and continues to influence its future. As technology and methods for archaeological discovery and preservation continue to advance, the conservation of ancient maritime artifacts will remain an essential endeavor, ensuring that the tales of our maritime ancestors endure for generations to come.

Future of Maritime Navigation and Technology

As we look toward the future, maritime navigation and technology present a promising and transformative landscape. The advent of advanced technologies has already begun revolutionizing the way maritime vessels navigate and operate at sea. One of the most significant developments on the horizon is the integration of artificial intelligence (AI) and autonomous navigation systems into maritime vessels, which has the potential to enhance efficiency, safety, and sustainability. These cutting-edge advancements are poised to redefine the future of maritime transportation and exploration.

With the evolution of maritime technology, intelligent ships are gaining momentum. Smart ships integrate innovative technologies, including IoT (Internet of Things), big data analytics, and remote monitoring systems, to optimize vessel performance, streamline operations, and minimize environmental impact. By leveraging real-time data and predictive analytics, smart ships can proactively address maintenance needs, manage fuel consumption, and mitigate operational risks, thereby ushering in a new era of intelligent and eco-friendly maritime transportation.

Furthermore, the future of maritime navigation encompasses developing next-generation propulsion systems that prioritize energy efficiency and environmental sustainability. This involves exploring alternative fuel sources, such as LNG (liquefied natural gas) and hydrogen fuel cells, to propel maritime vessels with reduced emissions and carbon footprint. Additionally, advancements in propulsion technologies, including electric and hybrid propulsion systems, have the potential to transform the maritime industry by offering cleaner and more efficient means of propulsion.

In navigation, the convergence of satellite-based systems, such as GNSS (Global Navigation Satellite System) and augmented reality (AR), holds immense promise for enhancing navigational accuracy, collision avoidance, and situational awareness at sea. By harnessing the power of these technologies, maritime navigation can achieve greater precision, reliability, and safety, setting new benchmarks for seamanship and maritime operations.

Looking ahead, the future of maritime navigation and technology is inexorably linked with the imperative of environmental stewardship. As the global community endeavors to address climate change and reduce the environmental footprint of maritime activities, technological innovations will play a pivotal role in fostering sustainable practices and mitigating the ecological impact of maritime navigation. As such, the path forward demands a concerted focus on advancing renewable energy solutions and implementing eco-conscious initiatives to uphold our oceans' and waterways' health and vitality.

In summary, the future of maritime navigation and technology is characterized by a convergence of innovation, sustainability, and seamless connectivity. Embracing this transformative trajectory holds the potential to redefine the maritime domain, elevating it into a realm marked by ingenuity, environmental responsibility, and unparalleled progress.

Chapter 13

Cultural Crossroads: The Flow of Ideas and Religion

The confluence of cultures in the ancient Gulf region is a testament to the enduring human endeavor for cross-cultural exchange and collaboration. As we embark on this exploration, we are propelled into an era where diverse civilizations intersected along the thriving trade routes, giving rise to pivotal moments of cultural assimilation and resistance. This chapter delves deep into the initial encounters between various ethnicities, religions, and traditions, unraveling the complex tapestry of ideologies and practices that coalesced in this remarkable region. The nexus of trade served as a meeting ground for traders, scholars, and religious emissaries, fostering dialogues that transcended linguistic and ideological differences. Amidst bustling marketplaces and vibrant ports, we witness the convergence of belief systems, philosophies, and artistic expressions, illuminating the interconnectedness of disparate yet symbiotic cultures. From the spirited debates in seaport taverns to the solemn rituals at ancient temples, the dynamic interplay

between faiths and customs shaped the collective consciousness of the Gulf's inhabitants. Our journey through time
unveils how these interactions facilitated material exchanges
and forged lasting imprints on the social fabric as communities grappled with the dichotomies of tradition and innovation. The saga of cultural assimilation and resistance unfolds
against a backdrop of commercial hunger and intellectual curiosity—propelling us to recognize the profound impact of this
confluence on the evolution of civilization. Through retelling
these transformative moments, we unravel the enigmatic web
of intercultural engagement, marveling at the resilience and
adaptability that propelled societies towards harmonious coexistence amidst diversity.

Historical Influence of Religion on Trade

Religion has played a pivotal role in shaping the trade dynamics of the Arabian Gulf throughout history. The convergence
of diverse religious ideologies has influenced the patterns of
commerce and exchange, creating a multifaceted tapestry of
economic interactions. From the early maritime routes that
connected ancient civilizations to the bustling trade hubs of
modern times, the interplay between religion and trade has
left an indelible mark on the region's commercial landscape.

The rise of Islam significantly transformed the trade networks of the Arabian Gulf. With the expansion of the Islamic
empire, trade flourished along the established routes under
the new Islamic order. The unification of regions under the
banner of Islam fostered an environment conducive to transre-
gional trade, as merchants could traverse vast territories with
relative ease. The spread of Islamic teachings also facilitated
cultural exchanges and economic collaborations, contributing
to the prosperity of Gulf trade.

Moreover, the coexistence of Christianity and Zoroastrianism alongside Islam in the region added layers of diversity to commercial activities. Traders representing different faiths engaged in cross-cultural interactions, amalgamating distinct religious practices and trading customs. This fusion of religious and trade practices resulted in the emergence of eclectic marketplaces where goods, ideas, and beliefs intertwined, enriching the commercial landscape of the Gulf.

Judaism's historical presence in the Arabian Peninsula has also left a notable imprint on trade. Jewish communities actively participated in various economic endeavors, contributing to the Gulf's intricate web of trade relations. Their influence extended beyond commerce, encompassing contributions to the region's intellectual and cultural milieu, thus shaping the interconnected history of religion and trade.

Beyond the monotheistic religions, the intricate philosophical systems originating from ancient Greece also significantly influenced the ideological underpinnings of trade in the Gulf. The exchange of philosophical ideas alongside material goods along the trade routes fostered intellectual enrichment and contributed to the development of vibrant market societies. This intellectual commerce complemented the material exchanges, elevating the Gulf's trade networks to realms transcending mere commercial transactions.

The historical interplay of religion and trade has fostered a dynamic environment where divergent belief systems have converged, intermingled, and evolved alongside commercial exchanges. This symbiotic relationship has contributed to the resilience and adaptability of the Gulf's trade networks, reflecting a rich tapestry woven from the threads of religious, cultural, and economic interactions.

Ideological Exchange via Maritime Routes

The maritime routes of the ancient Gulf were not just conduits for physical trade; they also facilitated a profound exchange of ideas and ideologies. The interconnectedness of civilizations through maritime trade routes allowed for disseminating religious beliefs, philosophical concepts, and cultural practices. The sailors and traders traversing these routes were not merely transporting goods but also carriers of knowledge, beliefs, and customs. As ships docked at diverse ports and harbors along the Gulf, they brought with them a blending of cultural and religious influences that left an indelible mark on the societies they encountered. The encounter between different faiths and cultures sparked ideological exchanges, fostering a dynamic tapestry of beliefs and practices. This exchange of ideologies was not limited to a one-way flow; it was a complex interplay of ideas, with each civilization contributing and assimilating elements from others. The open expanse of the sea served as a meeting ground for religious scholars, philosophers, and traders, leading to a rich exchange of thoughts and beliefs. Ideas that were once confined to specific regions found new shores through these maritime routes, enriching the spiritual and intellectual landscape of the Gulf.

The maritime routes were instrumental in shaping the religious and philosophical landscape of the Gulf. They provided avenues for the spread of Buddhism, Hinduism, and Jainism from the Indian subcontinent, intertwining these belief systems with the region's existing spiritual tapestry. The interactions with the Greco-Roman world further added layers of philosophical thought to the Gulf's cultural fabric. Additionally, the movement of empires, such as the Sassanian Empire, contributed to the cross-pollination of religious and philosophical ideals across the Gulf. The convergence of diverse religious and philosophical currents created a unique syncretic environment, giving rise to new cultural expressions and religious practices. The maritime routes thus served as conduits for the diffusion and coalescence of diverse ideological streams, setting the stage for the multi-faceted cultural mosaic that defines the Gulf region today.

The Spread of Islam and its Socio-Economic Impacts

The spread of Islam profoundly impacted the socio-economic landscape of the Arabian Peninsula and beyond. As the teachings of Islam traversed the maritime trade routes, they facilitated a spiritual transformation and brought about significant socio-economic changes that reshaped the fabric of society. The principles of Islamic finance, which prohibited usury and encouraged fair and ethical trade, catalyzed economic growth and stability in the region. The establishment of the Islamic caliphates further solidified these economic foundations, fostering a prosperous environment conducive to trade and commerce.

Coinciding with the rise of Islam was the expansion of trade networks, facilitated by the caliphates' support for commercial activities. This expansive trade network enabled the flow of goods, ideas, and technologies across diverse cultures, ultimately contributing to the flourishing of the economy. Moreover, the emphasis on social justice and equitable distribution of wealth within Islamic teachings influenced the development of socio-economic structures, fostering inclusive and sustainable practices that benefited communities at large.

The integration of Islamic jurisprudence, or Sharia law, into the legal and governance systems of the trading hubs along the maritime routes brought about a harmonious foundation for commercial interactions. Creating efficient marketplaces and fair trading regulations underpinned by Islamic ethics strengthened the integrity and reliability of the region's trade, enhancing overall economic prosperity.

Furthermore, the spread of Islam catalyzed advancements in various industries, such as agriculture, architecture, and craftsmanship. Islamic teachings fostered scientific and technological innovations, leading to advancements in irrigation techniques, architectural designs, and artistic pursuits, thereby enriching the cultural and economic tapestry of the Gulf region.

Adopting Arabic as a language of trade and scholarship further unified the diverse societies across the trade routes, enabling seamless communication and knowledge exchange. This linguistic unification played a pivotal role in the proliferation of ideas and the preservation of knowledge, augmenting the region's intellectual wealth and contributing to its sustained prosperity.

The spread of Islam and its profound socio-economic impacts shaped a vibrant and interconnected society characterized by prosperity, cultural exchange, and intellectual enlightenment. The enduring legacy of Islam's influence on the socio-economic dynamics of the Arabian Peninsula and its surrounding regions continues to resonate through the annals of history, underscoring the integral role of faith in shaping the economic and societal landscapes.

Christianity and Zoroastrianism: Minority Influences

Christianity and Zoroastrianism, while minority religions in the region, have played significant roles in shaping the cultural and religious landscape of the Gulf. The arrival of Christianity in the Gulf can be traced back to the early centuries AD when communities of Christians sought refuge in the Arabian

Peninsula. These Christian communities, often called the 'Nestorian Christians,' established themselves in regions such as modern-day Kuwait, Bahrain, and the eastern coast of Saudi Arabia. Their presence influenced the local customs, trade, and even art, leaving an indelible mark on the history of the Gulf. Zoroastrianism, an ancient religion with its roots in Persia, also found a place among the diverse religious tapestry of the Gulf. The faith, which emphasizes the dualistic struggle between good and evil, gained a following among the Persian communities in the region. With their distinct rituals and traditions, Zoroastrians contributed to the multicultural dynamics of the Gulf, enriching the societal fabric with their unique beliefs and practices. Both Christianity and Zoroastrianism, as minority influences, exemplify the openness of the Gulf's society to diverse religious expressions. This pluralism has not only fostered interfaith dialogue and mutual respect but has also led to the emergence of syncretic traditions that blend elements from various faiths. Through historical accounts, artifacts, and the enduring legacies of these minority influences, it becomes evident that they have left an enduring imprint on the Gulf's cultural, artistic, and intellectual spheres. In the contemporary era, recognizing and preserving their contributions serve as a testament to the enduring heritage of Christianity and Zoroastrianism in the region, reflecting the Gulf's commitment to embracing and celebrating its rich diversity.

Judaism in the Peninsula: Historical Echoes

Judaism holds a significant place in the historical tapestry of the Gulf Peninsula, its influence weaving through centuries of cultural exchanges and religious developments. Tracing its roots back to ancient times, Judaism emerged as a minority faith within the region, introducing a unique set of beliefs and practices that have left an indelible mark on the societal fabric of the Peninsula. Throughout history, Jews played pivotal roles in various aspects of Peninsula society, contributing to diverse fields such as trade, craftsmanship, and governance. Their presence added a rich layer of diversity to the cultural landscape of the Peninsula.

Introducing Judaism to the Peninsula brought forth a synthesis of traditions, fostering a cross-pollination of ideas and values. This dynamic exchange resulted in the emergence of hybrid cultural expressions, blending Jewish influences with indigenous customs and other incoming belief systems. Synagogues, communal gathering places, and ceremonial practices stood as a testament to the enduring presence of Jewish communities within the Peninsula, each serving as vibrant hubs of cultural interplay and spiritual enrichment.

Moreover, the historical echoes of Judaism in the Peninsula resonated beyond religious spheres, permeating into the realms of art, language, and intellectual discourse. Jewish scholars and thinkers played pivotal roles in facilitating dialogues between different communities, nurturing an environment of academic and philosophical exchange that enriched the collective wisdom of the Peninsula. The Hebrew language found resonance among linguistic circles, leaving its imprint on the diverse linguistic tapestry of the region and reflecting the intertwining of cultural threads.

Despite facing periods of both tolerance and adversity, Jewish communities steadfastly contributed to the vibrant mosaic of the Peninsula's social, economic, and intellectual spheres. Their legacy is a testament to the enduring spirit of cultural resilience and coexistence within the Gulf. Today, remnants of this historical lineage can be glimpsed in archaeological findings, traditional narratives, and the architectural imprints of generations past, reaffirming the lasting impact of Jewish heritage in shaping the multilayered identity of the Peninsula.

Philosophical Transmissions: From Greece to the Gulf

The cultural crossroads of the Gulf have served as a hub for trade and as a conduit for the exchange of philosophical ideas. The transmission of Hellenistic philosophy, particularly the works of Aristotle and Plato, fostered a profound impact on the intellectual landscape of the region. Greek thought permeated the Gulf through the intellectual pursuits of scholars and philosophers, shaping the ideological discourse of diverse societies. This era marked the convergence of Greek philosophy with indigenous beliefs and practices, leading to a rich tapestry of philosophical thought that defined the region's intellectual heritage. The adaptation and assimilation of Greek philosophical concepts into the Gulf's cultural milieu engendered a profound synthesis, giving rise to unique schools of thought reverberating through modern times. The study of ethics, metaphysics, and epistemology found fertile ground in the Gulf, catalyzing an intellectual flourishing transcending geographical boundaries.

Art and Architecture: Religions Carving History

The interplay between the Gulf region's religion, art, and architecture has carved a rich tapestry of history that fascinates scholars and enthusiasts alike. As trade routes facilitated the exchange of ideas and beliefs, diverse religious traditions influenced the artistic and architectural expressions across the Gulf's landscape. The convergence of Islamic, Christian, Zoroastrian, and Jewish influences has provided a nuanced lens to explore the evolution of art and architecture in the region.

Islamic art and architecture, characterized by intricate geometric patterns, arabesques, and calligraphy, have left an indelible mark on the Gulf's visual landscape. The grand mosques, with their ornate domes and minarets, stand as testaments to Islam's profound spiritual and artistic legacy in the region. Similarly, the ancient churches and cathedrals bear witness to Christianity's enduring imprint, displaying a blend of Byzantine, Romanesque, and Gothic architectural styles, reflecting the assimilation of diverse cultural influences.

Furthermore, the remnants of Zoroastrian fire temples and Jewish synagogues serve as poignant reminders of the historical coexistence of multiple faith traditions in the Gulf. The unique motifs adorning these sacred spaces reflect the syncretic nature of artistic expression, embodying the confluence of religious beliefs and cultural sensibilities.

Beyond religious edifices, the residential and commercial architecture of the Gulf also attests to the fusion of art and religious traditions, with intricately designed courtyards, decorative elements, and geometric motifs resonating with the spiritual and cultural ethos of the communities.

The evolution of art and architecture in the Gulf has not only been shaped by religious beliefs. Still, it has also influenced the societal fabric, serving as a visual testament to the coalescence of diverse identities and narratives. Through the study of art and architecture, one can discern the interconnectedness of religious communities and appreciate the enduring legacy of their creative expressions on the canvas of history.

In essence, the art and architecture of the Gulf encapsulate the interwoven narratives of religious pluralism, cultural exchange, and creative innovation, enriching the region's heritage with a captivating mosaic of visual and spatial experiences.

Linguistic Blend: The Evolution of a Cultural Linguasphere

Languages are not merely tools for communication; they are repositories of culture and history, capturing the essence of a society's heritage and values. In the Gulf region, the linguistic landscape is a tapestry woven from centuries of interaction, migration, trade, and conquest. The evolution of the cultural linguasphere in this region reflects the interconnectedness of diverse civilizations and the enduring impact of historical exchanges. Arabic, Persian, and Turkish are at the heart of this linguistic blend, each contributing to the rich mosaic of the Gulf's linguistic heritage. Arabic is the dominant language, deeply rooted in Islamic traditions and pivotal in shaping the region's religious, literary, and administrative spheres. Its influence extends beyond borders, connecting communities bound by a shared spiritual and intellectual legacy. Similarly, Persian, with its poetic eloquence and literary prowess, has imprinted itself on the Gulf's cultural fabric, leaving an indelible mark on art, literature, and intellectual discourse. As a testament to the enduring influence of Persian civilization, the echoes of its language reverberate across the Gulf, underscoring its significance in the region's historical evolution. Additionally, the Turkish language, influenced by the expansive reach of the Ottoman Empire, has left an imprint on the Gulf's linguistic tapestry, particularly evident in expressions, vocabulary, and place names. The intertwining of these linguistic strands embodies the cosmopolitan nature of the Gulf, reflecting a blending of cultures that transcends geographical boundaries. Furthermore, the Gulf's linguistic blend is perpetually evolving, shaped by waves of global migration, technological advancements, and the interplay of modernity with traditional customs. The inflow of expatriate communities has brought new languages and dialects to the region, adding further depth and diversity to the cultural linguasphere. The increasing globalization and interconnectedness of the Gulf have also led to the assimilation of English as a prominent language in business, education, and diplomacy. This linguistic fusion exemplifies the adaptability and openness of Gulf societies, as they navigate the complexities of a rapidly changing world while preserving their linguistic roots. The evolution of the Gulf's cultural linguasphere is a testament to the resilience of human expression and identity, encapsulating the spirit of coexistence and mutual enrichment amidst linguistic diversity.

Summation: Today's Gulf Through the Lens of History

Today, the Gulf is a region shaped by the convergence of various cultures and ideologies forged through centuries of interaction and exchange. The linguistic blend witnessed in the present day serves as a testament to the enduring legacy of historical influences that have left an indelible mark on the cultural fabric of the Gulf. As we navigate the complex tapestry of this region's history, it becomes apparent that the interplay of ideas and religious beliefs has not only defined the past but continues to resonate in the contemporary panorama. From the intricate patterns adorning traditional handicrafts to the nuanced dialects spoken across the landscape, the diverse inheritance of the Gulf speaks to a story of resilience and adaptation. Understanding the modern-day Gulf necessitates deeply exploring its historical roots, setting the stage for the contemporary synthesis of traditions and perspectives. The impacts of these ancient exchanges echo through the monuments that stand as testaments to bygone eras and the art forms that continue to encapsulate the spirit of cultural convergence. Within this rich historical context, we can truly comprehend the complexities and intricacies of today's Gulf.

The underlying currents of history have intertwined with the present, shaping the region into a mosaic of interwoven narratives. This summation offers a window through which the contemporary Gulf can be viewed - a vista where the echoes of the past reverberate alongside the vitality of the present. By scrutinizing the historical forces interwoven in the Gulf's narrative, we gain insight into the modern dynamics that define its cultural, social, and economic landscapes. Through the lens of history, the trajectory of the Gulf becomes illuminated, showcasing the enduring impact of cross-cultural fertilization and the enduring resilience of its people. This summation bridges the historical epochs and the contemporary milieu, inviting readers to engage with the narratives that have shaped and continue to shape the ever-evolving identity of the Gulf.

Chapter 14

The Caravans of the Desert: Trading and Traveling Across the Sands

Trade caravans have played a pivotal role in the economic development of desert societies for centuries, serving as the lifeblood of commerce and cultural exchange across vast and unforgiving landscapes. The emergence of desert caravans marked a significant turning point in the history of trade, providing a means through which valuable goods could be transported across arid expanses, often connecting diverse civilizations and facilitating the exchange of commodities, ideas, and knowledge. These caravans not only sustained local economies but also fostered cross-cultural interactions, contributing to the rich tapestry of human civilization. The significance of these journeys extended far beyond mere transportation of goods; they symbolized resilience, enterprise, and the enduring spirit of exploration. As merchants ventured into the dangerous deserts, braving harsh weather conditions, hostile terrains, and the ever-present specter of banditry, they forged paths to enable the flow of goods and prosperity. Through the intrepid efforts of traders, the once isolated and marginalized desert regions were integrated into extensive trade and exchange networks, fostering economic vitality and sociocultural dynamism. The advent of desert caravans catalyzed the flourishing of bazaars, trading posts, and market towns, becoming hubs of economic activity and societal congregation. This intricate web of trade routes facilitated the movement of goods such as spices, textiles, precious metals, and exotic produce and symbolized the interconnectedness of distant cultures, traditions, and aspirations. Moreover, the prevalence of these caravans engendered a unique sense of community and camaraderie among those undertaking the arduous vacations, leading to the establishment of oasis settlements, way stations, and rest areas that would grow into bustling centers of commerce and cultural confluence. The ingenuity and resourcefulness displayed by caravan travelers in overcoming the formidable challenges of traversing the desert terrain underscored their indispensable role in fostering economic growth and regional integration. Ultimately, the presence of trade caravans exemplified an enduring legacy of human enterprise and perseverance, transcending the physical boundaries of the desert to shape the very fabric of civilization.

Historical Context: Emergence of Desert Caravans

The emergence of desert caravans represents a fascinating intersection of history, geography, and human ingenuity. This pivotal point in time marked the rise of an intricate network of trade routes that connected distant civilizations and shaped the economic landscape of the ancient world. The roots of these caravans can be traced back to the early nomadic groups who, driven by necessity and opportunity, ventured into the vast deserts in search of resources and prosperity. As settlements flourished and trade demands grew, these nomadic journeys evolved into organized trading expeditions, giving birth to the legendary desert caravans. The historical context of these caravans further illustrates their profound influence over the development of societies and the exchange of goods, ideas, and cultural practices across diverse regions. Moreover, the strategic significance of these routes extended far beyond mere commercial transactions, serving as instrumental conduits for exchanging knowledge, technologies, and ideologies. The emergence of desert caravans is a testament to human civilization's resilience and adaptability, showcasing the ability to overcome geographical challenges and harness the potential of arid landscapes for mutual benefit. Understanding the historical context behind the emergence of these caravans provides invaluable insights into the interconnectedness of ancient civilizations and the enduring legacy of trade and exploration.

Major Trade Routes: Pathways Through the Sands

As the desert caravans emerged, so too did the need for established trade routes that would serve as the guiding pathways through the seemingly endless sands. These trade routes were not just simple navigational paths but lifelines connecting distant civilizations and cultures, facilitating the exchange of goods, ideas, and beliefs. One of the most renowned trade routes was the Incense Route, which linked the Arabian Peninsula with the Mediterranean region, enabling the transportation of precious spices, perfumes, and other exotic goods. This ancient network of trails and passages also played a crucial role in shaping the cultural and economic landscapes of the regions it touched. Another pivotal route was the Silk

Road, an extensive network of interconnected trade routes that spanned over 4,000 miles, facilitating the exchange of silk, spices, textiles, and other valuable commodities between East and West. The Silk Road fostered profound cultural exchanges, technological advancements, and the dissemination of knowledge across diverse civilizations. In addition to these prominent routes, other vital pathways emerged, such as the Trans-Saharan trade routes, which linked sub-Saharan Africa with North Africa and the Mediterranean world, enabling the exchange of gold, salt, slaves, and other commodities. These trade routes were not merely conduits for material goods but for the shared experiences of bazaars bustling with merchants, caravanserais offering respite, and oases providing sustenance. Moreover, these routes contributed to the diffusion of languages, beliefs, and philosophies, resulting in a rich tapestry of cultural interchange. Navigating these trade routes required immense skill and a thorough understanding of the desert's terrain. Caravan leaders became adept at utilizing natural landmarks, celestial navigation, and other indigenous methods to traverse through the shifting dunes and navigate the vast expanse of the desert. Often, these routes were difficult, fraught with natural hazards and unpredictable weather patterns, yet they remained essential arteries of commerce. As the desert caravans plied their way along these routes, they reshaped the geographic and cultural boundaries, leaving an indelible mark on the region's history.

Caravan Composition: Merchants, Camels, and Commodities

The composition of a desert caravan is a fascinating ensemble of humans, animals, and goods, each playing a crucial role in the intricate web of trade and travel. At the heart of this assembly are the merchants, who possess astute business acumen and an intimate knowledge of the trade routes that crisscross the arid terrain. These merchants often hail from diverse backgrounds, such as Bedouin tribes or urban centers, bringing unique insights and expertise in various commodities. Their leadership ensures the caravan's success through adept decision-making and establishing strategic partnerships.

Accompanying the merchants are the unsung heroes of the desert – the camels. Renowned for their resilience and ability to endure the harsh conditions of the desert, these majestic creatures are the backbone of the caravan's mobility. Beyond their physical strength, camels also offer a means of transporting goods, essential supplies, and even shelter in the form of traditional Bedouin tents. Their significance in the caravan cannot be overstated, as they ensure the safe passage of the merchants and their valuable cargo across vast stretches of barren land.

As for the merchandise carried by the caravan represents a rich tapestry of exotic goods sourced from distant lands. Spices, silks, precious metals, and other commodities are meticulously packed onto the camel caravans, constituting a visual testament to the interwoven fabric of global trade. Such cargo holds immense material value and serves as conduits of cultural exchange, carrying the essence of varied civilizations and igniting the imaginations of those encountered along the journey.

Assembling and organizing these elements into a harmonious unit requires meticulous planning and coordination. Each element – merchants, camels, and commodities – must seamlessly complement one another, forming a symbiotic relationship that enables the caravan to traverse the unforgiving landscape with purpose and efficiency. By exploring the intricate dynamics of the caravan's composition, we gain insight into the intricacies of ancient trade networks and the enduring spirit of human enterprise in the face of adversity.

Daily Life on the Move: Routines and Challenges

The daily life of a caravan in the desert is a testament to resilience, endurance, and the ability to adapt to an ever-changing environment. From the crack of dawn until twilight fades into night, the caravan members engage in a meticulously orchestrated series of routines and face numerous challenges as they traverse the vast, unforgiving expanse of the desert. Each day begins with the efficient packing of supplies, negotiation of trade deals, and ensuring the health and well-being of the camels, which serve as the lifeblood of the caravan. The arduous loading and securing of goods onto the camels requires precision and expertise, often taking several hours to complete. As the caravan sets off, the rhythmic swaying of the camels and the measured footfalls of the merchants create a hypnotic cadence, marking the start of another day's journey. However, the challenges are relentless, from navigating treacherous terrain and unpredictable weather to dealing with the ever-present threat of bandits and raiders. The scorching sun beats down mercilessly, and dust storms sweep across the landscape, obscuring the view and testing the resilience of both travelers and cargo. The constant vigilance required to protect the caravan from external threats adds complexity to an already demanding lifestyle. Despite these hardships, the caravan operates with remarkable efficiency and discipline, as each member fulfills their designated role with unwavering dedication. Along the way, daily rituals and traditions provide respite and camaraderie, fostering a sense of community amidst the isolation of the vast desert. As night falls, the caravan settles into a makeshift camp, where conversations around the crackling fire and the aroma of hearty meals offer brief glimpses of comfort and familiarity in an otherwise unfamiliar and challenging setting. In conclusion, the daily life of a desert caravan is characterized by a delicate balance between routine and unpredictability, where every moment presents a new trial or triumph, shaping the timeless narrative of trade and travel across the ancient sands.

Navigation Techniques: Stars, Landmarks, and Instincts

Navigation across the vast desert expanse relied heavily on a combination of celestial observations, recognition of landmarks, and innate instincts passed down through generations. As the desert offered minimal natural navigational aids, desert travelers developed a profound understanding of the night sky to chart their course. The stars, particularly Polaris, served as a guiding light, providing a fixed reference point for determining direction. In addition to stars, the position and movement of the moon and planets also aided in gauging time and direction, allowing caravans to navigate through the night. Furthermore, identifying specific formations and constellations helped determine the heading and distance traveled. The skill of reading the stars and interpreting their significance played a pivotal role in ensuring safe passage through the treacherous terrain. Landmarks such as prominent rock formations, unusual geological features, and distinctive dunes were crucial to successful navigation. These enduring markers served as reference points, guiding travelers along established routes and warning them of potential hazards. Moreover, accumulating shared knowledge about these landmarks facilitated the exchange of information among different caravan groups, contributing to safer and more efficient journeys. Beyond relying on external cues, the nomadic communities also instinctively understood the desert environment. Their acute awareness of subtle changes in the landscape, wind patterns, and animal behavior enabled them to anticipate impending weather conditions and locate vital resources, such as their camels' water sources and grazing areas. This innate connection with the environment gave them an intuitive sense of direction, allowing them to navigate the shifting sands and unforeseen obstacles. The masterful fusion of astronomical insight, landmark interpretation, and environmental intuition formed the backbone of desert navigation, emphasizing the resourcefulness and resilience of desert caravan travelers.

Trade Goods: From Spices to Textiles

The trade of goods in the ancient desert caravans was a fundamental aspect of economic exchange and cultural interaction. Caravans crossing the vast expanses of the desert were packed with a diverse array of commodities, each bearing its own history and significance. Among the most coveted trade goods were the exotic spices that journeyed across continents, tantalizing the senses and enriching the cuisines and cultures of distant lands.

Cinnamon, cloves, pepper, and nutmeg were highly sought after for their aromatic allure and culinary value. These precious commodities originated from distant lands, including the fabled Spice Islands of Southeast Asia and the lush plantations of the Indian subcontinent. Their inclusion in the cargo of desert caravans not only attested to the extent of trading networks but also highlighted the insatiable appetite for the rare and the refined.

Apart from spices, textiles formed another cornerstone of trade within the desert caravans. The fine fabrics and intricate weaves in faraway lands held an immense allure for merchants and consumers. Silk, cotton, and linen, woven into vibrant patterns and exquisite designs, captivated the imaginations of those who encountered them. Through these textiles, distant civilizations' stories unfolded, revealing their creators' artistic prowess and cultural depth.

Furthermore, the exchange of textiles facilitated the inter-weaving of traditions and identities, as garments and fabrics became conduits of regional styles and narratives. The rich tapestries of trade unfolded within the confines of caravans, enveloping the travelers in a sensory symphony of textures and hues. The impact of these textile treasures reverberated far beyond the points of exchange, embedding themselves within the fabric of societies and shaping the evolution of fashion and personal expression.

Moreover, the trading of goods extended beyond mere economic transactions; it symbolized the interconnectedness of disparate communities and the shared human desire for beauty, flavor, and distinction. The journey of spices and textiles across the deserts exemplified the resilience and in-genuity of ancient trade, transcending physical barriers and fostering a global tapestry of cultural exchange.

Cultural Exchange: Impact on Local Communities

The desert caravans served as conduits for more than just trade; they were also for cultural exchange. As these cara-vans crisscrossed the vast desert landscapes, they were crucial in disseminating ideas, beliefs, and practices across different communities. This cultural interchange was not confined to material goods but extended to knowledge, language, and customs, enriching the tapestry of desert life.

One significant impact of this cultural exchange was the amalgamation of diverse traditions within local communities.

Through interactions with merchants from distant lands, communities along the caravan routes were exposed to new cuisines, art forms, religious practices, and societal norms. This infusion of external influences contributed to the evolution of local cultures, fostering a unique blend of indigenous and foreign elements that resonated through generations.

Moreover, the interactions facilitated by the desert caravans fostered mutual understanding and tolerance among disparate communities. The exchange of ideas and experiences promoted a sense of interconnectedness, transcending geographical boundaries. It laid the foundation for a culture of open-mindedness and inclusivity, shaping the social fabric of the communities that thrived along these bustling trade routes.

Furthermore, the cultural exchange catalyzed intellectual growth within local societies. The encounters with diverse civilizations encouraged knowledge sharing in astronomy, medicine, and philosophy. This cross-pollination of intellectual pursuits engendered an environment of innovation, laying the groundwork for advancements in various disciplines. The resulting intellectual synergy enhanced the people's livelihoods and paved the way for enduring contributions to the collective body of human knowledge.

Beyond these tangible impacts, the cultural exchange brought about intangible transformations, fostering empathy and respect for diversity among the residents of the desert regions. It nurtured a spirit of curiosity and appreciation for differing perspectives, which permeated the consciousness of the local populace. The enduring legacy of this cultural exchange is reflected in the enduring ethos of hospitality, unity, and cultural diversity that defines the communities thriving amidst the arid expanses.

Essentially, the impact of cultural exchange propelled by the desert caravans transcends mere economic transactions. It kindled a veritable renaissance of ideas, values, and interconnectedness, sculpting the destinies of the local communities and leaving an indelible imprint on the annals of history.

Security Measures: Protecting the Caravan

In the desert's harsh and unforgiving landscape, security was paramount to safeguard the valuable goods transported across vast arid terrain. Protecting the caravan involved a multifaceted approach that combined the skillful use of manpower, strategic planning, and careful organization. One of the primary security measures employed was establishing a well-disciplined guard detail comprised of experienced and armed individuals adept at navigating the challenges posed by the desert environment. These guards maintained constant vigilance and defended the caravan against threats such as bandit raids or hostile encounters with rival trade parties.

Furthermore, the caravan would often adopt a defensive formation known as the 'caravan square' to deter attacks from all directions. This tactical arrangement involved positioning the camels and laden pack animals in the center of a protective ring formed by armed guards, creating a formidable barrier against external aggression. Additionally, the caravan leaders and merchants would collaborate with local tribal groups or seek the presence of military escorts to bolster their defense and ensure safe passage through contested territories.

The protection of goods also extended to concealing the most valuable commodities within the depths of the caravan, strategically distributed to minimize the risk of complete loss in the event of an attack. Moreover, the selection of routes and encampment sites was meticulously planned to avoid hazardous areas and leverage natural barriers for defense. Water sources along the journey were carefully chosen for sustenance and their potential to serve as defensive positions if necessary.

Implementing security measures necessitated a high level of discipline and coordination among the caravan members. Each individual had clearly defined responsibilities during heightened alertness, ensuring that every security aspect was thoroughly addressed. While the primary goal was to protect the caravan and its cargo, the safety and welfare of all participants, including men, animals, and supplies, remained a key priority.

Throughout history, the caravan's ability to navigate the problematic desert landscapes relied mainly on the efficacy of these security measures. As economic and political dynamics shifted over time, new challenges emerged, leading to significant changes in the methods used to safeguard caravans. Understanding the intricacies of securing these vital trade routes offers valuable insights into the resilience and resourcefulness of ancient civilizations.

End of an Era: The Decline of the Desert Caravans

The decline of the desert caravans marks a significant turning point in the region's economic and cultural landscape. As global trade dynamics evolved with modern transportation and communication, the traditional routes traversed by these storied caravans gradually fell out of favor. The rise of maritime trade and, eventually, air travel contributed to the waning significance of overland caravan routes. This shift led to a diminishment of the once-flourishing caravan trade and its associated way of life.

The diminishing relevance of desert caravans was not solely due to technological advancements in transport; shifting political landscapes and establishing nation-states also played a role. Border control measures and regulations imposed by emerging governments disrupted the fluidity of cross-desert trade, making the traditional routes less viable. Additionally, the discovery of oil in the region brought about an abrupt transformation of economic focus, reducing the emphasis on traditional trade networks and practices.

Simultaneously, societal and cultural changes further contributed to the decline of desert caravans. As modernization and urbanization took hold, the younger generations increasingly sought alternate livelihoods, moving away from the rigors of desert trade. The allure of conventional employment opportunities in burgeoning urban centers superseded the demanding and uncertain nature of desert commerce, leading to a dwindling pool of individuals willing to carry forward the legacy of the caravanners.

Despite these challenges, the lasting impact of desert caravans is ingrained in the cultural ethos of the region. Their influence can be seen in various aspects of contemporary society, from the preservation of traditional crafts and arts to the perpetuation of oral histories that recount the adventures and experiences of desert traders. Efforts to safeguard this rich heritage and revive interest in desert caravanning are evident through cultural initiatives and historical preservation endeavors undertaken by local and global organizations. While the era of the desert caravans may have drawn to a close, its indelible imprint on the collective memory endures, serving as a testament to the resilience and ingenuity of the intrepid desert traders.

Chapter 15

Life Before Black Gold: Daily Life and Community Structure

The period before the discovery of oil in this region is characterized by a distinct and intricate way of life deeply embedded in tradition, community, and resourcefulness. This era represents a time when daily routines and household activities were intricately connected to the geographical and historical fabric of the land, as well as the prevailing socio-economic structures. Understanding this historical context provides invaluable insight into the foundations that shaped the culture and identity of the communities within this landscape. The rhythms of life were guided by the unique challenges and opportunities presented by the surrounding environment, shaping the daily rituals and habits of the people in profound ways. Household activities were not merely chores but essential to the community's social and cultural tapestry. Within this framework, every action held significance beyond its immediate purpose, carrying traditions, beliefs, and values passed down through generations. Furthermore, the absence of modern technological conveniences required great ingenuity and collaboration among community members to sustain everyday life. Each facet of daily life reflected a harmonious relationship between humanity and its natural surroundings, from agricultural practices to domestic tasks. Understanding these elements allows us to appreciate the resilience and resourcefulness of the individuals who inhabited this region, setting the stage for the dynamic narratives that unfold within their daily lives.

Daily Routines and Household Activities

In the pre-oil era of the Gulf, daily life was intricately woven with a myriad of activities that formed the backbone of local communities. From dawn till dusk, household members engaged in diverse tasks that reflected the values, traditions, and necessities prevalent at that time. Daily routines were shaped by the specific needs of each family and community, often revolving around the cycles of agriculture, animal husbandry, maritime activities, and trade. Women played a vital role in managing domestic affairs, including food preparation, child-rearing, textile production, and tending to livestock. At the same time, men took on responsibilities such as farming, fishing, merchant pursuits, and protecting the community. The intricate balance of these roles contributed to the cohesion and sustenance of the entire social fabric. Household activities were interlinked with religious practices, cultural celebrations, and communal obligations, creating a tapestry of shared experiences and traditions. From preparing meals and crafting household items to preserving food for the future, every task carried a significance that transcended the tangible outcomes. Moreover, storytelling, music, and traditional games provided moments of leisure and entertainment, fostering bonds within families and neighborhoods. These daily routines and house-hold activities not only upheld the practical functioning of the society but also encapsulated the deeper ethos and essence of the Gulf's heritage.

Socio-Economic Structures in Local Communities

Local communities across the Gulf region are characterized by intricate socio-economic structures that have evolved over centuries. These structures are deeply rooted in tradition, cus-toms, and the unique geographical challenges of the region. At the heart of these structures is a complex web of kin-ship ties, social obligations, and economic interdependencies that shape the fabric of everyday life. Central to the socio-economic dynamic is the concept of mutual assistance and reciprocity, where individuals, families, and tribes collaborate to ensure the well-being of the community as a whole. This interconnectedness forms the basis of resource sharing, labor exchange, and collective decision-making within local socie-ties. This framework's traditional leadership systems and hier-archical arrangements are crucial in maintaining social order and mediating disputes. Moreover, these structures also define the distribution of resources, access to land, and control over natural assets, reflecting the historical resilience of local com-munities in adapting to their environment. Alongside these socio-economic intricacies, indigenous trading practices and commercial activities enrich the tapestry of community life. Traditional marketplaces serve as vibrant hubs for economic transactions and social interactions, preserving age-old barter-ing traditions while embracing modern trading techniques. The interplay between economic exchanges and social networking in these settings sustains local livelihoods and fosters a strong sense of communal identity. Furthermore, the diversification of economic activities within these communities showcases individuals' innovative spirit and adaptability, contributing to the dynamic evolution of the socio-economic landscape. As modern influences continue to shape these structures, a delicate balance is struck between preserving ancestral customs and integrating contemporary practices. Navigating this equilibrium demands an awareness of the historical significance of each social structure and its inherent value in sustaining community cohesion. In unpacking the multifaceted socio-economic structures of these local communities, one gains insight into the enduring heritage that has defined the Gulf region for generations.

Traditional Occupations and Crafts

The lifestyle of the ancient communities around the Gulf was intricately intertwined with various traditional occupations and crafts. These practices were not just means of livelihood but also embodiments of cultural heritage and expertise passed down through generations. The skills and knowledge associated with these traditional vocations formed the local economies' backbone, enhancing these communities' resilience and self-sufficiency. Among the most prominent occupations were those related to maritime activities, such as fishing, pearl diving, and boat building. The art of fishing involved intricate knowledge of tides, marine biodiversity, and mastery of various fishing techniques using nets, traps, and lines. Similarly, the difficult but rewarding practice of pearl diving required incredible physical prowess, deep-sea diving skills, and an intimate understanding of the native oyster beds. Another remarkable vocation was crafting dhows, the iconic wooden ships that played a pivotal role in the historical trade routes across the Gulf. The craftsmanship and techniques employed in dhow construction were a source of pride and identity for the communities who excelled in this trade. Apart from maritime pursuits, the communities also specialized in land-based occupations such as agriculture, animal husbandry, and oasis farming. The people's daily lives revolved around cultivating date palms, tending to livestock, and sustaining the ecosystem of the desert oasis. Additionally, the artisans in these societies were adept at creating intricate hand-woven textiles, pottery, jewelry, and metalwork. Each craft was not only functional but also infused with symbolic meanings and artistic expressions derived from the collective experiences and beliefs of the community. The longstanding tradition of passing on these skills within families and apprenticeships ensured the preservation of these invaluable crafts. These traditional occupations and crafts were integral to the fabric of everyday life, encompassing economic activities and spiritual and communal significance. They epitomized the symbiotic relationship between human ingenuity and the natural environment, showcasing the harmonious coexistence of the people with their surroundings. As modernization and globalization transform these societies, it is imperative to recognize and safeguard the legacy of these traditional vocations and crafts for posterity.

Agriculture and Food Practices

Agriculture was pivotal in shaping daily life and sustaining communities in the ancient Gulf civilization. The arid desert landscape posed numerous challenges for farming, yet resourceful irrigation methods such as falaj systems allowed settlers to cultivate crops in the oasis regions. Date palms were a cornerstone of agriculture, providing both sustenance and economic value through the trade of dates. The cultivation of fruits, vegetables, and grains also thrived in these fertile pockets, demonstrating the resilience and ingenuity of the local inhabitants. The agricultural calendar followed the rhythm of the seasons, with planting and harvesting dictated by the natural cycles and celestial movements. This intimate connection with the land fostered a deep reverence and gratitude among the people, reflected in rituals and ceremonies honoring the earth's bounty.

Food practices were intricately tied to cultural traditions and social gatherings. Meals often served as occasions for communal bonding, where aromatic spices and locally sourced ingredients took center stage. Culinary skills were passed down through generations, resulting in diverse and flavorful dishes that embodied the region's rich tapestry of flavors. Livestock, such as camels and goats, were integral to the pastoral way of life, providing sustenance, transportation, and materials for traditional crafts. The art of preservation was also highly developed, with techniques like drying, pickling, and fermentation ensuring food security during leaner seasons. These methods underscored the wisdom of the ancients, who recognized the value of self-reliance and sustainability in an unpredictable environment.

Furthermore, exchanging culinary practices and ingredients along ancient trade routes enriched the local cuisine, linking distant communities through shared gustatory experiences. From the vibrant souks brimming with exotic spices to the communal feasts celebrating weddings and festivals, food perpetuated a sense of unity and identity within the fabric of society. Additionally, the holistic approach to nourishment encompassed the physical, spiritual, and medicinal dimensions. Remedies derived from herbs and indigenous plants were integrated into culinary preparations, reinforcing the interconnectedness of agriculture, food, and holistic well-being. The agricultural and culinary heritage of the ancient

Gulf civilization thus stands as a testament to the harmony between human ingenuity and the natural world, reflecting a legacy of innovation and adaptation that continues to inspire us today.

Architecture and Housing

Architecture and housing were critical in shaping communities' daily lives and societal structures in ancient civilizations. The Gulf region's architectural heritage reflects a deep-rooted connection between people and their natural environment, with distinct features that have withstood the test of time. The traditional dwellings, characterized by their intricately designed courtyards, wind towers, and shaded passageways, were crafted to combat the harsh desert climate and create comfortable living spaces. Using locally sourced materials such as mud bricks, palm fronds, and coral stone showcases the resourcefulness and adaptability of the inhabitants. These historic architectural marvels continue to inspire contemporary designs, underpinning the rich cultural legacy of the Gulf.

The layout and construction of homes in the Gulf were tailored to foster community bonds and social cohesion. Courtyard houses across the region served as communal spaces for family gatherings, celebrations, and everyday interactions, emphasizing the interconnectedness of individuals within the community. Moreover, the architecture of these homes reflected an encompassing ethos of hospitality, where guests were welcomed and accommodated with graciousness and warmth. This cultural emphasis on communal living and shared spaces shaped the physical environment and influenced the social fabric of Gulf societies.

The significance of architecture extended beyond residential structures, encompassing monumental landmarks and public infrastructure that symbolized cultural identity and prosperity. Majestic forts, grand mosques, and vibrant marketplaces were testaments to the people's craftsmanship and artistic expression. These architectural wonders served as focal points for congregation and trade, fostering a sense of civic pride and collective identity within the diverse tapestry of the Gulf's population.

Contemporary architectural endeavors have harmonized modern innovations with age-old design principles as societies evolved. This fusion has catalyzed sustainable urban development characterized by innovative skyscrapers, eco-friendly neighborhoods, and avant-garde city planning. The architectural landscape continues to evolve, preserving the essence of tradition while embracing future advancements. Such a balance between heritage and progress underscores the resilience and adaptability embedded in the architectural narrative of the Gulf, serving as a testament to the enduring spirit of its inhabitants.

Community Governance and Social Order

In the historical context of the Gulf region, community governance and social order formed the cornerstone of a functional and harmonious society. The intricate network of tribes and local communities operated within a system of rules and norms that upheld stability, justice, and societal coherence. At the heart of these structures were tribal councils or 'Majlis,' where elders and influential members convened to discuss matters of significance and make decisions for the community's collective well-being.

The governance framework was deeply rooted in consensus, consultation, and mutual respect. Decisions were made with careful consideration for the voices of all members, fostering a sense of inclusivity and fairness. Disputes and conflicts were often mediated through customary laws and traditional mechanisms, emphasizing reconciliation and restoration of harmony rather than punitive measures.

Social order in this traditional context was intricately tied to the roles and responsibilities allocated to individuals within the community. Hierarchies were established based on age, wisdom, and contributions to the community, nurturing a sense of respect and deference towards elders and leaders. This hierarchical structure also extended to the division of labor, with distinct roles and duties for men, women, and younger members, aligning with cultural values and societal needs.

Additionally, the concept of 'Baraka' or divine blessing permeated community life, significantly shaping social interactions and governance. Leaders and influential figures were believed to possess 'Baraka,' endowing them with an aura of wisdom, foresight, and spiritual guidance. This conferred a moral responsibility upon them to lead with integrity, empathy, and a deep sense of duty toward their community.

Furthermore, the social order encompassed mutual support, solidarity, and communal obligations. Concepts like 'Ghair' emphasized the duty of mutual assistance among members, ensuring that individuals could rely on the collective strength and goodwill of the community in times of need. This spirit of interconnectedness and reciprocity wove a robust social fabric, fostering resilience, unity, and shared prosperity.

While the modern landscape has evolved, these foundational principles of community governance and social order continue to influence the cultural ethos of the Gulf, underscoring the enduring legacy of tradition and collective wisdom in shaping contemporary society.

Gender Roles and Family Dynamics

In the traditional society of the Gulf, gender roles and family dynamics significantly shaped the social fabric. The division of labor was clearly defined, with men primarily engaged in fishing, pearl diving, and trading. At the same time, women took on responsibilities within the household, including caregiving, food preparation, and textile work. However, it's essential to note that these roles, although distinct, were respected as equally valuable contributions to the well-being of the family and community.

The concept of family extended beyond the immediate nuclear unit, often encompassing multiple generations living together in close-knit arrangements. Such familial structures fostered a sense of community and mutual support, with elders guiding and imparting wisdom while younger members contributed through their labor and respect. This intergenerational cohesion was integral to upholding cultural traditions, values, and communal harmony.

Moreover, familial relationships were based on profound respect and reciprocity, with every member understanding their role within the intricate web of kinship. Traditional practices instilled a strong sense of duty and honor among family members, emphasizing the importance of loyalty, obedience, and unity. These values formed the cornerstone of the societal framework, ensuring stability and continuity across generations.

Regarding gender roles, while there were established norms, there also existed an underlying recognition of the complementary strengths and skills of both men and women. Women held esteemed positions as guardians of heritage, culture, and knowledge, passing down ancestral arts, crafts, and oral histories to subsequent generations. Thus, they greatly influenced preserving and perpetuating the region's rich cultural legacy. Conversely, men were responsible for safeguarding the family's material welfare and earning livelihoods through maritime trade, agriculture, or craftsmanship. This symbiotic relationship underscored the interdependence and mutual respect between genders.

The complexities of gender roles and family dynamics in the ancient Gulf society provide a captivating lens through which to comprehend the intricate tapestry of traditional life. As we delve deeper into these aspects, we gain profound insights into the shared humanity that unites us across time, revealing how the past continues to shape our present and future.

Educational Methods and Learning Paradigms

In ancient times, educational methods and learning paradigms were deeply rooted in the cultural traditions of the Gulf region. Education was primarily transmitted orally, with knowledge and skills passed down from generation to generation through storytelling, poetry, and communal gatherings. Young individuals learn about their history, values, and societal norms through these traditional forms of education. Additionally, elders played a pivotal role in mentoring and guiding the youth, imparting practical wisdom and moral teachings. The close-knit familial and communal structure fostered a highly personalized learning environment, allowing for individualized attention and support. Furthermore, skills such as navigation, fishing, trading, and craftsmanship were often taught through apprenticeships, providing hands-on experience and practical knowledge. The region's natural landscape also served as an essential educational resource, as nomadic Bedouin communities used their surroundings to teach survival skills, such as finding water sources and identifying edible plants. The interconnectedness between daily life and learning promoted a holistic approach to education, where practical knowledge was seamlessly integrated into the fabric of everyday existence. Additionally, educational methods were often intertwined with religious teachings, with mosques and madrasas serving as learning centers and spiritual guidance. Pursuing knowledge was valued as a sacred duty, and the Quran became a central source of learning, fostering literacy and intellectual development among the population. As societies evolved, formalized educational structures emerged, with specialized schools and academies catering to various disciplines, including mathematics, astronomy, and language studies. The diverse range of subjects reflected the multifaceted nature of knowledge, encouraging a well-rounded approach to learning. Furthermore, the exchange of ideas and intellectual discourse flourished in bustling trade hubs, where merchants, scholars, and travelers converged, creating a dynamic environment for intellectual growth. This convergence of educational influences allowed for the blending of diverse learning paradigms, enriching the cultural tapestry of the Gulf region. In essence, educational methods and learning paradigms in the ancient Gulf inherently reflected the interconnectedness between heritage, community, and the natural environment, shaping a comprehensive approach to nurturing intellectual curiosity and skill development.

Concluding Reflections

Considering the intricate tapestry of the ancient Gulf societies, the realm of educational methods and learning paradigms reveals a depth of cultural wisdom that resonates with timeless significance. This exploration illuminates the inextricable link between education, preserving tradition, and adaptive innovation within evolving communities. The diversity of teaching approaches, from oral traditions to hands-on apprenticeships, underscores an inherent resilience that has sustained these societies through generations.

Moreover, the broader implications of educational practices intersect with the interconnectedness of societal structures, influencing familial roles, social hierarchies, and regional distinctiveness. The transmission of knowledge and skills across diverse landscapes enriches individual lives and fortifies the communal fabric that defines these ancient cultures.

As we contemplate the enduring legacies of educational customs, it becomes evident that these methodologies have shaped the foundation of Gulf societies, fostering a collective ethos of shared wisdom and mutual respect. The interplay between traditional pedagogical techniques and modern advancements encapsulates a profound narrative of cultural continuity, wherein the past informs the present and, in turn, guides the future.

Lastly, this comprehensive examination of educational methods and learning paradigms invites thoughtful introspection on the role of education as an agent of societal cohesion and sustainable progress. It beckons us to recognize that the preservation of cultural heritage lies not solely in archaeological vestiges or historical records but equally in perpetuating knowledge and values through dynamic educational frameworks. The profound implications extend beyond academic pursuits to encompass the essence of identity, fostering an enduring legacy that nurtures the collective consciousness of Gulf communities and transcends geographical boundaries.

In conclusion, the intersection of education and tradition offers profound insights into humanity's rich tapestry, showcasing the resilience, adaptability, and unity woven into the historical fabric of the Gulf. By embracing the diverse modes of imparting knowledge and cultivating wisdom, these reflections serve as a testament to the enduring spirit of these ancient civilizations and provide invaluable lessons for contemporary society.

Chapter 16

Traditions and Celebrations

With its rich tapestry of cultures and landscapes, the Gulf region has given rise to diverse traditions and festivities deeply rooted in the unique geographical and cultural setting. The interplay between the vast desert expanses and the azure waters of the Arabian Gulf has profoundly influenced the customs and rituals practiced by the inhabitants of this region. The scorching heat and dramatic seasonal variations have fostered a deep reverence for the solar and lunar cycles, which form the cornerstone of many traditional celebrations. Moreover, the historical significance of the Gulf as a strategic hub for trade and cultural exchange has imbued contemporary festivities with a sense of continuity and heritage. As such, the region's long history of human habitation has left an indelible mark on the customs and practices observed during various festivals and commemorations. This profound connection to the land and its storied past continues to shape the vibrant tapestry of Gulf traditions, reflecting the resilience and adaptability of its people in the face of change and modernization.

Seasonal Festivals: Marking the Solar and Lunar Years

In the Gulf region, seasonal festivals play a pivotal role in marking the passage of time and celebrating the cyclical rhythms of nature. These festivals are deeply rooted in the ancient traditions of the indigenous people, reflecting their harmonious bond with the environment. The festivals mark the solar and lunar years, signifying the beginning of agricultural cycles and celestial events. As the sun moves across the sky, these festivals denote the changing seasons, from the vibrant spring blooms to the bountiful harvests of autumn. Each festival is meticulously planned and rich in symbolism, serving as a communal expression of gratitude, renewal, and hope for the future. The rituals performed during these festivals are imbued with deep spiritual significance, reinforcing the Gulf societies' cultural identity and communal bonds. Traditional music, dance, and decorative arts are intertwined to enrich the celebrations further, creating a captivating tapestry of sensory experiences. Through elaborate processions, vibrant cultural displays, and communal feasting, these festivals serve as a testament to the resilience and creativity of the Gulf communities. The interplay between tradition and innovation is evident in the adaptations made to the festivals over the centuries, showcasing the ability of the Gulf societies to embrace change while preserving their cultural heritage. The seasonal festivals provide a platform for transmitting ancestral knowledge and customs and offer a lens through which the evolution of the Gulf societies can be observed. Across the generations, these festive occasions continue to foster a profound connection to the land, the skies, and the interconnectedness of all living beings.

Rituals of Faith: Religious Celebrations Across the Gulf

Religion holds a significant place in the cultural tapestry of the Gulf region, with diverse faith traditions coexisting in harmony. The religious celebrations across the Gulf are vibrant and elaborate, offering a window into the deep-rooted spiritual beliefs and practices that have endured for centuries. Islamic festivals such as Eid al-Fitr and Eid al-Adha are celebrated with great fervor, marking the culmination of Ramadan and the annual pilgrimage to Mecca. The joyous atmosphere during these festivities is palpable, with communities coming together to share prayers, feasts, and acts of charity. Additionally, the Islamic New Year, known as Hijri, is commemorated with introspection and religious observance, providing an opportunity for spiritual renewal and gratitude. Beyond Islam, the region also embraces other faiths, each with its calendar of religious events. Christian festivals such as Christmas and Easter are honored by the Christian communities, often featuring special church services, traditional meals, and vibrant decorations. Similarly, the Hindu community marks festivals like Diwali and Holi, bringing the spirit of light, knowledge, and color to their celebrations. Moreover, the Jewish population observes important holidays like Hanukkah and Yom Kippur, signifying deep reflections, community gatherings, and expressions of devotion. These religious celebrations are integral to the Gulf's social fabric, fostering an environment of tolerance, understanding, and mutual respect among different religious groups. The rich tapestry of ritual, prayer, and festivity is a testament to the region's commitment to honoring diverse religious traditions within a collective spirit of unity and shared humanity.

Weddings in the Gulf: A Synthesis of Tradition and Celebration

Weddings in the Gulf region are rich tapestries woven with intricate traditions, symbolic rituals, and vibrant celebrations. These matrimonial ceremonies serve as a poignant reflection of the cultural legacy, familial ties, and communal bonds that define the essence of Gulf societies. Rooted in centuries-old traditions, the wedding customs in the Gulf stand as testaments to the deep reverence for heritage and the sanctity of union. The wedding journey commences with the intricate process of matchmaking, an age-old practice that aligns not just two individuals but also two families, uniting them in purpose and commitment. In the months leading up to the wedding, families engage in elaborate preparations, each step carrying profound meaning and significance. From selecting auspicious dates based on astrological considerations to creating sumptuous feasts, every aspect is meticulously planned to honor and uphold cherished customs. As the wedding day dawns, the air is saturated with anticipation and excitement. The ceremonial proceedings unfold amidst a backdrop of opulent decor, resplendent traditional attire, and the evocative melodies of traditional music. Guests from near and far gather to partake in the festivities, symbolizing the collective support and esteem bestowed upon the couple. Throughout the wedding rituals, symbols and gestures imbued with deep cultural significance permeate the proceedings, underscoring the reverence for tradition. Each moment encapsulates sustained heritage, from exchanging intricate, handcrafted jewelry to solemnizing vows in the presence of revered elders. Culinary indulgence forms an integral part of the celebration, with lavish spreads featuring traditional delicacies embodying Gulf cuisine's essence. The flavorsome dishes, infused with aromatic spices and time-honored recipes, elevate the festive ambiance, entwining sustenance with conviviality. The culmination of the wedding ceremony culminates with spirited jubilation as music, dance, and exuberant revelry unite the community in shared bliss. Beyond the ornate splendor and joyous revelry lies the profound symbolism of weddings in the Gulf — an embodiment of harmony, continuity, and the enduring legacy of tradition.

Culinary Tradishments: Food and Drink in Celebratory Contexts

In the Gulf, culinary traditions are central to celebrating various occasions, reflecting the region's rich and diverse cultural tapestry. These celebratory moments are infused with various flavors, aromas, and textures that evoke a deep sense of communal identity and heritage. Festivals and gatherings allow communities to showcase their distinctive culinary heritage, passing down time-honored recipes from generation to generation. The preparation of celebratory dishes often begins days in advance, with meticulous attention to detail and time-honored techniques. Each occasion carries its unique set of traditional delicacies, which are lovingly prepared and served with pride. From aromatic biryanis and slow-cooked stews to delicate pastries and refreshing beverages, the diversity and complexity of Gulf cuisine shine brightly during festive occasions. Furthermore, the significance of certain ingredients and methods reflects the historical and cultural narratives that have shaped the region's gastronomic landscape. Certain dishes are reserved exclusively for celebrations, symbolizing unity, prosperity, and the bonds of kinship. Throughout history, the exchange of culinary traditions has been integral to diplomatic relations and trade, showcasing the interconnectedness of cultures through shared gastronomic experiences.

The art of hospitality is deeply ingrained in Gulf culture, with guests being welcomed with an abundance of delectable offerings that signify warmth and generosity. Creativity flourishes within these culinary practices as individuals pay homage to their cultural roots while also adapting to modern influences. Traditional utensils and cooking vessels are irreplaceable in celebratory preparations, linking the present to the past. Whether it's the aromatic spices, the intricate layering of flavors, or the communal act of dining together, these culinary traditions continue to serve as a poignant expression of the region's identity and pride. Beyond nourishment, food and drink play a pivotal role in uniting communities, bridging generational gaps, and expressing gratitude. Each dish reflects the region's rich history, carrying with it the stories and traditions of centuries past, making every celebration more than just a feast but a living narrative of Gulf culture.

Music and Dance: Preserving Cultural Heritage Through Performance

Music and dance form an integral part of the Gulf's cultural fabric, serving to preserve and showcase the region's rich heritage. Traditionally, music and dance have been pivotal in narrating the people's stories, struggles, triumphs, and everyday experiences that bind communities together. In the context of celebrations, these art forms take on added significance, representing a continuation of age-old traditions and an expression of collective identity and joy.

The traditional music of the Gulf, often accompanied by Indigenous instruments such as the oud, rebab, and tabla, blends melodic intricacies with rhythmic complexities, offering a glimpse into the historical evolution and diversity of musical forms within the region. These musical compositions, whether vocal or instrumental, bear testimony to the ingenuity and artistry of Gulf composers and musicians, carrying the essence of the past while adapting to the contemporary landscape.

Dance, too, plays a significant role in upholding cultural inheritance. Each dance form in the Gulf narrates a tale, weaving together movements that capture the spirit of the land and its people. From lively group performances at weddings to elegant displays at social gatherings, dance remains a vibrant embodiment of regional customs and values. The intricate footwork and graceful gestures depict narratives of love, unity, and perseverance, echoing the sentiments that have sustained Gulf communities for generations.

Music and dance continue to evolve within this milieu, incorporating modern influences while safeguarding ancestral practices. Contemporary Gulf musicians and dancers adeptly infuse traditional elements with innovative expressions, ensuring the legacy endures in new and exciting forms. By mastering and adapting the rhythms and steps of yesteryears, they ensure that the essence of their cultural heritage remains undiminished, resonating with present and future audiences alike.

In this manner, music and dance serve as living embodiments of the Gulf's history and tradition, echoing through time and geography. They embody the resilience, beauty, and unity inherent in the region's collective story, forging connections between past and present, enriching celebratory occasions, and facilitating an ongoing dialogue between generations. The Gulf celebrates its heritage through music and dance, embracing its people's ever-changing yet enduring spirit.

Artistic Expression: Craftsmanship in Decorative Arts for Festivities

Artistic expression through craftsmanship is pivotal in the rich tapestry of Gulf traditions and celebrations. The decorative arts associated with festivities are imbued with cultural significance, encapsulating the essence of heritage and community. Across the region, skilled artisans create intricate works of art, showcasing their expertise in traditional crafts such as calligraphy, metalwork, ceramics, and textile embellishments. These crafts serve ornamental purposes and hold deep symbolic value, representing stories, beliefs, and values passed down through generations.

The meticulous process of crafting decorative pieces often involves a profound connection to history and shared narratives, as artisans draw inspiration from archival designs and ancestral techniques. Calligraphy, an esteemed art form in the Gulf, is utilized to inscribe meaningful verses and motifs onto various objects, infusing them with spiritual and philosophical meanings. Moreover, metalwork, particularly in creating ornate lamps, intricately detailed trays, and intricately patterned jewelry, exemplifies the artisan's skill and dedication to preserving age-old practices.

Ceramics, revered for their exquisite patterns and vibrant hues, emerge as central elements in festive décor, adorning homes and public spaces during celebratory occasions. The fusion of traditional methods with contemporary influences results in innovative and captivating designs, reflecting the adaptability and ingenuity of Gulf artisans. Furthermore, textile embellishments, such as embroidery and weaving, elevate the aesthetic appeal of ceremonial attire and adornments, amplifying the visual splendor of traditional costumes and accessories worn during festivities.

The beautiful marriage of artistic talent and cultural symbolism is evident in these handmade creations' intricate detailing and precision. Each piece serves as a testament to the enduring legacy of Gulf traditions, resonating with a timeless charm that transcends generations. As celebrations unfold, these masterfully crafted decorative arts become intrinsic components of the communal experience, infusing gatherings with grandeur and historical continuity. The cherished customs and rituals are intertwined with the mastery of artisans, culminating in an immersive celebration that honors the depth and diversity of Gulf heritage.

Dress and Adornment: Symbolism in Traditional Attire

The traditional attire of the Gulf region holds profound significance, reflecting both cultural heritage and societal values. Each garment and accessory carries a rich tapestry of symbolism, encompassing elements such as history, tradition, status, and identity. Traditional clothing in the Gulf serves as a visual narrative of the region's history and customs. Every style and pattern is steeped in heritage, from the flowing robes of the dishdasha to the vibrant dresses of women. Embroidery, color choices, and fabric textures are not merely ornamental; they speak volumes about the wearer's lineage, affiliations, and aspirations. As the Gulf societies have evolved over time, so has their attire, yet the essence of tradition remains interwoven with contemporary aesthetics.

Beyond aesthetics, traditional attire symbolizes social and cultural facets. The intricate designs and patterns are imbued with symbolism that varies between different tribes and regions. Additionally, using specific materials and adornments communicates various messages, signifying occasions, beliefs, or roles within the community. Thus, attire is a silent language, conveying sentiments, affiliations, and emotions.

Adornments are equally vital in traditional attire, with jewelry and accessories bearing significant meanings. From delicate filigree silverwork to mesmerizing gemstones, each piece represents craftsmanship and artistry, cultural pride and personal expression. Furthermore, these adornments often hold religious or spiritual significance, enhancing the wearer's connection to heritage and faith.

In modern times, the preservation and adaptation of traditional attire continue to be upheld to safeguard cultural identity. Fashion designers and artisans collaborate to blend heritage with contemporary fashion, ensuring that traditional attire remains relevant and revered. By understanding the symbolism and significance of dress and adornment, one can gain deeper insights into the complex tapestry of Gulf culture, appreciating the stories that garments and ornaments silently convey.

Children in Celebration: Roles and Rites of Passage

Throughout the Gulf region, children play integral roles in traditional celebrations and ceremonies, symbolizing the perpetuation of cultural customs and providing a glimpse into the community's future. Defined by traditions upheld for generations, the rites of passage for Gulf children mark significant milestones in their lives, shaping their identities and reinforcing the values inherent in their society. Each stage is honored through elaborate rituals demonstrating the deep-rooted significance of family, community, and heritage from birth to adolescence.

At birth, the arrival of a newborn is met with great joy and celebration, signifying hope and continuity. Newborns are welcomed into the world amidst vibrant festivities like 'aqiqah', a time-honored tradition where the infant's head is shaved, and an animal sacrifice is made to ward off harm and bring blessings. Families express their commitment to nurturing the child through such practices within cherished customs and spiritual beliefs.

As children grow, they partake in various coming-of-age ceremonies that mark adulthood. Among these, the 'Sohour' ceremony, held during Ramadan, signifies a child's first observance of fasting from sunrise to sunset, embodying discipline and devotion to faith. Additionally, the tradition of 'Henna' involves adorning the hands of young girls with intricate designs as they reach puberty, symbolizing femininity and fertility. These rites of passage emphasize the importance of maturity and responsibility, instilling in children a sense of pride in their cultural heritage and preparing them for adult roles within the community.

Gulf cultures place a high value on learning and knowledge acquisition in education. Children embark on their educational journey amid ceremonies that honor their initiation into the pursuit of wisdom. Whether it's the first day of school or the completion of a specific level of education, these moments are celebrated with enthusiasm, underscoring the communal reverence for intellectual development and the promise of a brighter future.

Through these robust traditions, Gulf communities nurture children as bearers of their heritage, imparting respect for their roots and fostering a deep sense of belonging. The evolution of these customs reflects a harmonious blend of tradition and modernity, demonstrating how the celebration of childhood remains a profound expression of cultural continuity and collective identity.

Conclusion: The Evolving Nature of Traditions and Celebrations

Throughout this exploration of Gulf traditions and celebrations, we have witnessed the deep-rooted significance of rituals and festivities in shaping the region's cultural identity. From marking seasonal changes to commemorating life's milestones, these customs reflect the rich heritage of the Gulf and embody the evolving nature of tradition in a contemporary context. As we observe the multitude of roles and rites of passage children experience within celebratory events, it becomes apparent that Gulf traditions are imbued with timeless values that continue to resonate across generations. The significance of these customs goes beyond mere symbolic gestures; they serve as powerful conduits for strengthening familial bonds, fostering communal unity, and transmitting cultural legacies. Despite the changing landscapes of modernity, Gulf traditions and celebrations persist in embracing the essence of cultural authenticity while adapting to contemporary interpretations. The interplay of tradition and modernity is evident in how festive occasions incorporate elements of artistic innovation, technological advancements, and an openness to diverse influences. This juxtaposition of the old and the new reflects a dynamic continuum of tradition, symbolizing the ability of Gulf cultures to preserve their roots while embracing the fluidity of adaptation. Through the lens of celebrations, we witness the evolution of customs and practices, encapsulating the harmonious coexistence of heritage and progression. In this way, tradition remains a living entity that evolves in response to societal shifts yet retains its core principles and values. The conclusion, therefore, is not a conclusion at all but a continuation—a recognition that the ever-evolving nature of traditions and celebrations in the Gulf reveals a profound resilience and adaptability that ensures their enduring relevance in an ever-changing world.

Chapter 17

Ties That Bind:
Family Dynamics
and Gender Roles

In exploring the intricate tapestry of Gulf family structures, it is essential to delve into the composition and size of traditional families that have long been the cornerstone of Gulf society. Historically, Gulf families were characterized by their expansive nature, often spanning several generations within a single household. The patriarchal system prevalent in these familial units underscored the authority and responsibility of the male head of the family, impacting the gender roles and dynamics within these structures. Moreover, the extended family network played a pivotal role in providing support and guidance, shaping the upbringing and socialization of the younger generations. Such arrangements fostered a sense of unity, interdependence, and shared responsibilities among family members. Alongside this, the concept of 'tribe' also had significant influence, as families often identified themselves with specific tribes, further intertwining kinship and societal dynamics. This interconnectedness extended beyond immediate relatives, encompassing distant cousins and even non-blood relations integrated into the familial fold. Regarding living arrangements, traditional Gulf families commonly resided in spacious homes accommodating the collective presence of numerous family members. Segregation along gender lines within households was a customary practice, underscoring the distinct roles and spaces allocated for men and women. Furthermore, these residences' architectural layout reflected the hierarchical structure within the family, with designated areas for communal gatherings, private quarters, and spaces reserved for the elderly. The physical environment thus mirrored the organization and values upheld within the family unit, signifying the fundamental role of the home as the nucleus of Gulf familial existence.

Historical Perspectives on Gender Roles

Throughout the history of the Gulf region, the roles and status of men and women within society have been deeply ingrained in cultural, religious, and tribal customs. Historical perspectives reveal a complex tapestry of gender dynamics that have evolved over centuries, influenced by various factors such as trade, religion, and prevailing social structures.

In ancient times, the Gulf region's societies often adhered to patriarchal systems, where men held positions of authority and power within the family and community. The economic activities of pearl diving, fishing, and trade were predominantly linked to male members, shaping their roles as breadwinners and providers. On the other hand, women assumed roles centered around domestic duties, childcare, and preserving cultural traditions within the family unit.

The advent of Islam played a significant role in shaping historical gender roles in the Gulf, providing a framework for societal conduct and familial responsibilities. While emphasizing respect for women and their roles as mothers and caretakers, Islamic teachings also delineated distinct gender roles and expectations within the community. The honor and protection of female family members became intertwined with notions of masculinity and chivalry, shaping the historical construct of gender roles throughout the region.

Key historical events and external influences further molded Gulf societies' perceptions of gender roles. The impact of colonialism and global trade brought shifts in traditional practices, introducing new ideas and challenging existing dynamics. As modernity and globalization took root, gradual transformations in gender roles emerged, especially concerning education, workforce participation, and leadership opportunities.

Moreover, revisiting historical gender roles allows us to understand the origins of prevailing attitudes and practices in contemporary Gulf societies. Elements of tradition persist alongside evolving perspectives, contributing to a nuanced understanding of how historical dynamics continue to influence present-day family structures and gender roles. By examining these historical perspectives, it becomes clear that gender roles are not static; they are subject to adaptation, reevaluation, and progressive change as societies navigate the complexities of modernization while honoring their cultural heritage.

Marriage and Kinship Patterns

Marriage and kinship patterns in the Gulf have been integral to the region's social fabric for centuries, serving as pillars around which families are structured and communities are bound. These patterns reflect intricate networks of relationships that extend beyond immediate familial units, encompassing broader kinship ties that form the basis of social organization. In the Gulf, marriage is not simply a union of individuals but an alliance between families, often perpetuating bonds and alliances forged over generations. The institution of marriage is deeply rooted in tradition and customs, with ceremonies and rituals bearing testament to the significance placed on matrimonial unions. Across different Gulf societies, there exist diverse marriage practices, each reflecting unique cultural norms and values. These traditions often incorporate elaborate rites and celebrations, symbolizing the merging of two individuals and their families and lineages. Kinship plays a crucial role in governing social interactions and obligations within Gulf communities. It extends beyond the nuclear family to encompass extended relatives, fostering a sense of interconnectedness and collective responsibility. The kinship system outlines rights, duties, and reciprocal obligations, shaping the dynamics of everyday life. Additionally, kinship structures guide inheritance laws, property rights, and decision-making processes within familial units, serving as a framework for distributing resources and responsibilities. Furthermore, the interconnectedness of kinship networks influences social hierarchies and power dynamics, contributing to the stability and continuity of Gulf communities. As the Gulf continues to evolve, contemporary challenges and global influences have begun to impact traditional marriage and kinship patterns, leading to societal norms and values shifts. This ongoing transformation necessitates a nuanced understanding of the interplay between tradition and modernity in shaping marriage and kinship dynamics, offering insights into the evolving landscape of interpersonal relationships and familial structures in the Gulf.

Childrearing Practices and Intergenerational Relationships

In the Gulf region, childrearing practices are deeply rooted in cultural traditions, emphasizing the importance of family unity and emotional support. From infancy to adolescence, children are nurtured within an environment that values respect for elders, discipline, and moral teachings. Intergenerational relationships play a pivotal role in shaping the identity and character of the young ones.

The nurturing of children begins from the moment they are born, with family members playing a collective role in their care. Grandparents, aunts, uncles, and older siblings all contribute to the child's holistic development, instilling core values and cultural traditions. This communal approach not only eases the burden on parents but also fosters strong bonds between the generations.

Throughout childhood, children are taught the importance of respecting their elders and upholding family traditions. They learn these values through oral storytelling, where grandparents and elders pass down tales of honor, bravery, and resilience. Such narratives serve as moral guidance and instill a sense of pride in one's heritage.

As they reach adolescence, children are encouraged to participate actively in familial and community activities, further reinforcing the interconnectedness of generations. Respect for elders and authority figures is emphasized, and their wisdom is revered. Additionally, children are groomed to take on roles of responsibility within the family structure, preparing them for adulthood and future leadership roles.

Intergenerational relationships are a cornerstone in transmitting cultural knowledge and values, ensuring that time-honored traditions are preserved and passed on to subsequent generations. Through these practices, families in the Gulf cultivate a sense of unity, continuity, and reverence for their rich cultural heritage.

Women's Roles within the Family and Society

In Gulf societies, women have historically played multifaceted roles within the family and broader social constructs. While traditional gender roles often cast women primarily as nurturers and caregivers within the domestic sphere, it is essential to recognize that women have also been pivotal in shaping their communities' cultural, educational, and economic landscapes. Within the family unit, women have traditionally been entrusted with raising children, passing down cultural traditions, and fostering a sense of unity and resilience. Their influence extends beyond the household, as women have been instrumental in preserving and enriching the artistic and artisanal heritage of the region. Women's contributions to literature, poetry, music, and handicrafts have served as a testament to their enduring impact on the cultural tapestry of the Gulf. In addition to their vital roles in upholding familial cohesion, women have also been active participants in community leadership and philanthropy, often initiating and organizing social initiatives and support networks to address local needs. Despite historical gender divisions, women have increasingly emerged as pioneers in education and professional pursuits, actively contributing to advancing various fields, including healthcare, education, entrepreneurship, and public service. As the region continues to undergo societal transformations, there has been a growing recognition of the importance of empowering women and fostering gender equality. This shift is reflected in efforts to enhance educational opportunities for girls, promote women's participation in decision-making processes, and eliminate gender-based barriers in the work-force. Such endeavors signify an evolving narrative that acknowledges and celebrates women's integral role in shaping the Gulf's familial and societal dynamics while highlighting the significance of ensuring equal opportunities and representation for future generations.

Men as Providers and Protectors

Traditionally, men have traditionally been regarded as their families' providers and protectors in the traditional Gulf society. This role is deeply ingrained in the cultural fabric, reflecting the historical emphasis on male responsibilities within the family unit. As providers, men have shouldered the responsibility of ensuring the financial sustenance and stability of the household. Historically, this has often involved engaging in professions such as fishing, pearl diving, trading, and, later, oil-related industries. The ability to provide for one's family has been a source of pride and honor for Gulf men, carrying a weight of cultural significance.

Alongside their role as providers, men are also seen as the primary protectors of the family unit. This includes safeguarding the physical, emotional, and material well-being of their loved ones. The concept of 'male protection' extends beyond the confines of the household, with men also assuming roles as guardians of their communities and traditions. Throughout history, Gulf men have been revered for their courage, resilience, and strength, qualities that were not only admired but also expected as part of their role as protectors. This societal expectation placed considerable pressure on men to exhibit bravery in the face of adversity and to defend their families against external threats.

While deeply rooted in history, these traditional roles have evolved significantly. While the essence of providing and protecting remains integral to the identity of Gulf men, societal shifts have gradually opened up new opportunities and expectations. With advancements in education, technology, and the workforce, men are redefining their roles as providers by actively participating in diverse professional fields, contributing to economic growth, and taking on domestic responsibilities. Moreover, the evolving perspectives on gender equality have encouraged a redefinition of the protection role, emphasizing mutual support and shared responsibility within the family unit.

The interplay between tradition and modernity has sparked conversations on the evolving nature of masculinity in the Gulf as men navigate the balancing act of preserving cultural heritage while adapting to contemporary dynamics. It is crucial to recognize and appreciate how the enduring spirit of providing and protecting has influenced the collective psyche of Gulf men, fostering resilience, unity, and a deep sense of familial commitment. This chapter sheds light on the multifaceted nature of men's roles as providers and protectors, highlighting the historical foundations, contemporary transformations, and future possibilities within the complex tapestry of Gulf family dynamics.

Cultural Rituals and Family Celebrations

In the Gulf region, cultural rituals and family celebrations significantly strengthen social ties and preserve traditions. These events serve as pivotal moments for communities to unite, reaffirm their collective identity, and pass down ancestral customs to future generations. One of the most cherished rituals is the celebration of Eid al-Fitr, marking the end of

Ramadan, the holy month of fasting. Families gather to offer prayers at mosques, share festive meals, and exchange heartfelt greetings, fostering a sense of unity and camaraderie. Additionally, the tradition of henna painting holds great cultural significance, particularly during weddings and other joyous occasions. The intricate application of henna on the hands and feet represents blessings, beauty, and protection, symbolizing the auspicious nature of the event. Moreover, the annual commemoration of National Day brings communities together to honor their country's history, displaying vibrant displays of traditional dances, music performances, and fireworks, showcasing pride in their heritage. Another poignant celebration is the 'Mawlid an-Nabi,' commemorating the birth of Prophet Muhammad. Devotees organize processions, recite poetry, and distribute charitable donations, reinforcing spiritual devotion and community solidarity. Families partake in elaborate feasts throughout these celebrations, where culinary specialties and traditional dishes become symbolic expressions of shared cultural heritage. Furthermore, multi-generational gatherings create an environment where elders pass down oral histories, folk tales, and wisdom, ensuring the continuum of customs and values. Therefore, these cultural rituals and family celebrations serve as a source of social cohesion and contribute to preserving the Gulf's rich cultural tapestry.

Educational Opportunities and Gender Expectations

Educational opportunities have significantly transformed in the Gulf region in recent decades. Traditionally, gender expectations played a major role in shaping access to education for boys and girls. Historically, boys were encouraged to pursue higher education and professional careers, while girls' educational paths were sometimes limited to domestic skills and homemaking. However, with societal shifts and a concerted effort towards gender equality, there has been a remarkable change in the perceptions of education and career options for both genders. This shift has made increasing educational opportunities accessible to all, regardless of gender. To promote equal educational opportunities, governments and institutions have implemented policies and programs to provide inclusive and quality education for all. The emphasis on gender equality in education has led to platforms and initiatives that actively encourage and support girls' participation in STEM fields and other traditionally male-dominated disciplines. Additionally, educational institutions play a pivotal role in fostering an environment promoting gender inclusivity and equity. Through targeted interventions, such as mentorship programs and scholarship opportunities, there is a conscious effort to eradicate any remaining disparities in educational access for boys and girls. This approach ensures a more diverse and skilled workforce in the future and contributes to overall societal progress and development. The evolving landscape of educational opportunities and gender expectations in the Gulf reflects a promising future where individuals, regardless of gender, can pursue their academic interests and professional aspirations without limitations or prejudices. As the region prioritizes education and gender equality, the unfolding narrative presents a powerful testament to the potential for meaningful and enduring change.

Challenges and Changes in Contemporary Family Dynamics

In the rapidly evolving Gulf countries, contemporary family dynamics encounter various challenges and changes that reshape traditional structures. With the advent of globalization and modernization, many Gulf families are navigating a delicate balance between preserving cultural values and adapting to external influences. One of the most pressing challenges is the impact of technological advancements on family cohesion. As digital connectivity becomes ubiquitous, families grapple with integrating electronic devices into quality bonding time, affecting interactions and communication. Moreover, the prevalence of social media presents new challenges in managing privacy and discerning the impact of virtual relationships on real-life connections. These developments have triggered a reevaluation of parenting practices and the establishment of boundaries within the family unit. Additionally, shifting economic dynamics have led to changes in traditional gender roles within households. As more women pursue higher education and career opportunities, there is a notable shift in the division of labor and decision-making processes in many families. This transition prompts the redefining of gender expectations and power dynamics within familial relationships. Furthermore, the influx of expatriate communities has introduced a mosaic of cultural influences, challenging established norms and fostering a sense of diversity within Gulf families. Integrating varying cultural practices and traditions can enrich cross-cultural experiences and potential conflicts as families strive to navigate this intercultural terrain. Amid these evolving dynamics, generational gaps and conflicting value systems often present internal tensions within families. The clash between traditional values upheld by older generations and the aspirations of younger members for greater autonomy and individual expression can create unique interpersonal challenges. Beyond internal dynamics, ongoing social, economic, and geopolitical transformations are also reshaping the broader societal context in which families operate. These external pressures introduce uncertainties and complexities, necessitating adaptability and resilience from Gulf families. In response to these changes, families adopt diverse strategies to preserve their cultural heritage while embracing progressive shifts. The evolving landscape of family dynamics in the Gulf mirrors a broader global trend toward redefining familial structures, gender roles, and interpersonal relationships. Navigating these challenges requires open communication, mutual respect, and a willingness to balance tradition and modernity.

The Evolving Landscape of Family and Gender in the Gulf

As we conclude our exploration of family dynamics and gender roles in the Gulf, we must recognize the evolving landscape that shapes these crucial aspects of society. The dynamics within Gulf families and the associated gender roles have undergone significant transformations. Influenced by globalization, urbanization, education, and changing social norms, the traditional structures are gradually adapting to accommodate modern realities. The convergence of tradition and progress presents the region's complex yet fascinating juxtaposition.

This evolution reflects a shifting paradigm where historical customs intersect with contemporary values, creating a uniquely Gulf blend. Traditional gender roles, once deeply entrenched and clearly defined, are now yielding to a more fluid and inclusive approach. Women, once confined to domestic realms, are increasingly entering the workforce and assuming leadership roles across various sectors. This represents not only a significant departure from the past but also an inherent acknowledgment of the invaluable contribution women make to the economic and societal fabric of the region.

Furthermore, family and its associated dynamics have progressed beyond conventional models, embracing diversity and pluralism. While the traditional joint family system still thrives, nuclear family units are becoming more prevalent. These shifts testify to the changing aspirations of Gulf societies and the corresponding need to adapt to new realities. It is imperative to note that such modifications do not negate the importance placed on family bonds and solidarity in the Gulf; rather, they reflect the resilience of these bonds amidst transformation.

The evolving landscape of family and gender in the Gulf is also intricately intertwined with educational advancements and increasing opportunities for both men and women. Education is pivotal in sculpting progressive attitudes toward gender equality and redefining familial expectations. As individuals gain access to knowledge and expertise, a paradigm shift occurs, fostering an environment conducive to greater equality and shared household responsibilities.

In conclusion, the Gulf's narrative of family dynamics and gender roles is marked by adaptation, evolution, and consolidation. As the region continues to navigate an era of rapid change and modernization, the intrinsic values and cohesion embedded within familial and gender constructs persist as pillars of stability and continuity. Embracing the duality of tradition and progression, Gulf societies stand at the cusp of a new era where familial relationships and gender roles navigate the delicate balance between heritage and innovation.

Chapter 18

Echoes of the Past: Traditions in a Changing World

Culture is an ever-evolving tapestry woven through time by the threads of tradition and innovation. Understanding the historical evolution of cultural traditions becomes imperative in the Gulf region as we navigate the complex landscape of socio-economic, technological, and global influences. The rich tapestry of Gulf traditions reflects a seamless blend of ancient practices and the dynamic forces of change. It is crucial to delve into the historical context that has shaped these traditions. Recognizing the historical trajectory of cultural practices allows us to appreciate the depth of their significance and the resilience of the communities that have upheld them throughout centuries. By exploring the historical roots of Gulf traditions, we gain insights into their adaptive nature, shedding light on how they have weathered tides of change while retaining their essence. This understanding also facilitates a nuanced comprehension of the challenges and opportunities of modernization and global integration. Moreover, it fosters an appreciation for the intergenerational transmission of knowledge, rituals, and customs, ensuring the preservation of cultural heritage amidst the current of progress. Through this exploration, we can discern the profound link between the past and present, recognizing the enduring spirit of cultural traditions in shaping identities and fostering social cohesion. This chapter aims to comprehensively examine the historical underpinnings of Gulf traditions, laying a foundation for understanding their evolution amid the transformative currents of the modern world.

Historical Context of Gulf Traditions

Throughout history, the Gulf region has been a melting pot of diverse cultures and civilizations, each leaving an indelible mark on the traditions and customs practiced by its inhabitants. The rich tapestry of Gulf traditions is woven with threads of ancient Bedouin customs, Islamic heritage, and influences from trade with neighboring regions and beyond. The nomadic lifestyle of the Bedouin tribes, rooted in self-sufficiency and resilience in harsh desert environments, has dramatically shaped the cultural norms and traditions of the region. Their practices, such as storytelling, poetry, hospitality, and communal solidarity, continue to endure as pillars of Gulf society. The arrival of Islam transformed the social fabric of the Gulf, bringing with it a code of conduct that emphasized unity, compassion, and charity. This spiritual influence permeated daily life, dictating social interactions, governance, and familial structures. Furthermore, the Gulf's strategic geographic location enabled it to become a vibrant hub for trade, fostering connections with far-reaching lands such as India, Persia, and East Africa. This exposure introduced a mosaic of cultural elements, including culinary traditions, handicrafts, and linguistic exchanges, all of which have contributed to the colorful patchwork of Gulf heritage. Additionally, once a cornerstone of the region's economy, the pearling industry brought prosperity and facilitated cultural exchange through interactions with divers and traders from distant shores. As the Gulf states underwent rapid modernization in recent decades, the historical context of their traditions became increasingly significant. Understanding the roots of these traditions provides valuable insights into the adaptive nature of Gulf societies and the challenges they face in preserving their cultural identities amidst globalization and technological advancements.

The Impact of Modernization on Cultural Practices

The Gulf region has undergone significant modernization, which has brought about substantial changes in traditional cultural practices. Urbanization, globalization, technological advancements, and shifts in societal norms have influenced this transformation. One of the most profound impacts of modernization on cultural practices is the modification of traditional lifestyles. With rapid urbanization and industrialization, there has been a noticeable shift from rural to urban living, altering daily routines and community dynamics. Globalization has led to increased connections with diverse cultures, resulting in the assimilation of external influences into traditional practices. As a result, indigenous customs have evolved to incorporate new elements, blurring the lines between tradition and modernity. Technological advancements have also played a crucial role in reshaping traditional cultural practices. While technological innovations have facilitated communication, transportation, and access to information, they have also challenged the authenticity and preservation of traditional practices. The proliferation of digital platforms and social media has fostered the dissemination of global trends, impacting traditional aesthetics, values, and rituals. Furthermore, the pervasiveness of technology has affected traditional occupations and craftsmanship, leading to a decline in specific skilled trades and artisanal practices. The impact of modernization on cultural practices extends beyond tangible aspects to encompass intangible heritage. Societal changes and evolving value systems have contributed to shifts in beliefs, rituals, and intergenerational transmission of cultural knowledge. As traditional practices intersect with contemporary lifestyles, there is an ongoing negotiation between preserving cultural identities and embracing progress. The tension between heritage conservation and adaptation to modernity poses a complex challenge for communities in the Gulf. It requires a balanced approach that respects the richness of tradition while acknowledging the need for dynamic evolution. Addressing the repercussions of modernization on cultural practices necessitates thoughtful consideration of the intersection between tradition, innovation, and sustainability. Embracing an inclusive dialogue that involves community stakeholders, scholars, policymakers, and cultural custodians is essential in navigating this transformative phase. Overall, understanding the multifaceted impact of modernization on cultural practices is crucial for cultivating a nuanced appreciation of the evolving cultural landscape in the Gulf region.

Technology: A Double-Edged Sword for Traditional Cultures

Technology has always been a catalyst for change, a force that can simultaneously empower and challenge traditional cultures. In the context of the Gulf region, technological advancements have brought about both opportunities and threats to the preservation of age-old traditions. The introduction of modern tools, communication devices, and digital platforms has revolutionized how people interact, work, and express themselves, affecting deeply ingrained customs and practices. While these innovations have facilitated connectivity and knowledge sharing, they have also posed significant challenges to the authenticity and continuity of traditional cultural heritage. The rapid evolution of technology has influenced various aspects of traditional lifestyles, from craftsmanship and storytelling to community dynamics and social rituals. One of the primary repercussions of technological integration is the potential dilution or distortion of indigenous knowledge and practices. As modern conveniences and global trends increasingly permeate traditional societies, the delicate balance between preserving heritage and embracing progress becomes more complex. However, it is crucial to recognize that technology can also serve as a valuable tool for documenting, revitalizing, and safeguarding endangered traditions. Through digital archives, virtual repositories, and multimedia platforms, communities can now leverage technology to preserve their unique customs and narratives for future generations. Moreover, technological innovation presents opportunities for the adaptation and sustainable development of traditional skills and crafts in contemporary contexts. While navigating the dual impact of technology on traditional cultures, it is essential to approach these changes with mindfulness and informed decision-making. Collaborative efforts between technology experts, cultural practitioners, and community leaders are key to ensuring that integrating modern tools and practices respects the intrinsic values and integrity of traditional heritage. By recognizing the nuanced nature of this relationship, traditional cultures can harness the benefits of technology while safeguarding their identity and legacy amidst the ever-changing currents of the modern world.

Case Studies: Adaptation of Traditions

In examining the adaptation of traditions within the context of rapid societal and technological changes, the study delves into specific case studies that highlight the complexities and nuances of this transition. Each case study serves as a microcosm, shedding light on the interplay of tradition, modernity, and the myriad factors influencing their evolution. One such case study revolves around the Gulf region's traditional art of pearl diving. Historically, pearl diving has been central to the cultural and economic fabric of the region, shaping its identity and traditions for generations. However, with the advent of modern technology and the discovery of oil, the pearl industry witnessed a sharp decline, leading to significant shifts in the social and economic dynamics of communities reliant on this practice. Yet, rather than fading into obscurity, the tradition of pearl diving underwent a remarkable transformation. Through concerted efforts in preserving the heritage and fostering sustainable practices, initiatives emerged to revitalize and adapt this age-old tradition to contemporary contexts. As a result, pearl diving evolved from a means of livelihood to a cultural symbol, celebrated through festivals and artistic expressions while embracing innovative techniques and diversifying its applications. Another compelling case study lies in the realm of nomadic desert traditions. The ancient Bedouin lifestyle, rooted in intimate knowledge of the desert and sustaining camels and oasis resources, faced unprecedented challenges in urbanization and globalization. However, instead of being overshadowed by modern conveniences, the traditions of the Bedouin community underwent a careful reimagining. While some aspects evolved to integrate with modern systems, preserving crucial elements of their lifestyle, others were consciously preserved as living museums and immersive experiences for locals and visitors. This adaptive preservation not only safeguards the legacy of the Bedouin way of life but also offers valuable insights into coexisting with progress without sacrificing heritage. These case studies reveal that adapting traditions is not merely about survival but also resilience, agency, and the enduring spirit of cultural heritage. They exemplify how traditions can transcend time and space, enriching contemporary societies and generating renewed appreciation for the profound wisdom embedded within them.

Cultural Preservation Amongst Rapid Development

As the Gulf region experiences rapid development and modernization, the preservation of cultural heritage becomes paramount. The collision between traditional practices and advancing technologies necessitates a deliberate effort to conserve and promote the region's rich cultural heritage. Amidst the gleaming skyscrapers and bustling urban centers, there is an increasing concern about the potential erosion of intangible cultural heritage passed down through generations. With the rise of globalized influences and unprecedented economic growth, there is a fear that the distinct traditions and customs of the Gulf could be at risk of fading into obscurity. However, concerted efforts are being made to safeguard and celebrate these invaluable heritage assets. Governments, NGOs, and cultural institutions actively engage in initiatives to document, preserve, and transmit traditional knowledge and practices. This includes establishing cultural centers, museums, and educational programs dedicated to promoting indigenous traditions. Additionally, there is a growing recognition of the importance of intangible cultural heritage, such as oral traditions, performing arts, social practices, rituals, festive events, and traditional craftsmanship, in shaping the identity of communities. Collaborative ventures with local communities are instrumental in ensuring their voices and expertise are central to the preservation and revitalization efforts. Furthermore, sustainable development programs are designed to integrate and support traditional practices within evolving socio-economic landscapes. The focus extends beyond mere conservation efforts to fostering an environment where cultural heritage is dynamically woven into contemporary life. By balancing preservation with innovation, the goal is to create a sustainable framework that respects the past while embracing the future. Through these multifaceted approaches, cultural preservation thrives amidst rapid development, reinforcing the deep-rooted legacy of the Gulf region for generations to come.

Role of Elders: Gatekeepers of Tradition

Elders play a pivotal role in preserving and safeguarding the rich cultural heritage of the Gulf region. With their deep understanding of traditional practices, wisdom, and experience, they act as the guardians and transmitters of invaluable customs, rituals, and knowledge passed down through generations. Their contributions are essential in maintaining the authenticity and integrity of the region's cultural identity amidst the rapid tide of modernization and globalization.

The elders serve as living repositories of historical narratives, oral traditions, and indigenous wisdom, which are integral to the fabric of the Gulf society. Through their storytelling prowess, they weave compelling tales that entertain and impart valuable lessons, ethical values, and social norms to the younger generation. By actively engaging with the youth, elders ensure the continuation of ancestral traditions, fostering a sense of pride and belonging among the community.

Moreover, the elders serve as advisors and mentors, offering guidance based on time-tested principles and unparalleled insights. Their role extends beyond mere preservation; it encompasses nurturing respect, resilience, and resourcefulness among the youth, instilling within them a profound appreciation for their heritage and lineage. By doing so, they bridge the generational gap, fostering mutual understanding and unity within the community.

In times of societal change and upheaval, the elders provide a stabilizing force, offering perspectives rooted in the enduring values of the past. Their counsel serves as an anchor, anchoring the community to its roots while navigating the complexities of a rapidly evolving world. This continuity ensures that the essence of tradition remains untouched, embodying a timeless link between the past, present, and future.

The elders' esteemed position is pivotal in upholding the Gulf's cultural legacy. Their inherent sense of responsibility and reverence for tradition foster a collective consciousness that transcends individual perspectives, binding the community together in a tapestry woven from shared history, customs, and beliefs. As gatekeepers of tradition, the elders stand as pillars of strength, preserving the precious inheritance of the Gulf for posterity and ensuring that its vibrant tapestry remains unblemished by the passage of time.

Youth and Tradition: Reinterpretation and Innovation

As the Gulf region continues to evolve in the face of modernization, the role of youth in reinterpreting and innovating cultural traditions is of paramount importance. In this rapidly changing landscape, the younger generation plays a pivotal role in shaping the future while upholding the essence of ancestral legacies. The interplay between tradition and innovation provides a dynamic platform for the youth to express their unique perspectives while safeguarding the rich heritage of the Gulf.

The fusion of traditional practices with contemporary ideas presents an opportunity for the youth to reinterpret age-old customs in ways that resonate with their modern lifestyles. By infusing creativity and fresh outlooks into time-honored traditions, the younger members of society breathe new life into cultural practices, ensuring their relevance for future generations. This process allows for a seamless transition of values and customs, bridging the gap between the past and the present.

Innovation, spurred by technological advancements and globalization, motivates young individuals to revitalize traditional crafts, music, dance, and storytelling techniques, thereby preserving the essence of their heritage in innovative art forms. Reviving traditional knowledge in domains such as herbal medicine, handicrafts, and culinary arts also serves as a powerful vehicle for cultural continuity and adaptation. Moreover, integrating sustainable practices into traditional activities not only honors the legacy of the past but also aligns with the current global emphasis on environmental stewardship.

The engagement of youth in reimagining and revitalizing cultural festivities, rituals, and ceremonies fosters a sense of belonging and cultural pride. Collaborative efforts between elders and young community members facilitate the transmission of wisdom and the cultivation of creativity, steering a harmonious balance between honoring the past and embracing the future. Moreover, the empowerment of youths as custodians of their heritage imparts a sense of ownership and responsibility, instilling confidence to carry forward the invaluable traditions of the Gulf.

While navigating the complex nuances of adapting tradition to contemporary contexts, the youth are tasked with preserving the authentic ethos of their culture. Understanding the historical significance behind each tradition bolsters their commitment to maintaining the integrity of inherited customs. This acknowledgment of cultural roots fosters a deep sense of identity and connection to the collective narrative, empowering the youth to steer the trajectory of their cultural evolution while respecting the wisdom of bygone eras.

Ultimately, the youthful endeavors in reinterpreting and innovating upon traditions serve as a testament to the enduring resilience of the Gulf's heritage. Through this harmonious blend of the old and the new, the younger generation avails themselves as the torchbearers of cultural continuity, perpetuating the timeless essence of the Gulf's traditions in an ever-changing world.

Strategies for Sustaining Cultural Heritage

Preserving the rich cultural heritage of the Gulf region amidst rapid modernization and globalization presents a monumental challenge. However, several strategies can be employed to ensure the sustained safeguarding of these traditions for future generations. Firstly, investment in educational programs and initiatives to increase awareness and appreciation of the region's cultural heritage is crucial. By integrating traditional teachings and practices into formal education, young individuals can develop a deep understanding and respect for their heritage. Additionally, fostering partnerships between governmental bodies, private enterprises, and cultural institutions can create sustainable funding mechanisms and strategic initiatives for cultural preservation. These collaborations can also support the establishment of museums and cultural centers dedicated to showcasing and celebrating the diverse traditions of the Gulf. Furthermore, implementing legal frameworks and policies aimed at protecting cultural artifacts and sites from exploitation and destruction is imperative. Strict regulations and enforcement mechanisms must be implemented to prevent the illicit trade and smuggling of valuable cultural assets. Moreover, empowering local communities to participate in the preservation and promotion of their heritage actively is essential. Community engagement programs involving residents in cultural activities, festivals, and events strengthen social cohesion and foster a sense of ownership and pride in traditional practices. Another critical aspect involves using digital technologies and multimedia platforms to document and disseminate cultural knowledge. Creating digital archives, virtual tours, and interactive resources can make cultural information accessible to a global audience while preserving it for posterity. Finally, promoting sustainable tourism practices that prioritize cultural sensitivity and respect for local customs can contribute to preserving heritage sites and traditional practices. By encouraging responsible tourism, the intrinsic value of cultural heritage is upheld while generating economic opportunities for local communities. In concert, these strategies form a comprehensive approach to sustaining the rich tapestry of the Gulf's cultural heritage in rapid change and development.

Conclusion: The Balance Between Progress and Preservation

Striking a delicate balance between progress and preservation is the essence of ensuring the sustainability of cultural heritage in the Gulf region. As demonstrated throughout this book, the rapid pace of modernization and technological advancement has posed significant challenges to traditional practices and customs. However, it has also opened new avenues for revitalizing and documenting these invaluable aspects of our heritage. In navigating this dynamic landscape, it becomes imperative to adopt a conscientious approach that respects the wisdom of the past while embracing the opportunities offered by contemporary developments.

The very concept of sustainability rests on the premise of finding equilibrium. Preserving cultural heritage does not imply stagnation or resistance to change; rather, it encompasses an active process of adaptation and evolution. It entails recognizing the intrinsic value of traditions and ensuring their continued relevance amidst evolving societal paradigms. This calls for a concerted effort to strike a harmonious chord between heritage conservation and progressive innovation. Such an approach is rooted in recognizing the enriching contributions of traditional practices to the identity, cohesion, and vitality of our societies.

Embracing the digital era, we find ourselves at a crossroads where technology can either serve as a catalyst for cultural commodification or as a powerful tool for safeguarding traditions. There lies an inherent responsibility in leveraging digital platforms and advanced technologies to disseminate, archive, and promote cultural heritage. By harnessing these tools effectively, we can bridge generational gaps, stimulate intercultural dialogue, and inspire a renewed appreciation for the depth and diversity of our shared legacy.

Crucially, the role of education emerges as a linchpin in this quest for equilibrium. Effective educational programs can instill a sense of pride and ownership in the younger generations, fostering an environment where tradition is perceived as an asset rather than an archaic relic. Furthermore, collaborative initiatives involving community members, scholars, and policymakers are essential in formulating comprehensive strategies for the sustainable preservation of cultural heritage.

In closing, achieving the delicate balance between progress and preservation demands a multifaceted approach that integrates tradition's adaptive spirit with contemporary society's dynamism. This equilibrium forms the cornerstone of a future where our cultural tapestry remains vibrant, resonant, and deeply cherished. Through such conscious, concerted efforts, we safeguard the timeless resonance of our heritage while propelling it toward a future illuminated by tradition and innovation.

Chapter 19

The Legacy Continues: From Ancient Times to Modern Prosperity

Throughout history, the Gulf region has been marked by significant and transformative economic shifts that have shaped its trajectory from ancient times to modern prosperity. Understanding the complex interplay of historical events, cultural evolution, and economic transformations is crucial to gaining insight into the region's current status and future direction. The continuing legacy of the Gulf's economic development can be seamlessly traced back to its ancient roots, where trade, commerce, and maritime activities laid the foundation for the region's profound influence on global trade routes. The rich historical tapestry woven by the Gulf's ancestors provides invaluable context for contemporary economic activities and is a guiding beacon for the future. By delving into the chronology of economic change, we can unravel the intricate web of commercial and cultural exchanges that have defined the Gulf's historical identity and continue to shape its present landscape. Recognizing this enduring link between past and present allows us to appreciate the resilience and adaptability demonstrated by the Gulf region in response to changing economic tides over the centuries. It underscores the deeply rooted connections that bind the region's economic heritage to its current state of prosperity and sets the stage for envisioning its future course. Further exploration of this dynamic continuum reveals the enduring relevance of historical ties, reaffirming their pivotal role in informing and influencing the contemporary economic fabric of the Gulf. Through this historical lens, one gains a broader perspective on the multifaceted interactions between culture, trade, and innovation, which have propelled the region forward. The forthcoming chapters will encapsulate this captivating journey through time, shedding light on the momentous events, actors, and forces that have driven the Gulf's economic transformation, culminating in its impressive modern prosperity.

Chronology of Change: The Gulf's Economic Transformation

The economic transformation of the Gulf region has been a remarkable journey marked by significant milestones and transitions over the centuries. Tracing back to ancient times, the Gulf states primarily relied on pearl diving, fishing, and trade routes for sustenance. As the global economy evolved, so did the Gulf's economic landscape. The historical shifts brought about by the discovery of oil reserves reshaped the socio-economic fabric of the region, catapulting it into a new era of prosperity.

Early economic activities in the Gulf focused on maritime trade, with bustling marketplaces and ports as critical hubs for commercial exchanges. The advent of the pearling industry further enhanced the region's economic standing, drawing attention from traders and adventurers seeking the coveted natural treasures. This era laid the groundwork for the Gulf's future economic prowess, influencing trade networks and cultural dynamics that endure today.

The discovery of oil reserves in the 20th century triggered a monumental shift in the Gulf's economic narrative. With the rise of oil production and exportation, the region experienced unprecedented wealth and development. This newfound economic vitality spurred infrastructural advancements, urbanization, and diversified investment opportunities, transforming the once-dormant landscapes into bustling metropolises and thriving economic centers.

As the world transitioned towards renewable energy and sustainable practices, the Gulf embarked on a path of diversification, expanding its economic portfolio beyond traditional hydrocarbon industries. Visionary leadership and strategic planning have steered the region towards embracing knowledge-based economies, fostering innovation, and nurturing entrepreneurship. Investments in technology, education, and sustainable development initiatives have positioned the Gulf as an emerging hub for global innovation and economic resilience.

Today, the Gulf stands as a testament to the power of adaptability and forward-thinking economic policies. The evolutionary chronicle of economic transformation within the Gulf underscores the region's ability to overcome challenges, capitalize on opportunities, and remain agile in a rapidly changing global landscape. The Gulf's commitment to sustainable growth and inclusive development continues to shape its economic destiny, reflecting a legacy of perseverance, ingenuity, and prosperity.

From Pearl Divers to Oil Barons: Diversification and Wealth

The dramatic shift from traditional industries, such as pearling and fishing, to the modern era of oil and gas extraction marks a significant economic transformation in the history of the Gulf region. The evolution from relying on natural resources found beneath the sea to harness the vast reserves of hydrocarbons beneath the desert sands has propelled the Gulf economies onto the global stage.

Centuries ago, the economy of the Gulf was sustained by the brave endeavors of pearl divers who risked their lives to harvest the treasures of the deep. This arduous and perilous occupation served as the backbone of the economy and held cultural significance, shaping the region's social fabric. However, with the discovery of substantial oil reserves, the economic landscape underwent a monumental shift, propelling the region into the forefront of energy production and global trade.

The emergence of oil and gas exploration and production provided a wealth of opportunities for the region, leading to unprecedented prosperity and development. The revenues generated from these valuable resources facilitated infrastructure projects, technological advancements, and widespread investments across diverse sectors, transforming the economic horizons of the Gulf nations. This transition from traditional maritime industries to becoming leaders in the global energy market exemplifies the adaptability and resilience of the Gulf societies as they embraced new avenues for prosperity.

Moreover, the strategic foresight of visionary leaders and policymakers spearheaded the diversification of economies beyond dependence on hydrocarbons. Recognizing the need to mitigate reliance on a single commodity, comprehensive economic strategies were formulated to promote non-oil sectors, such as tourism, finance, technology, and manufacturing. This deliberate effort to broaden the economic base and cultivate a knowledge-based society has ushered in an era of sustained growth and innovation, positioning the Gulf as a multifaceted hub of economic vibrancy and diversity.

The journey from the pearl diving expeditions to the development of robust oil and gas industries signifies a remarkable narrative of transformation and progress. It is a testament to the unwavering resolve and ingenuity of the Gulf communities, showcasing their ability to adapt to changing tides and evolve into dynamic, prosperous economies with a far-reaching global impact.

Innovations in Energy: The Role of Hydrocarbons

The Gulf's journey from a region renowned for pearl diving to one synonymous with oil wealth has been remarkable and transformative. The Gulf states were at the epicenter of a global economic shift as the world transitioned from traditional energy sources to hydrocarbons. The emergence of the oil industry spurred unprecedented advancements in energy production and consumption, redefining the region's role in shaping the modern world. The discovery and harnessing of vast hydrocarbon reserves laid the foundation for monumental changes, guiding the Gulf toward becoming a significant player in the global energy landscape. The strategic utilization of these resources has propelled the region's economic prosperity and generated far-reaching geopolitical implications. Moreover, the Gulf's innovative energy exploration, extraction, and distribution approaches have revolutionized how societies engage with and rely on hydrocarbons worldwide. The strategic deployment of advanced technologies and methodologies within the energy sector has accelerated the sustainable development and responsible utilization of hydrocarbon resources, contributing to a dynamic and resilient economy. Furthermore, formulating comprehensive energy policies and regulations has allowed the Gulf to effectively navigate the complexities of the global energy market, ensuring stability and adaptability in an ever-evolving industry. By continually reimagining its approach to energy, the Gulf has fostered an environment conducive to pioneering research and development, leading to profound breakthroughs in energy efficiency, carbon capture, and sustainable practices. The region has demonstrated a progressive outlook through ongoing investments in renewable energy initiatives, emphasizing the imperative of environmental stewardship and the pursuit of diversified, cleaner energy solutions. The commitment to leveraging hydrocarbons as a catalyst for innovation has fostered a culture of forward-thinking and resilience, solidifying the Gulf's position as an influential leader in the global energy arena.

Economic Visions and Policy Advances

The economic landscape of the Gulf states has undergone a profound transformation over the past century. From primarily relying on traditional industries such as pearling and fishing, the region experienced a remarkable shift with the discovery and subsequent utilization of hydrocarbons. This transition brought unprecedented wealth and necessitated strategic economic visions and policy advances to ensure sustainable development and prosperity for future generations.

One key aspect characterizing economic visions and policy advances in the Gulf has been the diversification of revenue sources. Many Gulf states have recognized the volatile nature of the oil market and have initiated ambitious economic diversification plans to reduce their dependency on hydro-carbons. These initiatives have focused on developing robust non-oil sectors such as tourism, finance, technology, and re-newable energy, aiming to create resilient economies less sus-ceptible to fluctuations in global energy markets.

Another cornerstone of economic visions and policy ad-vances has been the emphasis on strengthening innovation and entrepreneurship. Governments in the region have been actively promoting a culture of innovation and creativity, of-fering support for startups and small-to-medium enterprises (SMEs) through funding, infrastructure, and regulatory frame-works. This proactive approach aims to foster a dynamic entre-preneurial ecosystem, spurring economic growth, job creation, and the development of cutting-edge technologies.

Furthermore, the Gulf states have been at the forefront of implementing visionary policies centered on sustainable devel-opment and environmental conservation. With an awareness of the finite nature of hydrocarbon resources and a commitment to addressing global environmental challenges, governments have launched ambitious sustainability initiatives. These in-clude investment in renewable energy projects, stringent en-vironmental regulations, and conservation efforts to preserve the region's natural heritage for future generations.

In addition, economic visions and policy advances have pri-oritized social welfare and human capital development. Vari-ous programs and policies have been implemented to enhance education, healthcare, and housing, ensuring the well-being of citizens and residents. Furthermore, there has been a concerted effort to align educational curricula with the evolving demands of the job market, equipping the younger generation with the necessary skills and knowledge to contribute meaningfully to the diversified economy.

Moreover, the Gulf's economic visions and policy ad-vances have embraced technological integration and digital transformation as catalysts for progress. Adopting advanced technologies, digital infrastructure, and innovative city initiatives has enhanced public service efficiency and positioned the Gulf as a global hub for innovation and technological advancement.

As the Gulf continues to navigate the complexities of a rapidly evolving global economy, harmonizing economic visions and policy advances will play an instrumental role in shaping the region's socio-economic development trajectory. Through forward-thinking strategies, prudent governance, and a commitment to sustainable and inclusive growth, the Gulf states are poised to chart a resilient and prosperous course for the future, building upon the rich legacy of the ancient civilizations that once thrived in these lands.

Societal Shifts: Education and Employment Trends

The societal fabric of the Gulf region has been undergoing significant transformations in the spheres of education and employment. As the region continues to modernize and diversify its economy, a concerted effort has been to revamp and elevate education standards and address the workforce's evolving needs. One pivotal aspect underscoring these developments is the emphasis on quality education that aligns with global standards, fostering a generation equipped with 21st-century skills.

Education in the Gulf has seen a noteworthy evolution, transitioning from traditional models to modern pedagogical approaches. Recognizing the pivotal role of education in preparing the populace for the demands of a rapidly advancing world, governments and private entities have made substantial investments in educational infrastructure, curriculum development, and teacher training programs. Moreover, the focus has extended beyond primary and secondary education to encompass tertiary and vocational education, catering to the diverse interests and aptitudes of the youth.

Simultaneously, the employment landscape in the Gulf region has witnessed noteworthy shifts. With the economic diversification agenda gaining traction, there has been an increased impetus for fostering innovation, entrepreneurship, and knowledge-based industries. This has correspondingly led to a recalibration of the job market, with an augmented demand for individuals skilled in technology, engineering, finance, healthcare, and other specialized fields. The traditional reliance on expatriate labor has given way to initiatives to nurture local talent and create pathways for meaningful career advancements.

Furthermore, there has been a surge in programs and initiatives to integrate practical training and internships into academic curricula. These enable students to gain real-world experience and align their skills with industry requirements. This symbiotic relationship between academia and industry has enhanced graduates' employability and stimulated a culture of continuous learning and adaptability.

In this era of rapid globalization and technological disruption, the evolution of education and employment landscapes in the Gulf reflects a conscious endeavor to position the region as a hub of knowledge, innovation, and sustainable growth. The Gulf aspires to propel its society toward a prosperous and inclusive future by empowering its human capital through robust education and resilient employment opportunities.

Modern Infrastructure Development: A Leap into the Future

In the Gulf region, the modernization and development of infrastructure have played a pivotal role in shaping the trajectory of prosperity and progress. The strategic investments in advanced transportation networks, state-of-the-art utilities, and cutting-edge communication systems have transformed the physical landscape and propelled the region into a new era of connectivity and economic growth. The meticulous planning and execution of infrastructure projects have catered to the population's immediate needs and laid a solid foundation for sustainable development and global competitiveness. The futuristic urban skylines and world-class airports test the unwavering commitment to embracing innovation and leading the way into the future. Moreover, integrating smart technologies and sustainable practices within the infrastructure framework reflects a conscientious approach toward environmental preservation and efficient resource management. Adopting green building standards, renewable energy initiatives, and eco-friendly urban planning strategies exemplify the region's proactive stance in mitigating ecological impacts whilst fostering long-term resilience. Additionally, the burgeoning investment in digital infrastructure, including high-speed internet connectivity and e-governance platforms, has substantially augmented the region's digital readiness and knowledge-based economy, positioning it as a prominent player in the global digital landscape. Furthermore, the emphasis on developing robust logistical and industrial infrastructure has not only facilitated trade and commerce. Still, it has also attracted substantial foreign direct investment, fortifying the region's economic standing on an international scale. The seamless integration of multimodal transportation systems, world-class ports, and advanced warehousing facilities has exponentially enhanced the region's trade efficiency and supply chain competitiveness, bolstering its reputation as a pivotal hub in the global logistics network. With a forward-looking vision and unwavering commitment to excellence, the Gulf region continues to spearhead a paradigm shift in infrastructure development, heralding a new dawn of unparalleled progress and prosperity.

Cultural Renaissance: Arts and Heritage in the Modern Age

The modern age has witnessed a remarkable revival of cultural expression and artistic endeavors across the Gulf region. As the economic landscape evolved, so did the appreciation for and revitalization of traditional arts and heritage. The interplay of ancient traditions and contemporary innovation has engendered a burgeoning renaissance that celebrates the rich tapestry of Gulf culture. This resurgence in cultural consciousness has enriched the local populace and captivated international audiences, fostering a deeper understanding and appreciation for the Gulf's heritage. One of the defining features of this renaissance is the infusion of traditional arts with modern techniques, resulting in a harmonious blend of the old and the new. The craftsmanship passed down through generations is now being reinvigorated with cutting-edge tools and methodologies, leading to a vibrant spectrum of artistic manifestations. From calligraphy and weaving to pottery and metalwork, artisans preserve traditional crafts and reinterpret them in ways that resonate with contemporary sensibilities. Moreover, the modern age has renewed emphasis on promoting artistic education and patronage, enabling aspiring talents to hone their skills and contribute to the cultural renaissance. Institutions and organizations dedicated to preserving and promoting art and heritage have increased, providing platforms for artists to showcase their works and engage with diverse audiences. Furthermore, the integration of technological advancements has propelled cultural initiatives to new heights, facilitating the digitization of historical artifacts and enabling widespread access to the Gulf's rich heritage. Virtual exhibitions, interactive installations, and digital archives have broadened the reach of Gulf culture, inviting individuals from across the globe to partake in its timeless splendor. As such, the cultural renaissance in the modern age has not only invigorated traditional art forms but has also catalyzed a collective reawakening of pride and reverence for the Gulf's heritage. It stands as a testament to the resilience and adaptability of Gulf culture, ensuring that its legacy endures and thrives in the ever-evolving tapestry of human civilization.

International Relations: The Gulf on the Global Stage

The Gulf region has been a crucial player in international relations, strategically positioned at the crossroads of global trade routes and as a bridge between different cultures. Historically, the Gulf's significance as a trading hub has fostered deep connections with diverse nations across continents. Its strategic location has made it a pivotal player in global trade dynamics. Furthermore, the Gulf's extensive oil and gas reserves have positioned it as a key influencer in global energy markets. This interdependence has catalyzed diplomatic ties, with the region engaging in constructive dialogues and negotiations with major global powers, leveraging its resources for mutual benefit. Moreover, the Gulf's commitment to cultural preservation and promotion has sparked partnerships and collaborations with international entities to share its rich heritage and traditions with the world. As a result, the Gulf has emerged as a beacon of cultural diplomacy, fostering understanding and appreciation across borders. In recent years, the Gulf has actively contributed to global initiatives addressing environmental sustainability, technological innovation, and humanitarian causes, demonstrating proactive engagement on a global scale. Simultaneously, the Gulf has promoted regional stability and security, collaborating with international organizations to address common challenges and strengthen diplomatic alliances. Leveraging its position as a leading financial center, the Gulf has become an attractive destination for foreign investment, bolstering economic interdependence and fostering cross-border collaborations. The Gulf's commitment to education and knowledge exchange has facilitated academic and research partnerships with esteemed institutions worldwide, nurturing intellectual dialogue and fostering innovation. Looking ahead, the Gulf aims to play an increasingly influential role in global governance, contributing to developing sustainable policies and advocating for inclusive international cooperation. The Gulf continues to shape international relations in an ever-evolving global landscape, embodying a steadfast commitment to global progress and prosperity.

Conclusion: Reflecting on Prosperity and Challenges Ahead

As we reflect on the historical trajectory and the modern-day prosperity of the Gulf, it becomes evident that the region stands at a pivotal juncture. The legacy of ancient trade and cultural exchange has created a dynamic and diversified economy, propelling the Gulf onto the global stage. However, nuanced challenges warrant attention and strategic mitigation alongside this remarkable progress. The conclusion allows one to contemplate these contemporaneous realities and chart a course for a sustainable, inclusive, and prosperous future. Among the paramount considerations is fostering intercultural understanding and collaborative engagement in international relations. The Gulf's position on the global stage demands astute diplomacy and conscientious navigation of geopolitical complexities to secure enduring stability and fruitful partnerships. Furthermore, diversifying economic foundations from traditional industries to innovative sectors such as technology, renewable energy, and knowledge-based economies underscores the need for adaptive policies and foresighted governance. This shift allows the Gulf to pioneer sustainable development models and embrace technological advances while upholding environmental stewardship. Equally crucial is the push for comprehensive education reforms and targeted employment strategies to meet the evolving demands of a rapidly advancing society. As the Gulf evolves, investments in human capital and talent cultivation must be prioritized to ensure that the populace can actively participate in and benefit from the emerging socio-economic landscape. Acknowledging and addressing the intersectional dimensions of prosperity is integral, bridging the gaps between tradition and modernity, wealth and equitable opportunity, and cultural heritage and contemporary expression. In doing so, the Gulf can celebrate its rich legacy while embracing the promise of an inclusive and progressive future. Ultimately, the conclusion invites stakeholders across sectors to collectively steer the region toward a horizon of sustained prosperity, foremost by integrating the lessons of the past with the imperatives of the present and by constructively shaping a vision that harmonizes ambition with responsibility. The legacy of the Gulf must endure as an ever-evolving narrative of resilience, innovation, and forward-looking cooperation, underpinning a legacy that transcends time and echoes the enduring spirit of the region.

Chapter 20

Preserving the Past: Conservation Efforts in the Gulf

Heritage conservation stands as a testament to the rich tapestry of history woven through the landscapes and cultural heritage of the Gulf region. This vital practice holds immense significance in preserving the identity, traditions, and stories that have shaped the Gulf's historical narrative. The Gulf's historical sites serve as living testaments to the past, reflecting civilizations' triumphs, struggles, and milestones contributing to the region's unique identity. Through meticulous conservation efforts, these sites become conduits for understanding, connecting present and future generations with the legacy of their ancestors. Importantly, heritage conservation is not merely about preserving physical structures; it is about safeguarding intangible heritage, including traditions, languages, rituals, and craftsmanship, which are intrinsic to the regional culture. The Gulf's historical sites, ranging from ancient fortresses to vibrant marketplaces, embody the essence of the region's narrative, linking communities across time and space.

Highlighting the convergence of diverse influences, these sites encapsulate the fusion of indigenous customs and external interactions, underscoring the region's dynamic cultural exchange. Furthermore, heritage conservation is an essential tool for promoting sustainable tourism, contributing to the socio-economic prosperity of local communities. By safeguarding historical sites, the Gulf can showcase its profound legacy, attracting visitors keen on immersing themselves in the authentic tales of antiquity. Establishing a deeper connection to the past fosters a sense of pride and belonging among residents, instilling a profound appreciation for the shared heritage. As the Gulf continues to evolve within the global landscape, heritage conservation provides a platform for fostering cross-cultural dialogue and understanding. It enables the preservation of narratives that transcend boundaries, encouraging mutual respect and empathy. Through comprehensive conservation measures, the Gulf safeguards its historical sites for the benefit of present and future generations, ensuring that the echoes of the past reverberate dynamically throughout the ages.

Historical Sites of the Gulf

The Gulf region is home to a rich tapestry of historical sites that witness the civilizations and cultures that have thrived in this unique geographical setting. From ancient trading hubs to archaeological marvels, the Gulf's historical sites offer a glimpse into the social, economic, and cultural dynamics that shaped this region over millennia.

One of the most iconic historical sites in the Gulf is the ancient city of Gerrha, located in present-day Saudi Arabia. This once-thriving metropolis was at the heart of the Persian Gulf trade route and was renowned for its prosperity and influence as a trading center. The remains of Gerrha provide valuable insights into the ancient Gulf civilizations' commercial activities, architectural styles, and societal structure.

Another prominent historical site is the ancient port city of Dilmun, now part of Bahrain. Dilmun served as a vital hub for maritime trade and is celebrated for its distinctive burial mounds, which stand as testaments to the sophistication of the Dilmun civilization. Excavations at these mounds have yielded a treasure trove of artifacts, shedding light on the religious beliefs, economic activities, and daily life of the ancient Dilmunites.

Moving towards the UAE, the archaeological site of Al Baleed in Oman offers a fascinating insight into the role of this coastal city as a vibrant center of commerce and cultural exchange. Its well-preserved ruins and artifacts provide valuable evidence of the extensive trade networks and the cross-cultural interactions that characterized the mercantile activities of the Gulf.

The historical significance of these sites extends beyond their archaeological value; they are repositories of cultural heritage and embody the legacy of the civilizations that once flourished in the Gulf. As custodians of these historical treasures, the Gulf nations must prioritize their preservation and ensure that future generations can connect with their illustrious past. Through strategic conservation efforts and community engagement, these historical sites can continue to serve as living museums that narrate the tale of the Gulf's enduring legacy.

Legislation and Policies for Cultural Preservation

Preserving the rich cultural heritage of the Gulf region necessitates a comprehensive framework of legislation and policies specifically designed to safeguard historical sites, artifacts, and traditions. Implementing effective regulations is crucial in ensuring the conservation of the Gulf's heritage for future generations.

At the core of any successful preservation effort lies a robust legal infrastructure. Legislative measures are pivotal in protecting historical sites and artifacts and nurturing and promoting traditional practices. By enacting stringent laws and regulations, authorities can establish the necessary authority to monitor and regulate activities that may impact the integrity of historical and cultural assets. Notably, these legal measures should integrate provisions for penalties against violations and incentives to encourage active participation in preservation efforts.

Furthermore, policies tailored to cultural preservation should be all-encompassing, addressing diverse facets such as archaeological excavations, architectural conservation, folklore documentation, and the sustainable management of natural resources integral to cultural practices. Striking a balance between conservation and community development is imperative, as it ensures that heritage preservation aligns with the needs and aspirations of local inhabitants, fostering a sense of ownership and responsibility among the stakeholders.

Additionally, collaborative efforts at regional and international levels are vital in shaping cohesive policies that transcend national boundaries. Establishing partnerships with global organizations, sharing best practices, and adopting international charters contribute to converging strategies for heritage preservation. Such collaborations facilitate the exchange of expertise, technical knowledge, and financial support, enhancing the effectiveness of preservation initiatives across the Gulf region.

In essence, legislation and policies for cultural preservation act as guardians of the Gulf's diverse heritage, anchoring it firmly in the present while charting a course for perpetuity.

Role of International Bodies in Gulf Heritage Preservation

Preservation and conservation of the unique cultural heritage of the Gulf region is not just a national or local concern but a global responsibility. International bodies are pivotal in facilitating cooperation, providing expertise, and mobilizing resources to preserve Gulf heritage. This section explores the crucial role played by international organizations in safeguarding the rich historical and cultural legacy of the Gulf. For instance, the UNESCO World Heritage Centre has been instrumental in identifying and protecting sites of outstanding universal value in the Gulf region. Its conventions, such as the World Heritage Convention, contribute to developing effective strategies for conserving and managing cultural and natural heritage. Through collaboration with national authorities, UNESCO ensures that Gulf heritage sites meet the criteria for inscription on the World Heritage List, promoting their protection and sustainable management. Furthermore, international organizations like the International Council on Monuments and Sites (ICOMOS) and the International Centre for the Study of the Preservation and Restoration of Cultural Property (ICCROM) contribute significantly to capacity-building and technical assistance in preserving Gulf heritage. These organizations provide guidance on best practices for conservation, restoration, and the sustainable use of cultural resources while fostering international cooperation and knowledge exchange among experts in the field. Additionally, the involvement of international funding agencies and donors has been instrumental in supporting conservation projects in the Gulf. Collaborative initiatives between international organizations, national governments, and local stakeholders have successfully preserved iconic sites, ancient monuments, and traditional landscapes across the Gulf. The magnitude of the challenges facing Gulf heritage preservation underscores the importance of partnerships with international bodies, as they bring together expertise, experience, and financial support to ensure the sustainable safeguarding of the region's cultural legacy.

Community Involvement in Conservation Efforts

Community involvement plays a crucial role in the preservation of Gulf heritage. Engaging local communities in conservation efforts fosters a sense of ownership and responsibility, ensuring that the significance of the region's cultural assets is understood and valued by those directly impacted. Community engagement empowers individuals to actively safeguard their heritage, leading to a deeper appreciation and commitment to its preservation. One of the key aspects of community involvement is raising awareness about the importance of cultural heritage and the need for its protection. This can be achieved through educational initiatives, public outreach programs, and collaborative projects between local authorities and community groups. By providing opportunities for dialogue and participation, communities are better equipped to understand the challenges and opportunities associated with heritage preservation. Additionally, involving local residents in decision-making processes regarding conservation projects promotes transparency and inclusivity, reinforcing a collective dedication to protecting the Gulf's rich historical legacy. Community-led initiatives also contribute to the sustainable development of heritage sites, emphasizing conservation's social and economic benefits. The active involvement of local residents can result in innovative solutions that align with the needs and aspirations of the community, thus ensuring that preservation efforts are tailored to reflect the unique cultural identity of the Gulf. Furthermore, by integrating traditional knowledge and expertise from within the community, conservation strategies become more effective and culturally sensitive. This knowledge exchange between professionals and local practitioners fosters mutual respect and understanding, creating a collaborative framework for preserving cultural heritage. Leveraging community resources, such as traditional craftsmanship and indigenous practices, contributes to the authenticity of restoration and conservation work and strengthens the connection between traditions and contemporary society. Ultimately, community involvement in Gulf heritage preservation is a unifying force, fostering a collective sense of pride and responsibility toward safeguarding the region's cultural treasures for future generations.

Restoration Techniques and Challenges

Restoring ancient heritage sites in the Gulf region presents many challenges, intertwining technical, cultural, and environmental considerations. The intricacies of restoration demand a delicate balance between preserving the site's authenticity and implementing modern techniques to ensure longevity. One of the primary challenges lies in selecting appropriate restoration techniques that harmonize with the historical context while complying with ethical standards. Preservation specialists face the dilemma of maintaining the original architectural nuances and material integrity while addressing structural stability and weathering factors.

Moreover, the conservation process requires a comprehensive understanding of traditional building methods and artistic elements in the original construction. This requires extensive research and documentation to replicate the historical aesthetic and structure accurately. For instance, intricate carvings on historic structures demand skilled artisans who can meticulously recreate the designs using time-honored methods.

Another critical aspect is the impact of natural elements on preserving cultural relics. Climate variations, erosion, and seismic activities threaten the structural stability of heritage sites. Conservation efforts must integrate measures to fortify the structures against these challenges without compromising their original form. Implementing sustainable materials and reinforcing foundations become indispensable tasks in achieving long-term preservation goals.

Furthermore, restoration projects' financial and logistical complexities require judicious planning and resource allocation. Securing adequate funding, sourcing authentic materials, and orchestrating interdisciplinary collaboration between architects, historians, and conservation experts are formidable tasks. Additionally, navigating through bureaucratic procedures and obtaining necessary permits further contribute to the intricate challenges inherent in heritage preservation.

Given these challenges, the restoration community actively engages in knowledge exchange and skill development initiatives to address contemporary restoration issues. Collaborative platforms are vital for sharing best practices, fostering innovation in conservation technologies, and nurturing the next generation of preservation professionals. By embracing a holistic approach that acknowledges the diverse challenges of restoration, the conservation landscape can evolve to overcome barriers and safeguard the invaluable cultural legacy of the Gulf region.

Digital Archiving and Technological Contributions

Historic preservation in the Gulf region has embraced digital archiving and technological contributions to safeguard cultural heritage for future generations. The utilization of advanced digital archiving techniques, such as 3D scanning, high-resolution imaging, and virtual reality simulations, has revolutionized the preservation of historical sites, artifacts, and traditions. These technological tools enable detailed documentation of monuments, archaeological findings, and intangible cultural practices, providing an immersive platform for conservation and education. Digital archiving allows for the creation of accurate, interactive replicas that can be accessed and experienced remotely, transcending geographical boundaries and enhancing public engagement with the rich heritage of the Gulf. Moreover, integrating technology has facilitated the development of comprehensive databases and archives, ensuring the systematic preservation and accessibility of invaluable cultural resources. Digitizing historical records, manuscripts, and oral histories contributes to conserving the Gulf's diverse heritage and supports ongoing research and exploration. Furthermore, technological contributions extend to the monitoring and conserving of natural environments, including ecosystems and geological formations significant to the region's cultural identity. Remote sensing technologies and geographic information systems (GIS) aid in assessing and managing environmental resources, mitigating potential threats, and promoting sustainable practices. The incorporation of advanced technologies not only enhances the efficacy of preservation efforts but fosters interdisciplinary collaborations between heritage professionals, technologists, and local communities. As a result, digital archiving and technological contributions empower a dynamic approach to heritage conservation, embracing innovation while upholding the authenticity and significance of the Gulf's cultural legacy.

Case Studies: Successful Restoration Projects

In exploring the realm of heritage conservation, it is imperative to delve into specific instances where successful restoration projects have not only upheld the historical integrity of a site but also contributed to the preservation of cultural identity and enrichment of communities. These case studies exemplify the intricate processes and considerations involved in successfully restoring historic sites within the Gulf region, shedding light on the collaborative efforts and adaptive approaches essential for achieving sustainable conservation outcomes. One such exemplary case is the restoration of Al Jahili Fort in the United Arab Emirates. The project integrated traditional techniques with modern methodologies to revitalize the fort, a significant cultural landmark, and transform it into an engaging space for community gatherings and cultural events. The meticulous attention to detail and adherence to historical authenticity have ensured the preservation of architectural heritage and invigorated the local tourism sector, thus contributing to economic growth. Similarly, the restoration of Bahrain Fort is a testament to the harmonious amalgamation of archaeological research, architectural expertise, and public engagement. The project succeeded in reinstating the fort's structural stability while incorporating innovative interpretive elements to give visitors a rich understanding of its historical significance. Furthermore, the project's emphasis on community involvement through educational programs and outreach initiatives has fostered a sense of ownership among the local residents, instilling pride in their heritage and fostering socio-economic development. Additionally, the conservation of the Musandam Watchtowers in Oman presents an inspiring example of nurturing cultural legacy within a contemporary context. The careful preservation of these architectural marvels and the implementation of educational workshops and cultural exchanges have rejuvenated the surrounding village, empowering the inhabitants socially and economically. These triumphant cases underscore the pivotal role of collaboration between governmental entities, local communities, experts, and international partners in realizing the multifaceted benefits of heritage preservation. As we delve further into the discussion of successful restoration projects, we unravel the broader impact of conservation initiatives on local economies, social cohesion, and sustaining the living heritage of the Gulf.

The Socio-Economic Impact of Preservation

Preserving the cultural heritage of the Gulf region has substantial socio-economic implications that extend far beyond the realms of history and conservation. Conservation efforts to protect ancient sites, artifacts, and traditions contribute significantly to the region's socio-economic development.

First and foremost, cultural preservation enhances the tourism potential of the Gulf countries. As historical sites are conserved and made accessible to visitors, they become key attractions for tourists seeking authentic cultural experiences. This influx of tourism boosts the local economy and creates employment opportunities for individuals involved in the hospitality, transportation, and souvenir industries.

Furthermore, preserving heritage sites helps foster a sense of national and regional identity. These sites often symbolize pride and unity, instilling a sense of belonging and shared history among the local communities. This collective identity can increase social cohesion and stability, positively impacting society's well-being.

In addition, heritage preservation can directly impact the surrounding areas' real estate and property values. Well-maintained historic sites and culturally significant landmarks can attract property investors and developers, leading to infrastructural advancements and increased regional investments. As a result, the overall livability and attractiveness of the area improve, ultimately benefiting the residents and businesses.

Moreover, the conservation and maintenance of heritage sites provide opportunities for skill development and capacity building within the local workforce. By engaging in restoration and preservation projects, craftsmen, artisans, and skilled laborers gain valuable experience and expertise, which can be applied to other sectors, thus contributing to the overall human resource development in the region.

Finally, the socio-economic impact of preservation extends to international collaborations and partnerships. Gulf countries with well-preserved heritage sites are better positioned to engage in cultural exchange programs and collaborations with global organizations, fostering diplomatic and economic ties with other nations worldwide.

In conclusion, the socio-economic impact of heritage conservation in the Gulf region goes beyond preserving the past; it actively contributes to the area's sustainable development, cultural enrichment, and economic prosperity. By recognizing and leveraging these synergies, the Gulf countries can harness the full potential of their rich historical legacy for the benefit of present and future generations.

Future Directions in Heritage Conservation

As we navigate the intricate landscape of heritage conservation, it is imperative to envision the future directions that will shape this noble endeavor. The evolving field of heritage conservation calls for a forward-thinking approach that embraces innovation while upholding the sanctity of cultural legacies. One crucial aspect of future conservation efforts lies in integrating advanced technology. From state-of-the-art digital documentation techniques to cutting-edge preservation methods, the marriage of tradition and technology is pivotal in ensuring the continued safeguarding of our rich heritage. Embracing sustainable practices is also paramount in shaping the future of heritage conservation. By promoting environmentally conscious restoration and maintenance strategies, we can mitigate the ecological impact of our preservation endeavors while preserving our natural resources. Furthermore, fostering global collaborations and facilitating knowledge exchange among diverse cultural preservation communities will propel the field toward mutual learning and growth. Empowering local communities and indigenous groups in the conservation discourse is another indispensable facet of future directions in heritage conservation. Involving these stakeholders not only plays an essential role in preserving traditional knowledge and craftsmanship but also ensures that conservation efforts are culturally sensitive and inclusive. It is imperative to acknowledge that dynamic shifts in societal values and perspectives mark the trajectory of heritage conservation. Hence, engaging in ongoing dialogue and advocacy to raise awareness about the significance of heritage preservation is fundamental to steering the collective consciousness toward embracing and cherishing our shared cultural heritage. Moreover, nurturing the next generation of conservationists through educational programs and mentorship initiatives will foster continuity of passion and expertise in safeguarding our cultural legacy. Beyond the confines of academic circles, public engagement, and outreach programs play a pivotal role in cultivating a sense of ownership and pride in heritage conservation. We lay the groundwork for a more harmonious and conscientious society by fostering community involvement and shared responsibility for preserving cultural treasures. Ultimately, the future of heritage conservation hinges on our collective commitment to balance tradition with innovation, sustainability with progress, and inclusivity with preservation. By steering our concerted efforts toward these future directions, we can safeguard our cultural heritage as an enduring testament to the richness of human history and creativity.

Chapter 21

Legacy of the Future: Embracing Innovation in the Gulf

The Gulf region has undergone a remarkable evolution characterized by accelerated technological advancements. This phenomenon, driven by various factors, has reshaped the economic and social landscape and projected the region onto the global stage as a hub for innovation and progress. At the heart of this surge in innovation lies a combination of strategic vision, substantial investment, and a commitment to embracing cutting-edge technologies. The quest for diversification and reducing dependency on traditional industries has spurred a forward-looking approach that emphasizes the pivotal role played by technological innovation. Moreover, the region's leadership has recognized the intrinsic link between technological progress and sustainable development, channeling resources into research, development, and adopting state-of-the-art solutions across diverse sectors. The convergence of visionary leadership, a burgeoning young population eager to embrace change, and the formation of dynamic ecosystems for entrepreneurship have catalyzed a climate conducive to fostering innovation. This proactive stance stems from an aspiration to proactively address imminent challenges, leverage opportunities arising from globalization, and carve out a solid competitive position in the rapidly evolving global economy. The interplay of these dynamics has also heightened the region's appeal as a preferred destination for global talent, investments, and partnerships, thus fueling a cycle of innovation. Beyond economic aspirations, the commitment to innovation is rooted in a deep-seated cultural ethos that prizes knowledge acquisition, technological proficiency, and forward-thinking approaches. Promoting innovation in the Gulf transcends purely economic imperatives and aligns with a broader vision of societal progress and global influence. Consequently, the ongoing technological transformation represents the region's determination to chart a course toward sustainable prosperity and empowerment, with innovation as the cornerstone of this trajectory.

Historical Perspectives on Technological Advancements

The historical perspective on technological advancements in the Gulf region provides a fascinating journey through time, showcasing the innovative spirit that has long characterized this land. Dating back to ancient civilizations, the inhabitants of the Gulf have demonstrated an inherent curiosity and aptitude for technological progress. The region's strategic location as a trade and cultural exchange hub also contributed to the influx of diverse knowledge and inventions from neighboring and distant lands.

In the early periods, technological advancements were closely linked to fulfilling basic human needs and improving the efficiency of everyday tasks. From simple tools crafted for hunting and agriculture to developing water management systems and architectural marvels, the people of the Gulf epitomized resourcefulness and problem-solving skills.

One remarkable feat of historical and technological innovation in the Gulf was mastering maritime navigation. Early sailors honed their skills in shipbuilding, celestial navigation, and oceanography, enabling them to traverse vast distances across the seas in search of wealth and knowledge. The advent of sailing vessels revolutionized trade networks and fostered cultural exchanges that continue to influence the region's identity today.

Furthermore, the Golden Age of Islamic civilization significantly impacted the Gulf's development and diffusion of technology. Scholars and polymaths made profound contributions to mathematics, astronomy, medicine, and engineering. Their pioneering works laid the groundwork for groundbreaking innovations that enhanced the quality of life and propelled intellectual growth throughout the region.

As the age of colonization unfolded, the Gulf witnessed the integration of modern technologies introduced by European powers. This period set the stage for rapid transformations in various sectors, including transportation, communication, and energy. The introduction of industrial machinery, infrastructure, and scientific methodologies further reshaped the technological landscape of the Gulf, marking a pivotal era of convergence between traditional practices and emerging innovations.

In conclusion, the historical perspectives on technological advancements in the Gulf offer a compelling narrative of resilience, adaptability, and ingenuity. By exploring the legacy of past innovations, we gain valuable insights into the enduring relationship between technology and society in the Gulf, fostering a profound appreciation for the continuous quest for progress and innovation that defines the region.

Current Technological Landscape

The current technological landscape in the Gulf region is a testament to its commitment to innovation and progress. Rapid advancements in various fields, such as information technology, renewable energy, healthcare, and infrastructure, have positioned the Gulf as a hub for cutting-edge technologies and pioneering initiatives.

One of the most prominent aspects of the current technological landscape is the widespread adoption of smart city concepts. Cities across the Gulf embrace digitalization and employ innovative solutions to improve urban living standards. From intelligent transportation systems and energy-efficient buildings to advanced waste management and sustainable urban planning, the Gulf's cities are at the forefront of incorporating technology into their urban fabric.

Renewable energy has also emerged as a key focus in the Gulf's technological landscape. With abundant sunlight and strong winds, the region has significantly invested in solar and wind power projects to reduce its reliance on traditional fossil fuels and mitigate environmental impact. Developing large-scale solar parks and wind farms underscores the Gulf's commitment to sustainable, eco-friendly energy solutions.

Furthermore, the healthcare sector in the Gulf is experiencing a revolution driven by technological advancements. State-of-the-art medical facilities, telemedicine services, and digital health records are transforming healthcare delivery, making it more accessible and efficient for the population. Additionally, integrating artificial intelligence and robotics in healthcare diagnostics and treatment is paving the way for groundbreaking medical innovations.

In infrastructure development, the Gulf countries execute ambitious projects showcasing technological prowess. From high-speed rail networks and futuristic airports to iconic skyscrapers and advanced seaports, the region is redefining modern infrastructure through a fusion of architectural elegance and technological ingenuity.

Moreover, the Gulf's emphasis on research and development fuels breakthroughs in various sectors. Collaborations between academic institutions, research centers, and industry players yield innovations contributing to economic diversification and global competitiveness. These efforts foster homegrown talent and attract international expertise to participate in the region's technological evolution.

Overall, the current technological landscape in the Gulf reflects a dynamic and progressive environment that embraces innovation as a catalyst for sustainable development and prosperity.

Major Innovative Projects and Their Impacts

The Gulf region has witnessed a surge in major innovative projects across various sectors, each significantly impacting the socio-economic and technological landscape. One of the most notable innovative projects is the development of sustainable architecture that integrates traditional design elements with modern green technologies. This approach not only preserves the region's cultural heritage but also addresses the contemporary need for sustainability and energy efficiency. The impact of such projects extends beyond environmental considerations to encompass economic benefits and a heightened global profile for the Gulf. Additionally, advancements in renewable energy projects, such as solar and wind power initiatives, have redefined the energy sector, positioning the Gulf as a leader in clean energy production. These initiatives reduce the region's carbon footprint driving economic diversification and creating employment opportunities. Furthermore, the emergence of technology-driven intelligent cities and infrastructure projects is transforming urban landscapes, enhancing overall efficiency, and elevating the quality of life for residents. By leveraging innovations in IoT (Internet of Things), big data, and AI (Artificial Intelligence), these projects establish the Gulf as a hub for cutting-edge urban development. The impacts of such initiatives are far-reaching, driving technological adoption and fostering an ecosystem conducive to innovation and entrepreneurship. Moreover, the healthcare sector has witnessed remarkable advancements through state-of-the-art medical facilities with the latest diagnostic and treatment technologies. These pioneering healthcare projects have improved the quality of medical services and positioned the Gulf as a destination for medical tourism, contributing to the overall growth of the healthcare industry. As the Gulf continues to embrace innovation across various domains, the collaborative nature of these endeavors fosters cross-sectoral synergies, propelling the region onto the global stage as a pioneer of progressive innovation. The impacts of these significant innovative projects reverberate through societal, economic, and technological dimensions, painting a picture of dynamic transformation and sustainable progress.

Government Policies Supporting Technological Growth

Government policies are pivotal in creating an environment conducive to technological growth and innovation. Across the Gulf region, governments have recognized the importance of fostering a culture of innovation and have implemented various strategies to support technological advancement. One key aspect of government policy is establishing research and development (R&D) incentives. By providing tax credits, grants, and subsidies for R&D activities, governments incentivize businesses and organizations to invest in innovative projects and technological advancements. These incentives encourage private-sector innovation and contribute to the region's overall economic development. Furthermore, governments have also introduced initiatives to promote collaboration between industry and academia. Governments facilitate knowledge exchange and skill development by partnering with educational institutions and research centers, creating a talent pool crucial for driving technological innovation. Additionally, supportive regulatory frameworks are essential for technological growth. Governments have proactively revised regulations to accommodate emerging technologies and promote their adoption. This includes streamlining approval processes for new technologies and ensuring that intellectual property rights are protected, thus creating a conducive environment for entrepreneurs and innovators to bring their ideas to fruition. In addition to these initiatives, governments have also focused on building infrastructure to support technological growth. Investments in digital infrastructure, such as broadband connectivity and data centers, create the foundation for technological development and enable the widespread adoption of innovative solutions. Moreover, the Gulf region has further leveraged global expertise and resources through strategic partnerships with international organizations and other governments to enhance its technological capabilities. Overall, government policies supporting technological growth in the Gulf reflect a commitment to embracing innovation as a fundamental driver of progress and prosperity. By providing the necessary incentives, fostering collaboration, adapting regulatory frameworks, and investing in infrastructure, governments are paving the way for a future defined by technological excellence and sustainable development.

Role of Education in Fostering Innovation

Education plays a pivotal role in fostering innovation within the Gulf region. As countries strive to transition from resource-based economies to knowledge-based economies, there is an increasing emphasis on developing a highly skilled and innovative workforce through robust educational systems. The nurturing of innovative thinking starts in early childhood education, where a foundation for creativity, problem-solving, and critical thinking is laid. This foundation is further strengthened in secondary and tertiary education institutions, where students are exposed to diverse disciplines, encouraged to challenge conventional wisdom, and equipped with the skills necessary to thrive in an ever-evolving technological landscape.

In recent years, there has been a concerted effort by Gulf nations to invest in their education systems, recognizing that a well-educated populace is essential for driving innovation and sustainable development. This investment encompasses traditional academic subjects and strongly emphasizes science, technology, engineering, and mathematics (STEM) fields. By providing a vital STEM education, students are empowered to explore and pioneer advancements in various scientific and technological domains, thereby contributing to the overall progress of society.

Furthermore, higher education institutions in the Gulf have established research and innovation centers to foster a culture of creativity and ingenuity. These centers serve as platforms for collaboration between academia, industry, and government, fostering an environment that encourages the translation of research into practical solutions and commercial applications. Additionally, partnerships with leading international institutions have facilitated knowledge exchange and exposure to best practices, further enriching the educational experience and broadening horizons.

In line with the growing significance of digital technology and entrepreneurship, educational curricula are evolving to include courses focused on coding, digital literacy, and entrepreneurial skills. These initiatives aim to prepare students for the digital age and instill an entrepreneurial mindset, laying the groundwork for future innovators and industry leaders. Moreover, promoting lifelong learning and continuing education programs ensures that professionals remain agile and adaptable in the face of rapid technological developments, thus sustaining a culture of innovation across generations.

In conclusion, education is a cornerstone in the quest for innovation within the Gulf region. Education institutions are crucial in nurturing the next generation of innovators who will lead the region toward sustainable prosperity and global competitiveness by fostering a conducive environment for intellectual growth, critical thinking, and cross-disciplinary collaboration.

Private Sector Contributions to Technological Development

In the Gulf region, the private sector is pivotal in driving technological development and innovation. With a strong emphasis on economic diversification and investment in knowledge-based industries, private enterprises have been instrumental in fueling advancements across various sectors. One of the key areas where the private sector has made substantial contributions is renewable energy. Through strategic partnerships and initiatives, private companies have spearheaded the adoption of sustainable energy solutions, such as solar power and wind energy, contributing to the region's commitment to environmental sustainability and reduced dependence on traditional fossil fuels. Furthermore, private entities have actively invested in research and development, leading to breakthroughs in healthcare technologies, biotechnology, and pharmaceutical innovations. This has improved the quality of healthcare services and positioned the Gulf as a hub for medical advancements and treatment modalities. Moreover, partnerships between private firms and educational institutions have established advanced research centers and innovation hubs, fostering collaborations that drive technological progress. The private sector's engagement in information technology and digital transformation has been transformative, with investments in cutting-edge infrastructures, e-commerce platforms, and cybersecurity solutions, positioning the region as an emerging technology hub. These contributions have paved the way for enhanced connectivity, efficiency, and security in the digital realm. Additionally, private sector involvement in infrastructure development, urban planning, and smart city initiatives has propelled the integration of innovative technologies in shaping sustainable urban landscapes. Private entities have been at the forefront of propelling smart city endeavors from smart grid systems to intelligent transportation networks. However, it is essential to acknowledge the challenges that come with private sector contributions, including ensuring responsible and ethical use of technology, addressing potential disparities in accessibility, and mitigating cybersecurity risks. Nonetheless, with a collaborative approach involving governmental support, academia, and civil society, the private sector's role in technological development continues to be a driving force in shaping the future of the Gulf region.

Challenges Facing Innovation in the Region

The Gulf region, despite its progress in embracing innovation, is not without its challenges. One of the primary obstacles to technological advancement is the limited diversification of the economy. Relying predominantly on oil and gas revenues, the region faces the challenge of transitioning to a knowledge-based economy. This necessitates a shift in mindset, investment, and infrastructure to support diverse industries and innovations.

Additionally, while the Gulf region has made significant strides in technological adaptation, cybersecurity and data privacy concerns exist. As digital transformation accelerates, protecting sensitive information from cyber threats becomes increasingly critical. Governments and businesses must work together to implement robust cybersecurity measures and data governance frameworks to safeguard against potential vulnerabilities.

Furthermore, fostering an environment conducive to entrepreneurship and innovation remains crucial. Bureaucratic processes, outdated regulations, and limited access to funding can impede the growth of startups and innovative ventures. Developing streamlined regulatory frameworks, promoting venture capital investments, and cultivating a culture that celebrates risk-taking and creativity are essential in overcoming these hurdles.

Moreover, a skilled workforce is paramount for driving technological innovation. Investing in education and training programs that equip individuals with relevant skills for the digital age is imperative. Additionally, nurturing local talent and empowering women in technology-related fields can help address the existing skill gaps and enhance diversity in the innovation landscape.

Another challenge lies in balancing tradition with modernization. While acknowledging the importance of preserving cultural heritage, finding a harmonious integration of tradition and innovation is essential. Striking this balance requires inclusive dialogue, respect for cultural norms, and leveraging technology to preserve and promote traditional practices.

The complexity of geopolitical dynamics in the region also poses challenges to innovation. Volatility in political relationships and regional tensions can impact cross-border collaborations and investment prospects, hindering the seamless exchange of knowledge and technologies.

Overcoming these challenges demands strategic planning, collaborative efforts, and a forward-looking approach from all stakeholders—governments, private sector entities, educational institutions, and the wider community. The Gulf region can position itself as a hub for innovation by addressing these impediments and driving sustainable growth and prosperity.

Future Predictions and Emerging Technologies

In the rapidly evolving landscape of the Gulf, it is imperative to look ahead and contemplate the future of technological innovation. The region has witnessed remarkable progress in various spheres of technology, and this trajectory shows no sign of slowing down. As we gaze into the crystal ball of innovation, several key predictions emerge about the technological advancements that will shape the Gulf's future.

One notable area set to soar to new heights is renewable energy. With abundant sunlight and vast open spaces, the Gulf is primed to lead the world in solar energy production. The advent of cutting-edge solar panels and energy storage systems technologies promises to revolutionize the power sector, making the region a global trailblazer in sustainable energy solutions. Furthermore, integrating artificial intelligence (AI) and machine learning into energy grid management will optimize energy distribution and consumption, fostering greater efficiency and reducing environmental impact.

Another exciting prospect lies in the realm of smart cities. The Gulf boasts ambitious, smart city initiatives that envision interconnected urban centers leveraging data and technology to enhance the quality of life for residents. This includes advanced infrastructure for transportation, waste management, and public services, all interconnected through the Internet of Things (IoT). As these smart city projects unfold, they will elevate living standards and position the Gulf as a beacon of modern urban development on the global stage.

Moreover, the convergence of technology and healthcare presents a promising outlook for the future. Developments in telemedicine, personalized medical devices, and digital health platforms are poised to revolutionize healthcare delivery in the region. By harnessing the potential of telehealth services and remote monitoring, the Gulf can overcome geographical barriers and pave the way for widespread access to quality healthcare, thus improving the overall well-being of its inhabitants.

Furthermore, emerging technologies such as blockchain and quantum computing hold significant promise for advancing various sectors within the Gulf. Implementing blockchain technology in finance, logistics, and government services promises heightened security, transparency, and efficiency. Similarly, the potential of quantum computing to revolutionize data processing and cryptography opens doors to unparalleled computational capabilities, offering a competitive edge in scientific research and technological innovation.

In conclusion, the Gulf's landscape is poised for a technological metamorphosis, paving the way for groundbreaking developments that will redefine the fabric of society. By embracing these emerging technologies, the region will not merely adapt to change but will blaze a trail toward a more sustainable, connected, and innovative future.

Integrating Innovations with Cultural Values

In conclusion, integrating innovations with cultural values is imperative for the sustainable growth and development of the Gulf region. As the technological landscape continues to evolve rapidly, ensuring that these advancements are harmoniously integrated with the Gulf countries' rich cultural heritage and traditions becomes increasingly crucial. This integration preserves and celebrates the region's unique identity while embracing innovation's benefits.

At the core of this integration lies the need for a holistic approach that acknowledges and respects the cultural values intrinsic to the Gulf societies for centuries. It is essential to recognize that technology should not undermine or erode these values but rather enhance and complement them. By weaving new technologies into the fabric of traditional practices and beliefs, the Gulf nations can maintain their cultural authenticity while propelling themselves into unprecedented progress.

Furthermore, integrating innovations with cultural values requires a collaborative effort from various stakeholders, including policymakers, educational institutions, the private sector, and local communities. It demands thoughtful consideration of how innovative solutions can be tailored to align with cultural norms and societal expectations. Inclusive dialogues and partnerships can bridge the gap between modernization and tradition, fostering an environment where both can thrive harmoniously.

It is also important to emphasize that integrating innovations with cultural values is not just about preservation but also about transformation. The Gulf countries have a unique opportunity to demonstrate how ancient wisdom can coexist with cutting-edge technologies, creating a distinctive model for sustainable progress. By leveraging indigenous knowledge and adapting it to the digital age, the region can showcase how innovation and tradition are not mutually exclusive but complementary forces that can drive comprehensive development and prosperity.

In closing, integrating innovations with cultural values may present challenges and complexities, but the rewards are boundless. It is an opportunity to nurture a society rooted in its heritage yet forward-looking, one that cherishes its past while embracing the possibilities of the future. By striking this delicate balance, the Gulf region can emerge as a global exemplar of how innovation and tradition can interweave to create a legacy that resonates across time and space.

Chapter 22

Connecting Cultures: Embracing Diversity in the Gulf

The Gulf region is a testament to the rich tapestry of cultural diversity woven throughout centuries. As we delve into the historical influences on cultural diversity, it becomes evident that the Gulf has served as a crossroads for various civilizations, each leaving an indelible mark on the socio-cultural landscape. Extending back to ancient times, the region's strategic location at the intersection of major trade routes facilitated the exchange of goods, ideas, and cultural practices. This confluence of influences from the Mesopotamians, Persians, Greeks, Romans, and later Islamic empires has contributed to the multifaceted nature of the Gulf's contemporary society. Moreover, the recent demographic trends manifest a mosaic of ethnicities, languages, and religious beliefs, reflecting a dynamic interplay of historical legacies and modern complexities. Against this backdrop, exploring how these diverse threads have been intricately woven to form the intricate fabric of the Gulf's modern cultural landscape is imperative.

Historical Influences on Cultural Diversity

Today's rich tapestry of cultural diversity found in the Gulf region results from centuries of historical influences that have shaped the demographic, social, and cultural landscape. Throughout history, the Gulf has been a crossroads for trade, conquest, and migration, leading to a mosaic of traditions, languages, and belief systems. The ancient civilizations that thrived along the coasts of the Gulf were early catalysts for cultural exchange, with trade routes connecting regions as far as the Mediterranean, India, and East Africa. This vibrant interconnectedness laid the groundwork for the multicultural society in the region today.

The influence of various empires and dynasties, such as the Sassanids, Abbasids, and Ottomans, has also left an indelible mark on the cultural fabric of the Gulf. Each empire brought its customs, languages, and religious practices, contributing to the rich tapestry of cultural diversity that distinguishes the region. The arrival of Persian, Indian, African, and European traders and settlers over the ages further enriched the cultural amalgamation.

The spread of Islam across the Arabian Peninsula and beyond from the 7th century onwards played a pivotal role in unifying diverse tribes and communities under a shared faith while allowing for the preservation of regional customs and traditions. This blend of Islamic principles with existing cultures created a unique fusion of customs and practices, fostering a sense of unity amidst diversity.

Furthermore, the colonial era and the subsequent decolonization brought yet another wave of cultural interchange, as Gulf societies accommodated the influences of British, Portuguese, and Dutch administrations. The enduring imprint of these colonial legacies can be observed in the linguistic and architectural traces that still endure in the region today.

Throughout this historical trajectory, the Gulf has continuously assimilated various traditions, languages, and belief systems, resulting in the multiethnic and multicultural milieu characteristic of present-day society. Understanding the historical influences on cultural diversity provides invaluable insight into the complex tapestry of traditions, values, and customs that continue to define the Gulf as a vibrant hub of intercultural exchange.

Migration Waves: Shaping the Demographic Landscape

Numerous waves of migration have shaped the Gulf region, pivoting in the formation of its rich and diverse demographic landscape. From ancient times to the present day, the influx of various ethnic groups and communities has left an indelible imprint on the region's social fabric. Understanding the patterns and impacts of these migration waves is essential in grasping the complexity and dynamic nature of the Gulf's cultural mosaic.

The earliest migration movements can be traced back to the prehistoric era when nomadic tribes traversed the expansive deserts in search of fertile lands and water sources. These early populations laid the foundation for the indigenous communities that inhabit the region today. Subsequent waves of migration were propelled by trade, exploration, and conquest, leading to the integration of diverse ethnicities and cultural practices.

One of the most significant historical migrations was the expansion of Islamic civilization, which profoundly transformed the Gulf's social landscape. The migration of Arab tribes and the spread of Islam not only shaped the region's religious and linguistic identity but also contributed to the establishment of enduring societal norms and traditions.

The modern era has witnessed a surge in migrant populations driven by economic opportunities and labor demands. The development of the oil industry and the subsequent economic boom attracted diverse expatriate workers, leading to the coalescence of a genuinely multicultural society. Moreover, the Gulf's strategic geographical position has made it a focal point for global migration, resulting in the convergence of individuals from every corner of the world.

The demographic impact of migration waves extends beyond population statistics, influencing various facets of daily life. Cultural exchanges, culinary fusion, and artistic expressions bear testimony to the ongoing interplay between different migrant communities and indigenous populations. The blending of traditions and the emergence of hybrid identities reflect the interconnectedness of diverse cultures within the Gulf.

However, migration has also presented challenges, including socioeconomic disparities, cultural tensions, and integration issues. As the demographic landscape continues to evolve, policy-makers and community leaders are tasked with creating inclusive frameworks that honor the contributions of all segments of society while fostering a sense of unity and belonging.

In summary, the narrative of migration waves in the Gulf underscores the transformative power of human movement and interaction. The interwoven tapestry of cultures, histories, and aspirations is a testament to the resilience and adaptability of the region's inhabitants. Embracing diversity as a source of strength, the Gulf is a dynamic crossroads where migration waves continue to shape its evolving demographic landscape.

Language and Communication: Bridging Communities

Language is not merely a means of communication; it is the cornerstone of cultural expression and interconnectivity. The Gulf region's linguistic landscape is as diverse as its multicultural tapestry. Arabic serves as the lingua franca, uniting the region with its rich historical and literary significance. However, the dynamics of globalization and transnational interactions have given rise to a multilingual society where languages such as English, Urdu, Farsi, Hindi, and Malayalam coexist. This linguistic diversity reflects centuries of trade, migration, and cultural exchange, creating a vibrant melange of dialects and accents that enrich the social fabric.

Despite linguistic plurality's inherent beauty, it also challenges fostering effective communication and understanding among diverse communities. Language barriers can impede seamless integration and contribute to social fragmentation. Consequently, initiatives promoting language acquisition and multilingual proficiency are crucial in bridging the gap between ethnic and linguistic groups. Educational institutions and community organizations play a pivotal role in facilitating language learning programs that cater to the linguistic needs of different demographics, thereby fostering mutual comprehension and respect. Moreover, digital platforms and social media offer unprecedented opportunities for cross-cultural communication, transcending linguistic boundaries and empowering individuals to engage in meaningful dialogue regardless of their linguistic background.

The power of language extends beyond mere verbal communication; it encapsulates cultural values, etiquettes, and unique modes of expression that shape individual identity and communal belonging. Bilingualism and multilingualism promote cognitive flexibility and cross-cultural empathy, laying the groundwork for harmonious coexistence in a pluralistic society. Equipping individuals with the linguistic tools to navigate multicultural environments fosters intercultural competence, nurturing a shared sense of belonging while celebrating the richness of divergent linguistic heritages. Additionally, language acts as a bridge to heritage preservation, enabling future generations to connect with their ancestral roots and uphold traditional customs through oral traditions and vernacular expressions.

In essence, language and communication form the bedrock of societal cohesion, serving as conduits for intercultural understanding and cooperation. By embracing linguistic diversity and leveraging it as a unifying force, the Gulf region can embark on a trajectory of harmonious cohabitation, where linguistic plurality becomes a catalyst for inclusive societal development.

Religious Diversity and Its Impact on Society

The Gulf region is marked by a rich tapestry of religious traditions representing various faiths, including Islam, Christianity, Judaism, Hinduism, and Buddhism. This intricate mosaic of beliefs has significantly shaped the Gulf societies' social, cultural, and historical fabric. Religious diversity has been pivotal in influencing societal norms and customs, permeating various aspects of daily life, governance, and interpersonal relationships. The coexistence of multiple religious communities has fostered an environment where individuals from different backgrounds engage in dialogue, mutual respect, and peaceful cohabitation. This inclusive ethos has not only contributed to the development of a unique regional identity but has also served as a foundation for harmonious interactions and interfaith understanding.

Moreover, religious diversity has had a profound impact on the Gulf's arts, literature, and architectural heritage, leading to the creation of distinctive cultural expressions that reflect the synthesis of varied spiritual philosophies. The influence of different religious beliefs is evident in the design of sacred spaces, the celebration of religious festivals, and the proliferation of artistic forms that resonate with pluralistic values. This amalgamation of diverse religious influences has contributed to a dynamic and multifaceted cultural landscape characterized by a richness and plurality that exemplifies the spirit of unity amidst diversity.

One cannot overlook the role of religious pluralism in shaping the socio-political dynamics of the Gulf. The existence of multiple faith communities has necessitated the formulation of inclusive policies that safeguard individual freedoms, promote tolerance, and ensure equitable representation within public institutions. Moreover, religious diversity has spurred initiatives to foster interfaith dialogue, promote religious harmony, and address social justice issues, thereby underscoring the reciprocal relationship between spiritual beliefs and societal welfare.

In sum, religious diversity is a testament to the Gulf communities' open-mindedness, resilience, and adaptability. It embodies the values of acceptance, coexistence, and mutual enrichment, serving as a beacon of hope for the larger global community grappling with similar issues of religious plurality. Embracing religious diversity enriches the Gulf's cultural tapestry and reinforces its commitment to fostering a society where differences are celebrated and unity is forged through understanding and respect.

Cultural Integration in Urban Settings

Urban settings serve as dynamic hubs of cultural convergence, encapsulating a tapestry of traditions, beliefs, and customs from diverse backgrounds. In the context of the Gulf region, urban centers have emerged as epicenters of multicultural encounters, fostering an enriching environment conducive to cross-cultural integration. The cityscape pulsates with the thriving coexistence of various ethnic communities, each contributing to the vibrant mosaic of cultural expression that defines contemporary urban life. Amidst the bustling streets and towering skyscrapers, these diverse communities intermingle, creating a unique socio-cultural landscape reflective of the region's rich heritage and cosmopolitan ethos. The infusion of different cultural elements into urban settings has catalyzed a process of mutual enrichment, wherein traditions, languages, and culinary delights interweave to form a shared collective identity. As neighborhoods evolve into melting pots of diversity, residents engage in myriad everyday interactions that transcend traditional societal boundaries. These interactions nurture a spirit of inclusivity and mutual understanding, laying the foundation for cultural harmony and unity. However, the process of cultural integration in urban settings also presents its own set of challenges. Cultural misunderstanding or prejudice may arise from differences in social norms and practices. Urban communities must foster platforms for open dialogue and collaboration, enabling individuals to appreciate and learn from one another. Urban planners and policymakers are also critical in shaping inclusive urban environments by designing spaces that facilitate intercultural exchange and respect. Initiatives such as multicultural festivals, community workshops, and public art installations can serve as catalysts for promoting cross-cultural awareness and understanding.

Education also plays a pivotal role in nurturing cultural integration within urban settings. By incorporating multicultural curricula and programs that celebrate diversity, educational institutions can help instill values of empathy, respect, and appreciation for differences among future generations. Ultimately, the harmonious coexistence of diverse cultures within urban landscapes serves as a testament to the resounding success of multiculturalism, offering a blueprint for fostering inclusive societies. By embracing cultural diversity, urban settings emerge as epicenters of tolerance, cooperation, and collective progress, setting a precedent for global interconnectedness and shared humanity.

The Role of Education in Promoting Intercultural Understanding

Education is a powerful tool in shaping attitudes, beliefs, and behaviors, particularly in fostering intercultural understanding within diverse societies. Through a comprehensive and inclusive curriculum, educational institutions can play a fundamental role in nurturing respect for cultural diversity and promoting the principles of global citizenship. By integrating multicultural perspectives into various subjects, students gain valuable insights into different cultural traditions, practices, and customs, enhancing their capacity to empathize with and comprehend the experiences of individuals from varied backgrounds. Moreover, educational programs emphasizing critical thinking, empathy, and open-mindedness equip learners with the skills to navigate complex intercultural interactions with sensitivity and respect.

In addition to curriculum design, cultivating an inclusive and welcoming learning environment facilitates meaningful intercultural exchanges. Schools and universities can establish platforms for students from diverse cultural backgrounds to engage in dialogue, collaboration, and joint initiatives, fostering mutual understanding and appreciation. Furthermore, promoting cultural events, language courses, and exchange programs can allow students to immerse themselves in different cultural contexts, broadening their perspectives and breaking down barriers of misunderstanding and prejudice. Educators are also responsible for serving as role models by actively embracing cultural diversity and fostering an atmosphere of inclusivity, reinforcing the values of tolerance and mutual respect among students.

Beyond the classroom, partnerships between educational institutions, community organizations, and businesses can further advance the cause of intercultural understanding. Collaborative efforts may involve workshops, seminars, and outreach programs promoting cross-cultural communication and cooperation. By engaging with the broader community, educational institutions can contribute to creating a society that champions diversity and celebrates the richness of cultural differences. Ultimately, through the collective commitment of educators, learners, and stakeholders, education can create cohesive, harmonious, and inclusive societies where individuals from diverse backgrounds thrive and coexist in unity.

Challenges and Opportunities in Multicultural Policy Making

Multicultural policymaking is a complex and nuanced endeavor that requires a deep understanding of the diverse cultural tapestry within the Gulf region. As the Gulf states strive to embrace diversity and foster social cohesion, they encounter various challenges and opportunities in crafting and implementing effective multicultural policies. One significant

challenge lies in the delicate balance between preserving traditional cultural identities and integrating diverse communities
into a cohesive national framework. This entails the need for
policies that respect and celebrate cultural differences while
promoting common values and fostering a sense of belonging
for all residents. Moreover, policymakers must navigate the
interplay of historical tensions and contemporary geopolitical
dynamics, which can influence perceptions of cultural identity and national unity. There is also the critical task of building institutions and frameworks that can effectively address
discrimination, inequality, and the fair representation of diverse groups in decision-making processes. Equally pressing is
the need to recognize and accommodate the needs of minority communities, including language rights, religious practices,
and access to education and employment opportunities. Success in multicultural policymaking offers tremendous opportunities for societal enrichment and economic growth. By
harnessing the strength of cultural diversity, Gulf societies can
tap into a wealth of knowledge, skills, and perspectives that
contribute to innovation, entrepreneurship, and cross-cultural
collaboration. Embracing multiculturalism also opens doors to
enhanced diplomatic relations and global engagement, positioning the Gulf as a cosmopolitan hub that welcomes and
respects people from various backgrounds. Through proactive
policies, the Gulf states can showcase their commitment to
inclusivity and create vibrant, dynamic societies that attract
talent and investments worldwide. To achieve these aspirations, policymakers must engage in comprehensive dialogue
with community leaders, civil society organizations, and international partners to build consensus, exchange best practices,
and develop sustainable initiatives. With careful planning and
foresight, the Gulf can set an example for the world in cultivating harmonious coexistence and reaping the rewards of a truly
inclusive society.

Case Studies: Successful Models of Cultural Integration

In examining successful models of cultural integration in the Gulf region, it becomes evident that embracing diversity leads to unanticipated benefits for society. One prominent case study is the city of Dubai, where the expatriate population outnumbers the local Emirati community. Through deliberate policies and initiatives, Dubai has fostered an environment where individuals from diverse backgrounds coexist harmoniously while contributing to the city's growth and development. The government's commitment to tolerance and inclusivity has resulted in a thriving multicultural metropolis that serves as a testament to the potential of cultural integration. Another noteworthy example is the Kingdom of Bahrain, known for its rich history and openness to various cultures. The nation's ability to preserve its heritage while embracing global influences has positioned it as a model of coexistence and respect. By highlighting the contributions of different communities, Bahrain has created a vibrant social tapestry that continues to evolve while upholding traditional values. Beyond the urban landscape, the traditional Omani town of Al Hamra stands as a beacon of cultural preservation and integration. Its ancient architecture and close-knit community offer a glimpse into the past while showcasing the harmonious existence of varied cultural identities. The success of these case studies underscores the need for proactive measures to facilitate intercultural exchange, dispel stereotypes, and promote mutual understanding. By celebrating diversity through meaningful interactions, these communities have set a precedent for others seeking to harness the positive outcomes of cultural integration.

Towards a Unified Regional Identity

As we conclude our exploration of the diverse cultural tapestry that makes up the Gulf region, it becomes clear that the historical and contemporary models of cultural integration have laid the foundation for a unified regional identity. The case studies we've delved into offer powerful insights into the successful coexistence of various ethnicities, religions, and traditions, serving as beacons of hope for fostering unity in diversity. The rich fabric of this region's cultural heritage is interwoven with threads of inclusivity and mutual respect, creating a mosaic that defines its unique identity.

The path towards a unified regional identity hinges on embracing the collective experiences and aspirations of the diverse communities that call this region home. The Gulf can build a shared narrative that transcends individual identities and binds people together in a common tapestry of harmony by acknowledging and celebrating the multitude of traditions, languages, and customs. This concerted effort to recognize and respect the value each community brings to the whole is central to forming a cohesive regional identity.

Moreover, education plays a pivotal role in nurturing this unified regional identity. Institutions at all levels must emphasize the importance of understanding and appreciating various cultural practices, histories, and worldviews. By instilling the virtues of empathy and cultural intelligence in future generations, the region can aspire to create a society where diversity is tolerated and actively embraced as a source of strength and vitality.

However, we cannot overlook the challenges that accompany the pursuit of a unified regional identity. It requires a delicate balance between preserving the distinctiveness of individual communities while fostering a sense of belonging to the broader regional identity. Policymakers and leaders must navigate complex issues of governance, representation, and resource allocation to ensure that all cultural groups feel valued and included in shaping the region's collective destiny.

In traversing this journey towards a unified regional identity, the Gulf stands at a crossroads where the lessons of history intersect with the aspirations for a shared future. By learning from the past, acknowledging the present, and envisioning the future, the region can chart a course that honors its diversity while forging a unified regional identity that serves as a testament to the resilience and unity of its people.

Chapter 23

Legacy of the Sands: Embracing the Future

The historical journey of the Gulf region has been marked by extraordinary developments and pivotal moments that have significantly influenced the present state of modernization and technological advancements in the area. As we reflect on the rich history of this region, it becomes evident that the legacy of ancient civilizations and their innovative contributions continue to shape the contemporary landscape. The historical tapestry of the Gulf is woven with intricate threads of trade, cultural exchange, and resilience, laying the foundation for the remarkable progress witnessed today. From the ancient maritime trade routes that connected distant lands to the technologically advanced hubs thriving on innovation, the Gulf's historical journey serves as a compelling narrative that underpins the region's current trajectory. By acknowledging this historical continuum, we gain invaluable insights into the forces that have propelled the evolution of modernization and technological advancements in the Gulf. Therefore, a comprehensive exploration of the historical context provides an essential framework for understanding the interconnectedness of the past with present-day advancements, offering a profound appreciation for the enduring legacy that continues to inspire the future of the Gulf.

Modernization and Technological Advancements

In the wake of a rich historical legacy, the Gulf region has embraced modernization and technological advancements as key drivers of progress. This strategic shift towards leveraging cutting-edge technology and innovative solutions has propelled the region into a new era of development and growth. Embracing modernization has seen the integration of advanced systems across various sectors, including infrastructure, communication, energy, healthcare, and transportation. The adoption of digital technologies and smart infrastructure has not only enhanced operational efficiency but also elevated the region's global competitiveness. Furthermore, investments in research and development have led to breakthroughs in areas such as renewable energy, artificial intelligence, and sustainable urban planning. The pursuit of technological advancements has also catalyzed a paradigm shift in educational curricula, empowering the youth with vital skills for the future workforce. Additionally, embracing digital platforms has revolutionized how information is accessed and shared, fostering a culture of innovation and knowledge dissemination. The commitment to continuous improvement through technological advancement reaffirms the region's proactive approach to addressing contemporary challenges and seizing opportunities for sustainable growth. Moreover, modernization has cultivated an ecosystem fostering entrepreneurship, igniting a wave of startups and tech ventures redefining traditional industries and creating new economic opportunities. The convergence of global best practices with indigenous innovation has positioned the Gulf region as a trailblazer in pioneering tech-driven solutions that resonate on a global scale. As a result, the region continues to attract top talent and expertise from around the world, fueling a vibrant and dynamic landscape of creativity and progress. The journey of modernization and technological advancements signifies the region's unwavering commitment to shaping a future firmly rooted in sustainable development, propelled by innovation, and guided by a compelling vision for prosperity and progress.

Sustainable Development in the Gulf Region

The Gulf region has been at the forefront of sustainable development initiatives, recognizing the importance of preserving natural resources while pursuing economic growth. Sustainable development encompasses a holistic approach to addressing social, economic, and environmental concerns, and the Gulf countries have made significant strides in adopting policies and practices that promote sustainability. One notable aspect of sustainable development in the Gulf region is diversifying economies away from reliance on oil and gas by investing in renewable energy sources such as solar and wind power. This strategic shift reduces the carbon footprint and creates new opportunities for innovation and investment. Additionally, efforts to protect and conserve the region's rich biodiversity through establishing protected areas and conservation programs showcase the commitment to environmental stewardship. Integrating sustainable practices into urban planning and infrastructure development is another critical aspect of sustainable development in the Gulf region. Innovation in green building technologies, efficient waste management, and the promotion of public transportation are key components of creating environmentally friendly and resilient cities. Furthermore, sustainable development extends beyond environmental considerations to encompass social and economic dimensions. Initiatives aimed at enhancing education, promoting women's empowerment, and improving healthcare access contribute to the overall goal of sustainable development. These efforts foster human capital and promote social cohesion and inclusivity. Moreover, the Gulf region has increasingly recognized the importance of sustainable tourism in showcasing its cultural heritage while minimizing negative impacts on the environment and local communities. By embracing sustainable development, the Gulf region is positioning itself as a global leader in balancing economic prosperity with environmental and social responsibility. Through continued commitment to sustainable practices, the Gulf region is paving the way for a prosperous and harmonious future that benefits both present and future generations.

Educational Reforms and Their Impact

As the Gulf region continues its march towards a future of progress and innovation, educational reforms have emerged as a key driver of societal change. The integration of modern pedagogical methodologies, the nurturing of critical thinking skills, and the emphasis on STEM (Science, Technology, Engineering, and Mathematics) education have been pivotal in shaping the intellectual landscape of the region. Educational policies have evolved to align with global best practices, integrating digital literacy and computer science into curricula to prepare the youth for the demands of the 21st-century knowledge economy.

Furthermore, the Gulf region has witnessed a concerted effort to elevate the quality of higher education institutions, fostering environments conducive to research, innovation, and collaboration. Investments in state-of-the-art infrastructure, laboratories, and academic resources have lured distinguished faculty members and researchers, creating hubs of excellence that resonate far beyond national borders. Leveraging partnerships with leading international universities, these institutions have become crucibles for fostering talent, driving intellectual discourse, and nurturing visionary leaders equipped to navigate an increasingly complex and interconnected world.

The impact of these educational reforms reverberates across myriad facets of society. By empowering the new generation with advanced skill sets and equipping them with a global perspective, the transformative potential of education catalyzes economic diversification and sustainability. Beyond the economic realm, it engenders a populace imbued with intellectual curiosity, empathy, and a commitment to lifelong learning—the cornerstones of a vibrant civic society. Moreover, educational institutions have become incubators for creativity and cultural dynamism, preserving and promoting the region's rich heritage while fostering cross-cultural dialogue and understanding.

However, challenges persist, necessitating ongoing introspection and adaptation. Ensuring accessibility and inclusivity across all segments of society, addressing skill gaps, and harmonizing educational outcomes with evolving market demands remain imperative. Moreover, an adaptive and forward-looking educational ecosystem is paramount in an era characterized by technological disruptions and rapid societal transformations. Continual synergy between academia, industry, and policymakers is vital to charting a sustainable trajectory for the educational sector while fortifying the region's position within the evolving global knowledge landscape.

Thus, educational reforms and their enduring impact underscore the Gulf region's commitment to embrace the future and architect it—a testament to the region's unwavering resolve to cultivate a progressive, enlightened, and inclusive society.

Economic Strategies for Future Prosperity

In looking toward the future prosperity of the Gulf region, it is imperative to analyze and implement robust economic strategies that align with the evolving global landscape. The interplay of geopolitical dynamics, technological advancements, and shifting consumer behaviors necessitates a forward-thinking approach to foster sustainable economic growth and mitigate potential challenges. Critical to this endeavor is diversifying the economy beyond traditional sectors such as oil and gas, embracing innovation, and nurturing entrepreneurship.

A paramount component of future economic prosperity involves investing in human capital and fostering a knowledge-based economy. This entails allocating resources to education, research and development, and skills training to cultivate a dynamic and adaptable workforce capable of driving innovation across various industries. By harnessing the potential of emerging technologies and promoting a culture of continuous learning, the Gulf region can position itself at the forefront of global innovation and knowledge creation.

Moreover, leveraging the opportunities presented by sustainable development is essential for shaping the economic trajectory of the Gulf. Introducing environmentally conscious policies, renewable energy initiatives, and sustainable urban planning ensures environmental stewardship and opens new industries and employment opportunities. Embracing sustainable practices safeguards the region's natural resources and bolsters its attractiveness for foreign investment and tourism.

Strategic partnerships and international collaborations are instrumental in fortifying the Gulf's economic resilience. By fostering robust trade relations, engaging in bilateral and multilateral agreements, and pursuing mutually beneficial partnerships, the region can amplify its economic footprint on the global stage. Proactive engagement with international markets, tapping into emerging economies, and actively participating in cross-border infrastructural projects can further enhance the region's economic relevance and influence.

Lastly, adopting agile economic policies that align with contemporary market trends and global developments is pivotal for future prosperity. Cultivating a conducive business environment, streamlining regulatory frameworks, and incentivizing private sector participation can galvanize economic diversification and growth. At the same time, proactive risk management strategies, contingency plans, and forward-looking fiscal policies serve as bulwarks against economic volatility and external shocks.

In summary, embracing economic diversification, prioritizing human capital development, championing sustainable practices, nurturing international collaborations, and implementing adaptive economic policies form the bedrock of the strategic blueprint for securing future prosperity in the Gulf region.

Cultural Heritage in Contemporary Society

Cultural heritage is the timeless link that binds society to its roots, shaping identities and fostering a sense of belonging. In contemporary Gulf society, the preservation and celebration of cultural heritage hold profound significance amid the rapid transformations witnessed in recent decades. As urban landscapes evolve and economies diversify, a growing need exists to safeguard and promote traditional art forms, craftsmanship, and customs unique to the region. Embracing this legacy enriches the social fabric and facilitates cross-generational understanding, contributing to cultivating a cohesive community ethos. Within contemporary Gulf society, cultural revival initiatives are gaining momentum. Traditional music, dance forms, and oral storytelling are experiencing a resurgence, providing a platform for intergenerational transmission of knowledge and reinforcing cultural continuity. Furthermore, museums and cultural institutions play an integral role in nurturing appreciation for historical artifacts and indigenous art, serving as vital custodians of the Gulf's rich heritage. Integrating cultural education into modern curricula is imperative, ensuring that future generations inherit a deep appreciation for their ancestral legacy. Preserving and promoting cultural heritage safeguards authenticity during rapid change and allows communities to navigate contemporary challenges while staying rooted in timeless practices. Moreover, integrating traditional architectural styles and urban planning principles preserves visual heritage and fosters a connection to the past within dynamic urban spaces. This deliberate fusion of tradition and modernity emphasizes respect for heritage while embracing innovation. Additionally, encouraging traditional crafts and artisanal skills ensures the continuity of art forms that have defined the Gulf's cultural landscape for centuries. By empowering local artisans and celebrating their expertise, contemporary Gulf society can uphold its rich artistic traditions while fostering economic sustainability. Cultural heritage bridges the past and present, guiding societies towards sustainable development and fostering a collective pride in their unique identity. As the Gulf navigates the complexities of modernization, the preservation and reinvigoration of cultural heritage provide a roadmap for balanced progress, helping to shape a harmonious future where tradition and innovation coexist seamlessly.

Environmental Challenges and Responses

The Gulf region has undeniably faced environmental challenges that necessitate proactive responses to preserve its natural resources and ecological balance. One prominent issue is the impact of rapid urbanization and industrialization on the region's delicate ecosystems. As urban centers expand and industries multiply, energy and water resources demand increases, placing significant strain on the environment.

Furthermore, the fragile marine ecosystem is under pressure from various sources, including overfishing, habitat destruction, and pollution. Once sustainable, traditional fishing practices are now threatened by modern techniques and excessive exploitation. Additionally, the depletion of marine resources directly threatens the livelihoods of coastal communities that have long depended on fishing for sustenance and trade.

Another critical concern is the escalating pollution levels, particularly in densely populated urban areas. Air and water pollution from industrial activities, vehicular emissions, and waste disposal pose substantial risks to public health and the natural environment. These pollutants degrade air and water quality, harm wildlife, and disrupt the delicate ecological balance.

In response to these environmental challenges, the Gulf region has begun implementing initiatives to address and mitigate these issues. Renewable energy projects, such as solar and wind power, are being embraced as sustainable alternatives to mitigate the environmental impact of traditional energy sources. Furthermore, conservation efforts and protected area management are being enhanced to safeguard vulnerable habitats and species amidst rapid development.

Moreover, there is an increasing focus on promoting sustainable agriculture, fisheries, and industry practices to minimize the ecological footprint and preserve natural resources for future generations. Collaborative regional agreements and international partnerships have been forged to address transboundary environmental issues and foster collective action for conservation and environmental sustainability.

Environmental research and technology advancements are pivotal in monitoring and addressing environmental concerns. Cutting-edge innovations in waste management, pollution control, and environmental monitoring enable informed decision-making and more effective responses to environmental challenges.

Finally, raising public awareness and fostering environmental stewardship through education and advocacy are crucial in addressing environmental challenges. By nurturing a culture of environmental responsibility and sustainability, communities can actively contribute to protecting and conserving their natural surroundings, empowering individuals to become champions of environmental stewardship.

While the Gulf region faces grave environmental challenges, the concerted efforts and evolving strategies towards sustainable development and environmental stewardship offer hope for a harmonious coexistence with nature, ensuring a legacy of environmental integrity for future generations.

International Relations and Regional Stability

The concept of regional stability in the Gulf region has been intricately linked to international relations for centuries. As the global political landscape evolves, the strategic significance of this region continues to attract widespread attention from major powers, leading to complex diplomatic dynamics that influence the socioeconomic and geopolitical fabric of the Gulf. In today's interconnected world, the relationships between Gulf states and major international players are central to regional stability and the broader global order. The multifaceted nature of these relationships is shaped by factors such as energy security, trade dynamics, military cooperation, and cultural exchange. The Gulf states must navigate these relationships with foresight, diplomacy, and an acute awareness of historical contexts. Alongside traditional alliances, emerging partnerships and evolving power dynamics call for astute diplomatic engagements while safeguarding the region's autonomy and collective interests. The interplay of economic interdependence and strategic alignments further underscores the intricate nature of international relations in the Gulf. These interactions impact regional policies, security architectures, and the region's overall stability. Furthermore, the Gulf states' involvement in international organizations and forums provides platforms for dialogue, negotiation, and consensus-building, serving as conduits for addressing common challenges and fostering mutual understanding. However, it is imperative to acknowledge the potential vulnerabilities and frictions that can arise in international relations. Tensions stemming from ideological differences, territorial disputes, and external interventions necessitate a reasonable approach to conflict resolution and mitigation efforts. Building sustainable regional stability requires a delicate balance of respecting sovereignty, engaging in constructive dialogues, and promoting inclusive frameworks for cooperation. Moreover, the resilience of the region's sociopolitical landscape hinges upon the ability of the Gulf states to leverage their diplomatic acumen and navigate the complexities of international relations while upholding principles of mutual respect and non-interference. The Gulf region can reinforce its role as a bastion of stability and prosperity by proactively engaging in global partnerships and advocating for collaborative solutions to shared challenges. Pursuing regional stability through balanced international relations is pivotal for preserving the Gulf's distinct identity, fostering economic growth, and contributing to a harmonious global order.

Health Initiatives and Public Well-being

Promoting public health and well-being is a crucial aspect of societal development in the Gulf region. As part of ongoing efforts to enhance the quality of life for all residents, various health initiatives have been implemented to address emerging challenges and improve healthcare services. With a focus on preventive care, the region has prioritized public health interventions to combat non-communicable diseases (NCDs) such as diabetes, cardiovascular diseases, and obesity. Additionally, advancements in medical research and technology have facilitated the establishment of state-of-the-art healthcare facilities, leveraging innovation to achieve better patient outcomes and experience. Collaborative partnerships between government entities, private healthcare providers, and international organizations have played a pivotal role in shaping the healthcare landscape, fostering cross-sector synergies and knowledge exchange. Furthermore, community engagement and awareness campaigns have been instrumental in promoting healthy lifestyle choices and raising consciousness about mental health and wellness. Integrating traditional healing practices with modern medicine has also contributed to a more holistic approach to healthcare, respecting cultural beliefs while embracing evidence-based treatments. In addressing public well-being, socioeconomic disparities and access to healthcare services have been key focal points, with inclusive policies ensuring equitable distribution and affordability of medical care. Embracing the future entails an unwavering commitment to advancing healthcare infrastructure, nurturing a skilled workforce of healthcare professionals, and upholding

ethical standards safeguarding patient rights and dignity. Moreover, the convergence of digital health technologies, telemedicine, and artificial intelligence presents new opportunities to
revolutionize healthcare delivery and empower individuals to
take control of their health. As the region continues to embrace modernization while remaining grounded in its cultural
heritage, pursuing comprehensive healthcare solutions is a testament to a visionary approach to fostering resilience, vibrant
communities, and a prosperous future.

A Vision for the Future

   As we conclude this exploration into the legacy of the Gulf
region, it becomes paramount to envision a future that integrates the diverse elements of cultural heritage, sustainable
development, and technological advancement. Modern society's complexities present challenges and opportunities; we
can navigate the path toward a prosperous future through a
cohesive vision. With health initiatives and public well-being
at the forefront, the holistic vision for the future of the Gulf
emphasizes the crucial role of education in fostering enlightenment and progress. Education lays the foundation for a society's prosperity and resilience, providing the knowledge and
skills to address contemporary challenges. Therefore, investing
in educational reforms is key to nurturing future generations
capable of steering the region toward greater heights. In con-
junction with educational reforms, modernization and technological advancements will catalyze growth and innovation.
Embracing emerging technologies and sustainable practices
will bolster economic strategies and contribute to environmental preservation. Recognizing the intricate interplay between
economic progress and ecological equilibrium, sustainable development becomes imperative in charting the future course

of the Gulf. Emphasizing the preservation and promotion of cultural heritage within contemporary society forms another integral aspect of the envisioned future. Through embracing cultural diversity and traditional values, the Gulf community can safeguard its rich history while adapting to the evolving global landscape. This preservation is a source of inspiration and identity, harmonizing the past, present, and future. Environmental challenges further compel the region to cultivate responsible stewardship and prompt collective responses to mitigate potential threats. By promoting efficient resource management and conservation efforts, the Gulf can confront environmental challenges head-on, securing the well-being of current and future generations. International relations and regional stability intersect closely with this vision, advocating for harmonious cooperation and mutual understanding among nations. Fostering diplomatic ties and collaborative partnerships will fortify the region's place in the global arena, engendering peace, security, and progress. Finally, the comprehensive approach to nurturing the future vision of the Gulf encompasses health initiatives and public well-being. Prioritizing accessible healthcare, preventive measures, and community welfare programs vitalizes the social fabric, ensuring individuals' sustained vitality and happiness. In closing, the vision for the future of the Gulf revolves around unity amidst diversity, innovation alongside tradition, and progress rooted in sustainability. It is a vision that harmonizes the past, present, and future, steering the Gulf toward an era of enduring prosperity, cultural vibrancy, and global significance.

Next volume in this collection: Colonial Legacies And The Birth Of Modern Gulf States

Bibliography

Abazov, R. (2008). International Trade and the Beginning of the Great Silk Road. 28–29.

Abdalla, N. N. I., & Alhassan, S. E. (2024). The Influence of Urbanization on Social Dynamics in Yemen: Insights from Environmental and Climate Data. Journal of Engineering Research and Reports.

ABDALLAH, A. M., & MOHAMED, A. B. A.-R. (2023). A COMPARISON BETWEEN THE CANAANITE AND SAWIAN CIVILIZATIONS. RIMAK International Journal of Humanities and Social Sciences.

Abdellatif, S., Halalat, K. I. A., & Aboraya, M. E. (2023). The Representations of Pearl Fishing and Trade Heritage by University's Youth in the UAE. Dirasat Human and Social Sciences.

Abdellatif, S., Ibn Hedi Missaoui, & Missaoui, K. (2020). Cultural Heritage between Rooting and Continuity: Crossed Views of Pearls in the Emirates.

Abdussamad, E. M., Pillai, N., Mohammed, O., & Jayabalan, K. (2010). Sardines of the Gulf of Mannar ecosystem - fishery and resource characteristics of major species. Indian Journal of Fisheries, 57, 7–12.

Abi, N. N., & Norfu'adi, M. (2023). Socio-Economic Conditions of the Arabian Peninsula Before Islam. ARRUS Journal of Social Sciences and Humanities.

Abokhodair, N., Hodges, A., & Vieweg, S. (2017). Photo Sharing in the Arab Gulf: Expressing the Collective and Autonomous Selves. In Conference on Computer Supported Cooperative Work.

Abozaid, A. M. (2021). The Rise of Small States in the Arabian Gulf: The Case of UAE and Qatar: A Historical Sociology Perspective.

Abraham, R. (2022). Identity Formation, Social Media and Migrants 2.0: Case Study of Second Generation Malayali Migrants in the Gulf. Asian Journal of Middle Eastern and Islamic Studies, 16, 497–507.

Abu-Amero, K., González, A., Larruga, J., Bosley, T., & Cabrera, V. (2007). Eurasian and African mitochondrial DNA influences in the Saudi Arabian population. BMC Evolutionary Biology, 7, 32–32.

Adib-Moghaddam, A. (2006). The International Politics of the Persian Gulf: A Cultural Genealogy.

Adnan, M., & Fatima, B. (2015). Globalization of Central Asia. Journal of Political Studies, 22, 437.

Aerde, M. (2022). Crossing oceans: Interdisciplinary research and ancient trade routes. Journal of Roman Archaeology, 35, 441–449.

Agarwal, R. (2014). Persian Gulf 2013: India's Relations with the Region. Indian Foreign Affairs Journal, 9, 72.

Agiùs, D. (2002). In the Wake of the Dhow: The Arabian Gulf and Oman.

Agiùs, D., Cooper, J., Semaan, L., Zazzaro, C., & Carter, R. (2016). Remembering the Sea: Personal and Communal Recollections of Maritime Life in Jizan and the Farasan Islands, Saudi Arabia. Journal of Maritime Archaeology, 11, 127–177.

Ahmad, D. S. (2018). The Arabian Mission in Kuwait, 1910–67: Effects of Modern Medicine on Women's Healing Practices and Ideals of Womanhood. Gender & History, 30.

Ahmed, A. M. T. K. (2023). The Ottoman – British Rivalry in the Arabian Gulf Area (1840 – 1872 A.D.) Ottoman Reports as a Source. Dirasat Human and Social Sciences.

Ahmed, A. O. (2020). Historical relations between the arab gulf countries and Russia. 90, 66–71.

Ahmed, A. T., Gohary, F. E., Tzanakakis, V., & Angelakis, A. (2020). Egyptian and Greek Water Cultures and Hydro-Technologies in Ancient Times. Sustainability.

Ahmedov, V. M. (2022). The Role of Nationalism in Arab-Iranian Relations: Historical and Ideological Dimensions. Oriental Courier.

Aigul, T., Zibagul, I., & Saira, S. (2015). The Great Silk Road as Cultural Phenomena. 3, 1–12.

Ajirlou, A. G., Farhadi, S., & Jahed, M. A. (2014). Historical and Legal Investigation of the Persian Gulf.

Akıncı, İ. (2020). Culture in the 'politics of identity': conceptions of national identity and citizenship among second-generation non-Gulf Arab migrants in Dubai. Journal of Ethnic and Migration Studies, 46, 2309–2325.

Akyeampong, E. (2010). For Prayer and Profit: West Africa's Religious and Economic Ties to the Gulf 1960s to the Present. Journal of African Development.

Al-Ahmadi, Dr. H. Y. Y., & Rahman Mohammad Jailan, Prof. A. (2023). Factors influencing the development of Ottoman construction in Levant during the period from 1550-1800 Aleppo and Damascus as a Model. Yemen University Journal.

Al-Busaidi, K. (2013). Banana domestication on the Arabian Peninsula: A review of their domestication history. Journal of Horticulture and Forestry, 5, 194–203.

Al-Hind: The Making of the Indo-Islamic World, Vol. II. The Slave Kings and the Islamic Conquest, 11th–13th Centuries. By André Wink. pp. xii, 427. Leiden, E. J. Brill, 1997.

Al-Kaisi, M. (2022). The Iraqi Folkloric Tradition of Mājīnā: The 'Trick-or-Treat' of Mesopotamia. Folklore, 133, 200–223.

Al-Khalifa, H. (2017). The Friday mosque of the Arabian Gulf: defining its spatial and formal languages, 1975-2010.

Al-Majnouni, M. A. A. A. (2020). The method of historical writing for western travelers in Al-Ahsa of 1328- 1353 AH/ 1910- 1934 AD: منهج الكتابة التاريخية عند الرَّحالة الغربيين في منطقة الأُحْسَاءَ من الفترة 1328ـ1353هـ/ 1934ـ1910م. Journal of Humanities and Social Sciences, 4.

Al-Mohannadi, A., & Furlan, R. (2018). THE PRACTICE OF CITY PLANNING AND DESIGN IN THE GULF REGION: THE CASE OF ABU DHABI, DOHA AND MANAMA. International Journal of Architectural Research: ArchNet-IJAR.

Al-Nasr, T. (2011). Gulf Cooperation Council (GCC) Women and Misyar Marriage: Evolution and Progress in the Arabian Gulf. Journal of International Women's Studies, 12, 43–57.

Al-Noaimi, H. (2021). Militarism and the Bedouin: Intersections of colonialism, gender, and race in the Arab Gulf. Security Dialogue, 52, 529–545.

Al-Otaibi, M. (2023). The Security Situation in Najd During the Twelfth Century AH / Eighteenth Century AD. Jordan Journal for History and Archaeology.

Al-Quraini, A. J. (1997). The Arab Gulf Cooperation Council (AGCC) is not Just an Organization for Security, But it is an Organization for Cooperation in All Fields.

Al-Raeeini, M. H. M. (2014). The Political Situation in the North of the Arabian Peninsula and Its Impact on the Yemen and Indian Trade. International Journal of Innovation and Applied Studies, 9, 1582–1588.

Al-Rawi, A. (2009). The Mythical Ghoul in Arabic Culture. Cultural Analysis, 8, 45.

Al-Salem, M. (2014). The role of human experience in enhancing Arab traditional identity awareness in interior design education in Kuwait.

Al-Suwaidi, A. (1993). Developments of the Legal Systems of the Gulf Arab States. Arab Law Quarterly, 8, 289–301.

AL-Zaqroot, K. I. (2012). Religion in the southern Arabian Peninsula and its relationship With two Religions Judaism and Christianity before Islam. Al-Anbar University Journal For Humanities.

Al–Taie, A. (1993). Khaldoun Hasan Al-Naqeeb, Society and State in the Gulf and Arab Peninsula: A Different Perspective, trans. L. M. Kenny, emended by Ibrahim Hayani, under the aegis of the Project of Translation from Arabic (London: Routledge, 1990). Pp. 227. International Journal of Middle East Studies, 25, 539–541.

Alami, R. (2008). Economic Co-operation in the Gulf: Issues in the Economies of the Arab Gulf Co-operation Council States. Middle Eastern Studies, 44, 166–167.

Albahar, A. K. (2016). Thaj Civilizations Influenced the Civilization of the Arabian Peninsula and some neighboring areas. Journal Of Arabic And Human Sciences, 10.

Alfheeaid, H. (2023). Nutritional profile and energy density evaluation of common traditional meals in Arabic Gulf region. European Review for Medical and Pharmacological Sciences, 27 2, 532–539.

Alieva, M. A., Keldibaeva, N. B., & Ibragimova, A. I. (2024). Epics on the Great Silk Road: the influence of agriculture on literature and culture. BIO Web of Conferences.

Almahmoud, S. (2015). THE MAJLIS METAMORPHOSIS: Virtues of Local Traditional Environmental Design in a Contemporary Context.

Almarhoon, N. M. (2015). Arab regional politics in the oil-rich Gulf Arab states and Labor Migrants, Refugees. Journal for Studies in Management and Planning, 1, 431–441.

Almathen, F., Charruau, P., Mohandesan, E., Mwacharo, J., Orozco–ter-Wengel, P., Pitt, D., Abdussamad, A. M., Uerpmann, M., Uerpmann, H., Cupere, B., Magee, P., Alnaqeeb, M., Salim, B., Raziq, A., Dessie, T., Abdelhadi, O., Banabazi, M. H., Al-Eknah, M., Walzer, C., ... Burger, P. (2016). Ancient and modern DNA reveal dynamics of domestication and cross-continental dispersal of the dromedary. Proceedings of the National Academy of Sciences of the United States of America, 113, 6707–6712.

Alotaibi, D. M. (2017). Ibn Sa'ud and Britain : early changing relationship and pre-state formation 1902-1914.

Alotaibi, M. I., Elsamad, G., Aljardahi, A. N., Alghamdi, A. N., Alotaibi, A. I., Alorabi, H. M., Alzahrani, K. M., & Abdel-Moneim, A. S. (2023). Changes in dietary and lifestyle behaviors and mental stress among medical students upon Ramadan diurnal intermittent fasting: a prospective cohort study from Taif/Saudi Arabia. BMC Public Health, 23.

Alsayer, D. M. (2018). The "Right to the City" in the Landscapes of Servitude and Migration, from the Philippines to the Arabian Gulf, and Back. Mapping Migration, Identity, and Space.

AlShehabi, O. (2019). Policing labor in the empire: the modern origins of the Kafala sponsorship system in the Gulf Arab States. British Journal of Middle Eastern Studies, 48, 291–310.

Álvarez-Martí-Aguilar, M. (2023). A Major Earthquake and Tsunami in the Gulf of Cadiz in the Sixth Century B.C.? A Review of the Historical, Archaeological, and Geological Evidence. Seismological Research Letters.

Alzahrani, H. J. M. (2021). Emancipation of slaves in Saudi Arabia: تحرير الرقيق في المملكة العربية السعودية. 5, 114–125.

Amin, A., & Mousa, M. (2007). Merits of anti-cancer plants from the Arabian Gulf region.

Aqil, K., & Казим, A. (2018). Pearl industry in the UAE region in 1869-1938: its construction, reproduction, and decline. 18, 452–469.

Arabic Historical Dialectology. (2018). Oxford Scholarship Online.

Archaeology and Material Culture of Nabataea and the Nabataeans. (2021). Biblical Studies.

Armajani, J. (2000). HERIBERT BUSSE, Islam, Judaism, and Christianity: Theological and Historical Affiliations, trans. Allison Brown, Princeton Series on the Middle East (Princeton, N.J.: Markus Wiener Publishers, 1998). Pp. 207. International Journal of Middle East Studies, 32, 155–157.

Artzy, M. (1994). INCENSE, CAMELS AND COLLARED RIM JARS: DESERT TRADE ROUTES AND MARITIME OUTLETS IN THE SECOND MILLENNIUM. Oxford Journal of Archaeology, 13, 121–147.

Asadov, F. (2024). Silk Road in the aftermath of Arab conquest: Trade routes traversing Azerbaijan.

Asgari, S. (2024). THE SILK ROAD AS A COMMON PART OF THE HISTORY OF IRAN AND KAZAKSTAN. KAZAKHSTAN ORIENTAL STUDIES.

Baibussinova, N. K. (n.d.). GULF COUNTRIES TRADE RELATIONS WITH THE UNITED STATES.

Baig, R. (2024). THE ENGLISH LANGUAGE IN THE GULF: A LINGUA FRANCA REDEFINING IDENTITY AND OPPORTUNITY. The Journal of English Language and Literature.

Bar-Oz, G., Galili, R., Fuks, D., Erickson-Gini, T., Tepper, Y., Shamir, N., & Avni, G. (2022). Caravanserai middens on desert roads: a new perspective on the Nabataean–Roman trade network across the Negev. Antiquity, 96, 592–610.

Bauman, A., Baird, A., & Cavalcante, G. H. (2011). Coral reproduction in the world's warmest reefs: southern Persian Gulf (Dubai, United Arab Emirates). Coral Reefs, 30, 405–413.

Bayirhan, İ., & Gazioğlu, C. (2021). New Maritime Trade Routes in the Arctic Region: one of the Strongest Alternatives to the Suez Canal. International Journal of Environment, 8, 397–401.

Beaujard, P. (2019). The Ancient Routes of Trade and Cultural Exchanges and the First States (Sixth–Second Millennium BC). 19–272.

Bell, L., Johnson, J. H., & Whitcomb, D. (1984). The Eastern Desert of Upper Egypt: Routes and Inscriptions. Journal of Near Eastern Studies, 43, 27–46.

Benoist, A. (2008). The Iron Age Culture in the United Arab Emirates, between 1100 BC and 250 BC. 29, 31–41.

Bergjan, S. (2022). Ancient Geographers and Modern Travelogues in the Early Seventeenth Century. The Difference between Hugo Grotius's Bewys van den waren Godsdienst (1622) and De veritate religionis christianae (1627–40). Grotiana.

Beydoun, Z., As-Saruri, M., & Baraba, R. (1996). Sedimentary Basins of the Republic of Yemen: Their Structural Evolution and Geological Characteristics. Oil & Gas Science and Technology-Revue De L Institut Francais Du Petrole, 51, 763–775.

Bienkowski, P., & Millard, A. (2001). Dictionary of the Ancient Near East. American Journal of Archaeology, 105, 105.

Bin, & Song. (2023). The Social and Cultural Exchange and the Conversions of Different Religions along the Trade Routes When Trading Groups Intermingled. SHS Web of Conferences.

Bingham, J. M. (2003). The Usborne Internet-Linked Encyclopedia of the Ancient World.

Bishara, F. (2022). Circulation and Capitalism in a Maritime Bazaar: Notes from a Pearl Merchant's Chest. Comparative Studies of South Asia, Africa and the Middle East, 42, 107–117.

Biygautane, M. (2015). Analysis of the Impact of the Cultural and Institutional Characteristics of the Gulf Cooperation Council States on Entrepreneurship: Opportunities and Challenges. 222–234.

Blenkey, N. (2000). WHEN TRAVEL TRADE DREAMS MEET MARITIME REALITIES.

Blevis, R., Bar-Oz, G., & Zohar, I. (2019). The role of Red Sea Parrotfish (Scaridae) as Trade Indicators in the Negev Desert during the Byzantine-Islamic Transition Period.

Blevis, R., Bar-Oz, G., Tepper, Y., & Zohar, I. (2021). Fish in the desert: Identifying fish trade routes and the role of Red Sea parrotfish (Scaridae) during the Byzantine and Early Islamic periods. Journal of Archaeological Science: Reports, 36, 102808.

Blom, R., Crippen, R., Elachi, C., Clapp, N., Hedges, G., & Zariņš, J. (2006). Southern Arabian Desert Trade Routes, Frankincense, Myrrh, and the Ubar Legend. 71–87.

Blom, R., Crippen, R., Hedges, G., & Zariņš, J. (1997). Application of Space Technology to Discovery of Ancient Desert Trade Routes in the Southern Arabian Peninsula.

Boahen, A. A. (1962). The Caravan Trade in the Nineteenth Century. The Journal of African History, 3, 349–359.

Boboeva, S. (2020). Historical Toponyms Along 'Termez - Iron Gate' Trading Way. 6, 347–355.

Borhan, B. (2021). Sinews of war and trade: shipping and capitalism in the Arabian Peninsula. British Journal of Middle Eastern Studies, 50, 804–806.

Bosworth, C. (1997). The Nomenclature of the Persian Gulf. Iranian Studies, 30, 77–94.

Bouchaud, C., Tengberg, M., & Prà, P. D. (2011). Cotton cultivation and textile production in the Arabian Peninsula during antiquity; the evidence from Madâ'in Sâlih (Saudi Arabia) and Qal'at al-Bahrain (Bahrain). Vegetation History and Archaeobotany, 20, 405–417.

Boudiaf, Dr. B. (2018). On Ecology and Culture: Analogy between Contemporary and Traditional Architectures in the Gulf Region.

Bowen, J. (1998). What Is "Universal" and "Local" in Islam? Ethos, 26, 258–261.

Breakey, J. (2021). Sinews of War and Trade: Shipping and Capitalism in the Arabian Peninsula. Cambridge Review of International Affairs, 34, 765–767.

Bsheer, R. (2015). The Superlative City: Dubai and the Urban Condition in the Early Twenty-First Century. Arab Studies Journal, 23, 428.

Burgersdijk, D. (2019). Palmyra on the Silk Road. Terrestrial and Maritime Trading Routes from China to the Mediterranean. 51, 246–257.

Carter, R. (2005). The History and Prehistory of Pearling in the Persian Gulf. Journal of The Economic and Social History of The Orient, 48, 139–209.

Chattopadhyay, A. (2022). A Study of Aromatic Woods in Seventeenth-Century India: Circulation of Aloewood and Sandalwood through Facilitating Port Cities and Trade Networks. Crossroads.

Chaudhuri, K. N. (1985). Trade and Civilisation in the Indian Ocean: Emporia trade and the great port-towns in the Indian Ocean.

Cherkas, B., & Novytska, N. (2023). The Interests of the Gulf Monarchies in the Horn of Africa. Przegląd Politologiczny.

Choi, S. (2022). Growing Pains of Emerging Gulf Cities: A Review of The New Arab Urban. Georgetown Journal of International Affairs, 23, 272–276.

Church, S. K. (2024). Interplays and Interactions on the Maritime and Overland Silk Roads in the First Millennium. The Medieval History Journal.

Çiçek, M. T. (2016). Negotiating power and authority in the desert: the Arab Bedouin and the limits of the Ottoman state in Hijaz, 1840–1908. Middle Eastern Studies, 52, 260–279.

Çinar, E., Geusz, K., & Johnson, J. (2015). Historical Perspectives on Trade and Risk on the Silk Road, Middle East and China. Topics in Middle Eastern and North African Economies, 17.

Claire, S., & Tallet, P. (2013). A Road to the Arabian Peninsula in the Reign of Ramesses III. 27, 511–518.

Cobb, M. (2013). THE RECEPTION AND CONSUMPTION OF EASTERN GOODS IN ROMAN SOCIETY. Greece and Rome, 60, 136–152.

Cobb, M. M. (2021). "Barbarians" and Blemmyes: Who Was in Control of the Red Sea Port of Berenike in the Late Antique Period? Journal of Late Antiquity, 14, 267–293.

Collins, R., & Burns, J. (2013). A History of Sub-Saharan Africa: East Africa and the Indian Ocean world. 96–113.

Connan, J. (1999). Use and trade of bitumen in antiquity and prehistory: molecular archaeology reveals secrets of past civilizations. Philosophical Transactions of the Royal Society B, 354, 33–50.

Covert, A. (2016). From Ocean to Desert: Analysis of Prehistoric Shell Through Type, Use, and Trade Routes to Petrified Forest National Park.

Crabtree, S. (2007). Culture, Gender and the Influence of Social Change amongst Emirati Families in the United Arab Emirates. Journal of Comparative Family Studies, 38, 575–588.

Culture and Customs of the Arab Gulf States | Retrieved June 20, 2024, from https://www.researchgate.net/publication/375106738_Culture_and_Customs_of_the_Arab_Gulf_States

Dabrowski, V., Bouchaud, C., & Tengberg, M. (2015). Local harvesting and importation of wood in the Oman peninsula at the end of Antiquity: recent charcoal analyses from a burnt building at Mleiha (U.A.E, 2nd -3rd century AD).

Dabrowski, V., Bouchaud, C., Tengberg, M., & Mouton, M. (2021). Crop processing, consumption and trade of Asian rice (Oryza sativa L.) in the Arabian Peninsula during Antiquity: earliest evidence from Mleiha (third c. AD), United Arab Emirates. Archaeological and Anthropological Sciences, 13.

Daineh, T. M. B. (2018). ECONOMIC AND CULTURAL COOPERATION BETWEEN GULF COOPERATION COUNCIL AND ARAB.

Dakhteh, S. M. H., Ranjbar, S., Moazeni, M., Mohsenian, N., Hossein, Delshab, Moshiri, H., & Waerebeek, K. (n.d.). On the presence of humpback whales in the Persian Gulf: rare or rarely documented?

Dangre, G. (2024). From Ancient Paths to Modern Highways: Mapping the Evolution of World Trade Routes and their Crucial Role in Today's

Global Supply Chains Gaurav Dangre. INTERNATIONAL JOURNAL OF SCIENTIFIC RESEARCH IN ENGINEERING AND MANAGEMENT.

Darabi, J. (2014). The government's role in relations between Iran and the Arabian Peninsula, in the Sassani era.

Demichelis, M. (2021). Arab Christian Confederations and Muhammad's Believers: On the Origins of Jihad. Religions.

Demirel, S. (2022). THE EFFECT OF GLOBALIZATION IN THE GULF COUNTRIES AND THE CHANGING ROLES OF WOMEN: A COMPARA-TIVE STUDY ON ARABIA, THE UNITED ARAB EMIRATES AND QATAR.

Diallo, I. (2012). Intercultural teaching in the Arab Gulf region: Making a case for pedagogy that takes into account the epistemic context and the scholastic traditions of Muslim students. International Journal of Pedagogies and Learning, 7, 211–217.

Dong-qia, X. (2013). The channel of cultural exchange, spread and diffusion: A case study of the Silk Road in China. Journal of Northwest University.

Doszhanova, A. (2023). Intercultural communication on the territory of Eurasia: historical and cultural heritage of the Great Silk Road. Uchenyy Sovet (Academic Council).

Drège, J.-P., & Bührer, E. M. (1989). The Silk Road Saga.

Eaaswarkhanth, M., Haque, I., Ravesh, Z., Romero, I. G., Meganathan, P. R., Dubey, B., Khan, F., Chaubey, G., Kivisild, T., Tyler-Smith, C., Singh, L., & Thangaraj, K. (2010). Traces of sub-Saharan and Middle Eastern line-ages in Indian Muslim populations. European Journal of Human Genetics, 18, 354–363.

el–Aswad. (2021). Oriental Images and Ethics. British Empire and the Arab Gulf (1727–1971). A Perspective from Historical Anthropology. Anthropos?

Elias, H. (2024). The Southwest Silk Road: artistic exchange and trans-mission in early China. Bulletin of the School of Oriental and African Studies.

Elsheikh, A. (2024). Enhancing the Efficacy of Assistive Technologies through Localization: A Comprehensive Analysis with a Focus on the Arab Region. Nafath.

Emmanouela Grypeou, Mark Swanson, and David Thomas, eds. The Encounter of Eastern Christianity with Early Islam, The History of Christian-Muslim Relations (Leiden: E. J. Brill, 2006). Pp. 344.

Eum, I.-R. (2023). A Study on the Networking Space in the Gulf Region: Focusing on Diwaniya Case in Kuwait. The Institute of Middle Eastern Affairs.

Ffrench, G., Hill, A., & Jusatz, H. J. (1971). Regional studies in geographical medicine. Vol. 4. Kuwait: urban and medical ecology. A geomedical study.

Finlayson, C. (2002). The Women of Palmyra–Textile Workshops and the Influence of the Silk Trade in Roman Syria.

Floor, W. (2010). The rise and fall of Bandar-e Lengeh: the distribution center for the Arabian Coast, 1750-1930.

Foltz, R. (2000). Religions of the Silk Road: overland trade and cultural exchange from antiquity to the fifteenth century. The American Historical Review, 105, 1273.

Fox, M., Bibi, F., & Hill, A. (2008). Jacketing the desert sands.

Frank, A. (2012). The Children of the Desert and the Laws of the Sea: Austria, Great Britain, the Ottoman Empire, and the Mediterranean Slave Trade in the Nineteenth Century. The American Historical Review, 117, 410–444.

Fraser, M., & Golzari, N. (2009). Human Habitation: Architecture, Settlement and Cultural Identity in the Persian Gulf Region.

Fürtig, H. (2007). Conflict and Cooperation in the Persian Gulf: The Interregional Order and US Policy. Middle East Journal, 61, 627–640.

G.I., S., & K., A. (2021). Developmental Historiography of the Ancient Silk Road. African Journal of Culture, History, Religion and Traditions.

Gairola, S., Shaer, K. I. A., Harthi, E. K. A., & Mosa, K. A. (2018). Strengthening desert plant biotechnology research in the United Arab Emirates: a viewpoint. Physiology and Molecular Biology of Plants, 24, 521–533.

Ganai, M. (2016). A Case of India and Iran, Political Relationship since Gulf War to 2001. International Affairs and Global Strategy, 44, 59–61.

Garcia, Z. (2015). Davidson, Christopher. The Persian Gulf and Pacific Asia: From Indifference to Interdependence. The Journal of Third World Studies, 32, 267.

Garoo, A. A. (2018). Rise and fall of Maritime Hubs in Pre-Islamic Arabia. Journal of Arts and Social Sciences [JASS].

Gawlikowski The Sacred Space in Ancient Arab Religions. (2019).

Gawlikowski, M. (2018). The Indian trade between the Gulf and the Red Sea. Polish Archaeology in the Mediterranean.

Găzdac, C., Josanu, V., Spantidaki, S., & Scafuro, A. C. (2022). Journal of Ancient History and Archaeology.

George, A. (2015). Direct Sea Trade Between Early Islamic Iraq and Tang China: from the Exchange of Goods to the Transmission of Ideas. Journal of the Royal Asiatic Society, 25, 579–624.

Ghaffar, N. A. (2013). Development of Creative and Innovative Thinking through Studying the Design of the Art of Drafting Metal Ornaments to Emphasize the Arab Cultural Identity in the Arabian Gulf States.

Ghaly, M. (2014). Domesticating Genomics In The Arab World: Islamic Religio-ethical Deliberations. 2014.

Ghasemi, T., Vahdani, S., & Tarrah, J. (2015). Determination of texture characteristics of coastal sediments in east of Bandar Abbas. 6, 515–520.

Golkowska, K. U. (2014). Arab Women in the Gulf and the Narrative of Change: the Case of Qatar. International Studies. Interdisciplinary Political and Cultural Journal, 16, 51–64.

Grasso, V. (2023). Pre-Islamic Arabia.

Gregoricka, L. A. (2013). Geographic origins and dietary transitions during the Bronze Age in the Oman Peninsula. American Journal of Physical Anthropology, 152 3, 353–369.

Gresh, G. F. (2015). Gulf Security and the U.S. Military: Regime Survival and the Politics of Basing.

Grigor, T. (2015). Review: Architecture and Globalisation in the Persian Gulf Region, by Murray Fraser and Nasser Golzari, eds. Journal of the Society of Architectural Historians, 74, 509–511.

Guy, J. (2019). Shipwrecks in Late First Millennium Southeast Asia: Southern China's Maritime Trade and the Emerging Role of Arab Merchants in Indian Ocean Exchange. Early Global Interconnectivity across the Indian Ocean World, Volume I.

Haase, F.-A. (2013). The Representation of the Arabian Peninsula Before the Establishment of the Gulf States: The Contemporary Areas of 'Oman,' 'United Arab Emirates,' 'Saudi Arabia,' and 'Bahrain' in a Diachronic Study of Ethnonyms and Toponyms in Historical Arabic and English Sources.

HABIB, B. M. (2023). THE BABYLONIAN KING NABONAIDH'S CAMPAIGN ON THE NORTHWEST OF THE ARABIAN PENINSULA. RIMAK International Journal of Humanities and Social Sciences.

Habib, K. S. (2016). Music and Traditions of the Arabian Peninsula: Saudi Arabia, Kuwait, Bahrain, and Qatar by Lisa Urkevich (review). Notes, 72, 748–751.

Hamdani, A. (2012). Common Ground between Judaism, Christianity, and Islam: An Islamic View of the Monotheistic Path to Morality. 269 –277.

Hameed, A., Arif, A., & Anwar, A. (2022). Potential of Islamic Tourism in District Mansehra, Khyber Pakhtunkhwa Pakistan: A Case Study of Naukot Monument Attributed to Sayyid Ali Hamadani. Global Sociological Review.

Hamlin, R., Alhejji, H., & Patel, T. (2023). Perceived managerial and leadership effectiveness within multinational corporations in Saudi Arabia: The role of Islamic and Wasta values. Human Resource Development Quarterly.

Hancock, J. (2021). Land of punt and the incense routes. Spices, Scents and Silk: Catalysts of World Trade.

Hansen, V. (2021). Silk Road cities and their co-existing legal traditions. Research Handbook on International Law and Cities.

Hawker, R. (2004). IMAGINING A BEDOUIN PAST: STEREOTYPES AND CULTURAL REPRESENTATION IN THE CONTEMPORARY UNITED ARAB EMIRATES.

Haynes, J. (1999). Religion, globalization and political culture in the Third World.

Held, A. (1989). Contributions of ancient civilizations. 3–6.

Held, C., Cummings, J., & Cotter, J. V. (1989). Middle East Patterns: Places, Peoples, And Politics.

Higham, C. (2004). Encyclopedia of Ancient Asian Civilizations.

Hollifield, Eds. J., Foley, N., & Thiollet, H. (2023). Illiberal Migration Governance in the Arab Gulf.

Holloway, M. F. (1959). Patterns of Library Service in the Middle East.

Hord, J. K. (2001). The Comparability of Ancient and Modern Civilizations. Comparative Civilizations Review, 44, 3.

Horner, N. A. (1978). Present-Day Christianity in the Gulf States of the Arabian Peninsula. International Bulletin of Mission Research, 2, 53–60.

Hosaka, S. (2011). Japan and the Gulf: a historical perspective of pre-oil relations (Special feature: Gulf studies in Japan: new trend, perspective, and approach). 4, 3–24.

Howard, M. C. (2012). Transnationalism in Ancient and Medieval Societies: The Role of Cross-Border Trade and Travel.

Ibrahim, I. (2017). The History of Traditional Medicine in the Arab Region. 4.

Ibrahim, M. (2018). Monotheistic religious currents and their impact on the Arab mentality In the peninsula before Islam. ALUSTATH JOURNAL FOR HUMAN AND SOCIAL SCIENCES.

Ingham, B. (2005). Dialect, Culture & Society in Eastern Arabia: 1 Glossary. By Clive Holes. pp. 573, Leiden, Brill, 2001. Journal of the Royal Asiatic Society, 15, 93–95.

Insoll, T. (2016). The Land Of Enki In The Islamic Era: Pearls, Palms and Religious Identity in Bahrain.

Insoll, T. (2021). Marine Shell Working at Harlaa, Ethiopia, and the Implications for Red Sea Trade. Journal of African Archaeology.

Institut, T., Islam, A., Kediri, N., Taufiqurrahman, S. S., Politik, S., & Islam, M. (2023). The Quranic Text Approach: A Review of Watt and Crone's Theses on the Emergence of Islam. Canonia Religia.

Ismail, M., & Hussein, S. (2018). Population aging and long-term care policies in the Gulf region: a case study of Oman. Journal of Aging & Social Policy, 31, 338–357.

Iy, Q. (1983). Urbanization in contemporary Arab Gulf states. 50, 170–182.

Jabado, R., Ghais, S., Hamza, W., & Henderson, A. (2015). The shark fishery in the United Arab Emirates: an interview-based approach to assess the status of sharks. Aquatic Conservation-Marine and Freshwater Ecosystems, 25, 800–816.

Jain, P. (2019). Indian Trade Diaspora in the Arabian Peninsula: An Overview. 267–280.

Jargy, S. (1989). Sung Poetry in the Oral Tradition of the Gulf Region and the Arabian Peninsula.

Joyner, C. (1990). The Persian Gulf War.

Juchniewicz, K. (2023). Aynuna: A Case Study of the Changing Functions of a Hijazi Coastal Settlement from the Nabatean to the Early Islamic Period. Études et Travaux.

Kanchana, R. (2018). Is the Kafala Tradition to Blame for the Exploitative Work Conditions in the Arab-Gulf Countries? 61–79.

Kazerouni, A. (2013). Le miroir des cheikhs : musée et patrimonialisme dans les principautés arabes du golfe Persique.

Kehinde, M. (2013). Trans-Saharan Slave Trade. 1–4.

Keohane, A. (1991). Bedouin: Nomads of the Desert.

Khajehpour-Khoei, B. (2002). Mutual Perceptions in the Persian Gulf Region. 239–251.

Khalaf, S. (2000). Poetics and politics of newly invented traditions in the Gulf: Camel racing in the United Arab Emirates. Ethnology, 39, 243–261.

Khalifa, F. A. (2015). Urban Sustainability and Transforming Culture in the Arabian Gulf: The Case of Bahrain.

Khan, A., & Major, M. (2020). From residential village to heritage marketplace: evaluation morphological transformation and their use consequences over time in the historic settlement of Al-Wakran, Qatar. Proceedings of the 56th ISOCARP World Planning Congress.

Khashabh, A. S. A., & Akhmedova, N. (2023). The rise of Qatar in the international arena: causes, factors, consequences. RUDN Journal of World History.

Kolster, J. (2015). North Africa - Working paper - Trade Volume and Economic Growth in the MENA Region: Goods or Services?

Kozah, M. (2022). New Evidence for an Early Islamic Arabic Dialect in Eastern Arabia? The Qaṭrāyīth ("in Qatari") Spoken in Beth Qaṭraye. Journal of Near Eastern Studies, 81, 71–83.

Kubo, M., & Tsuda, S. (2022). The Golden City on the Edge: Economic Geography and Jihad over Centuries.

Kučera, F. (2013). Arab Horse in the Culture of Orient. 12.

Lado, S., Elbers, J., Doskocil, A., Scaglione, D., Trucchi, E., Banabazi, M. H., Almathen, F., Saitou, N., Ciani, E., & Burger, P. (2020). Genome-wide diversity and global migration patterns in dromedaries follow ancient caravan routes. Communications Biology, 3.

Landen, R. (2020). The Changing Pattern of Political Relations between the Arab Gulf and the Arab Provinces of the Ottoman Empire. The Arab Gulf and the Arab World.

Landry, D. (2009). 'Rewriting the Sea from the Desert Shore: Equine and Equestrian Perspectives on a New Maritime History.'

Larry, F. (2019). Discursive assessment practices in a special school for girls identified with a disability in one Arabic-speaking Gulf-Arabian country.

Law, R., & Underwood, K. (2012). Msheireb Heart of Doha: An Alternative Approach to Urbanism in the Gulf Region. 1, 131–147.

Lightfoot, M. (2014). Building a knowledge society on sand – When the modernist project confronts the traditional cultural values in the Gulf. 24.

Liu, X. (2010). The Silk Road in World History.

Lombard, P., & Boksmati-Fattouh, N. (2020). Cultural diffusion and its impact on heritage representation in the Kingdom of Bahrain. Museums of the Arabian Peninsula.

Looney, R. (2007). The Arab World's Uncomfortable Experience with Globalization. Middle East Journal, 61, 341.

M, Dr. F. B. (2021). Early Arab trade with India: With special reference to Kerala. International Journal of History.

Maclean, M. (2015). Tribal Modern: Branding New Nations in the Arab Gulf. Arab Studies Journal, 23, 423.

Magee, P. (2005). Investigating cross-Gulf trade in the Iron Age III period: chronological and compositional data on Burnished Maroon Slipped Ware (BMSW) in southeastern Arabia and Iran. Arabian Archaeology and Epigraphy, 16, 82–92.

Mahmoud, A. (2017). DOES PERSIAN/ARABIAN-GULF COMPARATIVE LITERATURE EXIST? AN EXPLORATION OF THE PRACTICES OF COMPARATISTS IN THE GULF COUNCIL COUNTRIES. 19, 107–118.

Maisel, S., & Shoup, J. (2009). Saudi Arabia and the Gulf Arab States Today: An Encyclopedia of Life in the Arab States.

McDonald-Toone, E. C. (2019). "Curating the region": exhibitions, geopolitics & the reception of contemporary and modern art from the Arab world & the Middle East.

McIntosh, J. (2005). Ancient Mesopotamia.

Megahed, N. (2016). Education and the reverse gender divide in the Gulf States: Embracing the global, ignoring the local. International Review of Education, 62, 659–660.

Menoret, P. S. (2014). Cities in the Arabian Peninsula: Introduction. City, 18, 698–700.

Miyake, R., & Rumi, O. (2012). A Study on the Trading Routes Connecting the Red Sea and Ethiopia as Serial Heritages. 49, 23–38.

Moore, A. (2011). Elasmobranchs of the Persian (Arabian) Gulf: ecology, human aspects, and research priorities for improved management. Reviews in Fish Biology and Fisheries, 22, 35–61.

Morton, M. (2015). THE BURAIMI AFFAIR: OIL PROSPECTING AND DRAWING THE FRONTIERS OF SAUDI ARABIA. Asian Affairs, 46, 1–17.

Moscatelli, M., Raffa, A., & Shipstone, A. U. (2023). Revitalisation of urban spaces by women architects: enhancing cultural heritage in the gulf region. Archnet-IJAR.

Moussa, N. M. K. (2019). The contribution of the domesticated camel and advanced irrigation techniques (the horizontal well/Falaj system) to the Iron Age economy and settlement patterns of the Oman Peninsula and Arabia. Journal of General Union of Arab Archaeologists.

Mouton, M., & Schiettecatte, J. (2014). In the desert margins. The settlement process in ancient South and East Arabia.

Musvver, A. (2019). India's Commodity Trade with Saudi Arabia: A Panel Data Approach. Indian Journal of Economics and Development.

Nadjmabadi, S. (2009). The Arab Presence on the Iranian Coast of the Persian Gulf. 129–145.

Naeem, Z. (2011). Emerging Trend of Waterpipe Use in Saudi Arabia— International Journal of Health Sciences, 5 2, V–VI.

Naufal, G., & Genc, I. (2012). History of Labor Migration to the Gulf.

Near Eastern Languages and Civilizations. (2022).

Noss, D., & Grangaard, B. R. (1993). A History of the World's Religions.

Nusair, I. (2012). Gender and Violence in the Middle East (review). The Middle East Journal, 65, 699–700.

Onsman, A. (2011). It is better to light a candle than to ban the darkness: government-led academic development in Saudi Arabian universities. Higher Education, 62, 519–532.

Op, S. (2022). Translations and Literary Exchanges between Kerala and Middle-East. SMART MOVES JOURNAL IJELLH.

Özoral, B. (2022). The Effect of Globalization in the Gulf Countries and the Changing Roles of Women: A Comparative Study on Arabia, The United Arab Emirates and Qatar. Süleyman Demirel Üniversitesi Vizyoner Dergisi.

Pasha, A. (2018). Arabs and Euro-Asian maritime contacts. 3.

Pasternak, M. D., & Erickson-Gini, T. (2023). The Secret in the Desert: Preliminary Conclusions from the Excavation of a Unique Burial Complex in the Negev Highlands. Tel Aviv, 50, 3–20.

Pike, K. (2018). Disney in Doha: Arab Girls Negotiate Global and Local Versions of Disney Media. Middle East Journal of Culture and Communication, 11, 72–90.

Pirotta, M. (1994). Cultural aspects of medical practice in Saudi Arabia. Medical Journal of Australia, 161.

Potter, L. (2017). Society in the Persian Gulf: Before and After Oil.

Potts, D. (1993). Rethinking some aspects of trade in the Arabian Gulf. World Archaeology, 24, 423–440.

Qutub, I. (1983). Urbanization in contemporary Arab Gulf states. Ekistics; Reviews on the Problems and Science of Human Settlements, 50 300, 170–182.

Raffa, P. (2019). Between Absolute and Fluid Space: the Representation of the Oasis.

Ramadan, L. N. (2016). The Role of Women Artists in Qatar and the Representation of their Work in Mathaf: Arab Museum of Modern Art. 2016.

Rasheed, M., & Al–Rasheed, L. (1996). The Politics of Encapsulation: Saudi Policy towards Tribal and Religious Opposition. Middle Eastern Studies, 32, 96–119.

Reece, G. (1954). The Horn of Africa. International Affairs, 30, 440–449.

Renzi, M., Intilia, A., Hausleiter, A., & Rehren, T. (2016). Early Iron Age metal circulation in the Arabian Peninsula: the oasis of Tayma as part of a dynamic network.

Researching Dress and Identity in Saudi Arabia: - "What a strange power there is in clothing" - Isaac Bashevis Singer - Asfar. (n.d.). Retrieved June 20, 2024, from https://asfar.org.uk/researching-dress-and-identity-in-saudi-arabia-what-a-strange-power-there-is-in-clothing-isaac-bashevis-singer/

Reus, E. L., Amrousi, M. E., & Paleologos, E. (2020). Modern Heritage and the Living City: Arab Identity and Modernization in the Architecture of Abu Dhabi. Journal of Arabian Studies, 10, 90–115.

Reyaee, S., & Ahmed, A. (2015). Growth Pattern of Social Media Usage in Arab Gulf States: An Analytical Study. 4, 23–32.

Ricks, T. M. (1970). Persian Gulf Seafaring and East Africa: Ninth-Twelfth Centuries. International Journal of African Historical Studies, 3, 339–357.

Roll, I. (2005). Imperial Roads Across and Trade Routes Beyond the Roman Provinces of Judaea-Palaestina and Arabia: The State of Research. Tel Aviv, 32, 107–118.

Ruiz, L. S. (2017). The artisanal shark fishery in the Gulf of California: Historical catch reconstruction and vulnerability of shark species to the fishery.

Sabah, M. A., Grilec, A., & Simončič, K. N. (2024). Crafting Tradition and Innovation: Gulf Sandals. Koža & Obuća.

Sachedina, A. (2022). Assimilating the Heterogeneity of Migrant Populations through a National Past: Transforming a Shīa Minority Community in Post-Nationalist Oman. Anthropological Quarterly, 95, 839–868.

Saffaie, W. M. (2018). The Inscribed Metal Pots in the West of the Arab Gulf (Mleiha and Al- Fueda), Mesopotamia and Ancient Egypt: A Comparative Study. Asian Social Science.

Sakr, N. (2018). 'Smarter, stronger, kinder': Interests at stake in the remake of Iftah ya Simsim for Gulf children. Middle East Journal of Culture and Communication, 11, 9–28.

Salama, A. M., & Wiedmann, F. (2013a). Evolving urbanism of cities on the Arabian Peninsula. Open House International, 38, 4–5.

Salama, A. M., & Wiedmann, F. (2013b). Unveiling urban transformations in the Arabian Peninsula: dynamics of global flows, multiple modernities, and people-environment interactions. Open House International, 38, 1–114.

Salih, Abdelrahim. "Music and Dance of the Middle East". Retrieved June 20, 2024, from https://chrysalis-foundation.org/wp-content/uploads/2019/06/Music_and_dance_in_the_Midde_East.pdf

Salimi, A. (2012). Trends in Religious Reform on the Arabian Peninsula. 161–173.

Samin, N. (2014). Our Ancestors, Our Heroes: Saudi Tribal Campaigns to Suppress Historical Docudramas. British Journal of Middle Eastern Studies, 41, 266–286.

Santini, R. H., & Wulzer, P. (2024). The Evolution of the Gulf: History and Theories Of a Complex Subregional System. Middle East Policy.

Saud, M. K. (2024). Components of Society in the Gulf Cooperation Council Countries. European Journal of Theoretical and Applied Sciences.

Schlumberger, O. (2012). Desert Dreams: The Quest for Arab Integration from the Arab Revolt to the Gulf Cooperation Council (review). The Middle East Journal, 66, 754–756.

Schorle, K. (2014). Long-distance trade and the exploitation of arid landscapes in the Roman imperial period (1st - 3rd centuries AD).

Schuhn, L. (2021). Arab Gulf Monarchies as an Epistemic (Online) Community Revisited Diffusion, Competition, and Survival in the Aftermath of the Arab Uprisings.

Schwall, C., Brandl, M., Börner, M., Lindauer, S., Deckers, K., David-Cuny, H., Yousif, E. A., Jasim, S., & Horejs, B. (2024). Kalba: research on trade networks of a prehistoric coastal community on the Gulf of Oman, United Arab Emirates. Antiquity, 98.

Scott, C. (2011). A Long Walk in the Desert: A Study of the Roman Hydreumata along the Trade Routes between the Red Sea and the Nile.

Segal, A. (1985). Shivta-A Byzantine Town in the Negev Desert. Journal of the Society of Architectural Historians, 44, 317–328.

Segal, E. (2020). Palm Dates, Power, and Politics in Pre-Oil Kuwait. All Things Arabia.

Seland, E. H. (2011). The Persian Gulf or the Red Sea? Two axes in ancient Indian Ocean trade, where to go and why. World Archaeology, 43, 398–409.

Semaan, R. W., Lindsay, V., Williams, P., & Ashill, N. J. (2020). Special Session: Drivers of Female Luxury Consumption in the Gulf Region: An Abstract. 189–190.

Seray, H. B. (1996). Christianity in the East of the Arabian Peninsula. Aram Periodical, 8, 315–332.

Serjeant, R. (1981). Sheila A. Scoville: Gazetteer of Arabia: a geographical and tribal history of the Arabian Peninsula. Vol. I: A–B . vii, 733 pp., Graz: Akademische Druck- u. Verlagsanstalt, 1979. ÖS 980. Bulletin of the School of Oriental and African Studies, 44, 372–373.

Shamsi, S., Dixon, C., Hossan, C., & Papanastassiou, M. (2015). Coaching Constructs and Leadership Development at an Oil and Gas Company in the United Arab Emirates. 23, 13.

Shan, D. (2022). Occupational safety and health challenges for maritime key workers in the global COVID-19 pandemic. International Labour Review (Print), 161, 267–287.

Sheng, A. (2010). Textiles from the Silk Road: Intercultural exchanges among nomads, traders, and agriculturalists. The Expedition, 52, 33–43.

Siddiqui., Dr. ZakeraA. (2016). The Rise of Islam. International Journal of Approximate Reasoning, 4, 1849–1851.

Sidebotham, S. (2011). Berenike and the Ancient Maritime Spice Route.

Simpson, I., Aburizaiza, O. S., Siddique, A., Barletta, B., Blake, N., Gartner, A., Khwaja, H., Meinardi, S., Zeb, J., & Blake, D. (2014). Air quality in Mecca and surrounding holy places in Saudi Arabia during Hajj: initial survey. Environmental Science and Technology, 48 15, 8529–8537.

Sinclair, C. (1987). M. S. El-Azhary, ed., The Impact of Oil Revenues on Arab Gulf Development (London: Croom Helm, 1984). Pp. 203. International Journal of Middle East Studies, 19, 491–492.

Sooud, S. (2019). Re-engaging with the Gulf Modernist City: Heritage and Repurposing Practices.

Stahl, D. (2016). The British Invasion and Occupation of Ottoman Iraq/enemy on the Euphrates: The British Occupation of Iraq and the Great

Arab Revolt, 1914 1921/desert Hell: The British Invasion of Mesopotamia. Arab Studies Journal, 24, 206.

Stančius, A., & Grecevičius, P. (2022). Influence of Ancient Mesopotamian Aesthetics of Gardens/Parks and Water Installations on the Development of Landscape Architecture. Athens Journal of Architecture.

Storbeck, D. (2011). Indian Labour Migration to the Arab Gulf States. The Impact of a Growing Interdependence. 42, 21–46.

Subhi-Yamin, T. (2009). Gifted Education in the Arabian Gulf and the Middle Eastern Regions: History, Current Practices, New Directions, and Future Trends. 1463–1490.

Tayeh, R., Mohammed, H., Campbell, T., & Malley, G. (2012). Gulf States' Perspectives on Invasion. 413–420.

Thabit, A. (2020). Iraq's alternatives in light of the challenges surrounding the security of the Arabian Gulf: the challenges of security of navigation in the Strait of Hormuz. Tikrit Journal For Political Science.

Thomas, J., Raynor, M., & McKinnon, M. (2014). Academic integrity and oral examination: an Arabian Gulf perspective. Innovations in Education and Teaching International, 51, 533–543.

Tiliouine, H., & Meziane, M. (2017). The History of Well-Being in the Middle East and North Africa (MENA). 523–563.

Tosland, B. (2020). European architects at the confluence of tradition and modernity in the Persian Gulf, 1954-1982.

Ulrich, B. (2023). The Medieval Persian Gulf.

Varisco, D. (1989). The Arab Gulf States Folklore Centre: A Resource for the Study of Folklore and Traditional Culture. Middle East Studies Association Bulletin, 23, 157–167.

Vasconcellos, M. S. L. D. (2009). Dubai: Where the East meets the West.

Vyazemskaya, K. (2020). Louvre Abu-Dhabi: At the Crossroads of Civilizations. Oriental Courier.

Ward, S. M. (1990). A fragment from an unknown work by al-Ṭabarī on the tradition 'Expel the Jews and Christians from the Arabian Peninsula (and the lands of Islam).' Bulletin of the School of Oriental and African Studies, 53, 407–420.

Weier, J. (2017). Market Orientalism: Cultural Economy and the Arab Gulf States. Geografická Revue, 108, 489–491.

Winterhalter, C. (1981). Indigenous housing patterns and design principles in the Eastern Province of Saudi Arabia.

Wood, J. (1991). Desert sounds—international broadcasting in the Arab world.

Wyatt, D. J. (2019). Cargoes Human and Otherwise: Chinese Commerce in East African Goods During the Middle Period. Early Global Interconnectivity across the Indian Ocean World, Volume I.

Xiao-yong, Y. (2011). Development of the United States and the Gulf Region the Evolution of Relations between Peoples and Nations(I). Journal of Hubei University for Nationalities.

Yang, J. (2023). Gender Norms and Perceptions in Islamic World: A Study of the Travel Account of al-Sirafi. Advances in Social Development and Education Research.

Yaphe, J. (1996). Islamic Radicalism in the Arabian Peninsula: Growing Risks.

Yoshitake, M. (2014). Arab. Bedouin of the Syrian Desert: Story of a Family.

Yunis, A. (2021). Film and Visual Media in the Gulf.

Yunis, A., & Hudson, D. (2021). Introduction. Middle East Journal of Culture and Communication.

Zahlan, R. (2016). Rethinking Gulf Museology Identity and Museums in Doha and Abu Dhabi John Durovsik New museums in Qatar and the United Arab Emirates have stimulated scholarly interest.

Zaidan, E., & Abulibdeh, A. (2020). Master Planning and the Evolving Urban Model in the Gulf Cities: Principles, Policies, and Practices for the Transition to Sustainable Urbanism. Planning Practice & Research, 36, 193–215.

Zogo, S. C. (2016). Gwyn Campbell and Elizabeth Elbourne (Eds.). 2014. Sex, Power and Slavery. African Studies Quarterly, 16, 183.

Байбусинова, Н. К. (2020). Gulf countries trade relations with the United States. 93, 71–81.

Нуридинова, Т., & Удовенко, О. (2019). On Interfaces on the Great Silk Road: Historical Examples of Relations Between Middle Asia and China. The Language and Culture.

About the authors

The GEW Social Sciences group within GEW Reports & Analyses (The Voice of the Mediterranean) is responsible for researching and analyzing contemporary social trends. The objective is to produce relevant reports and thought-provoking books that enlighten readers on current societal issues, whether locally, regionally, or globally.

The Unit's commitment to academic excellence is reflected in its works, as it constantly strives to deepen our understanding of the complex social dynamics shaping our world.

The Editor

Hichem Karoui (Hisham al Karoui) is a renowned expert in the Middle East and the Gulf, where he has lived and worked regularly since 2011. First, he was the Head of the Political Unit—head of Online Academic Publishing—at the Doha-based Arab Center For Research and Policy Studies (ACRPS), and later, he was a senior Consultant for the Diplomatic Institute at the Ministry of Foreign Affairs in Qatar.

Since 2020, he served as Executive Director of the London-based Gulf Futures Center (which became Gulf Futures For

Studies and Consulting) and as Senior Researcher and Editor at the GEW Reports & Analyses.

He has published over fifty books in three languages (English, Arabic, and French), not considering the edited books, reports, and several important articles and academic papers.

He holds a PhD in sociology from Paris III Sorbonne University.

A Masters in Middle-East-Mediterranean Studies, 2 Maitrises (Masters One), one in Arabic and the other in English, all from the same University.